NORVAL MORRISSEAU

NORVAL MORRISSEAU

Man Changing into Thunderbird

Armand Garnet Ruffo

Douglas & McIntyre

For Heather and Alex

And in memory of Norval Morrisseau,
Selwyn Dewdney,
and Jack Pollock

Douglas and McIntyre (2013) Ltd.
P.O. Box 219, Madeira Park, BC, V0N 2H0
www.douglas-mcintyre.com

Edited by Pam Robertson
Text design by Mary White
Indexed by Nicola Goshulak
Printed and bound in Canada

Douglas and McIntyre (2013) Ltd. acknowledges the support of the Canada Council for the Arts, which last year invested $153 million to bring the arts to Canadians throughout the country. We also gratefully acknowledge financial support from the Government of Canada and from the Province of British Columbia through the BC Arts Council and the Book Publishing Tax Credit.

Library and Archives Canada Cataloguing in Publication

Ruffo, Armand Garnet, 1955-, author
    Norval Morrisseau : man changing into thunderbird / Armand Garnet Ruffo.

Includes index.
Issued in print and electronic formats.
ISBN 978-1-77162-046-8 (hardcover).--ISBN 978-1-77162-158-8 (softcover).--
ISBN 978-1-77162-047-5 (html)

    1. Morrisseau, Norval, 1931-2007. 2. Painters--Canada--Biography.
II. Title.

ND249.M66R83 2014   759.11   C2014-905399-1
                                                   C2014-905400-9

"We are a living people and a living culture. I believe we are bound to move forward, to experiment with new things and develop new modes of expression as all peoples do."
—*Daphne Odjig, Potawatomi, artist*

"There are images, songs and words that will appear at your death like familiar birds to accompany you on your journey to the sky."
—*From "sudden awareness" by Joy Harjo, Muscogee Creek, poet and musician*

Contents

Introduction   1

I ◉ BIZHIG

Destiny   11
Binawiigo (In the Beginning)   14
I Used to Draw   17
Veronique   20
Conversion   24
Sister Lorenzia   25
Wonder Boy   27
Vision Quest   30
Instruction   33
Nanaboozho   37
Copper Thunderbird   41
Harriet   44
Archaeologist of the White Man   48

II ◉ NIIZH

Red Lake   57
Patrons   59
Grandfather Stories   64
Constable Bob   68
The Amazing Morrisseau   71
Mining for Gold   79

An Encounter with Genius   82

Success   91

Devil Thirsty   96

On Ne Sait Jamais   98

A Fickle Public   101

Culture Shock   104

Big as Christmas   108

An Incredible Journey   118

Legends of My People   121

Celebrating Canada's 1967 Centennial   125

Windigo and Other Tales   127

Victoria and the Bear   131

Flying High   133

The Ojibway Art Circuit   139

Perfection   147

Hail Noble One   150

P&M What-Not-Shop   154

Legally Separated   159

III   ⊙   NISWI

Penance   165

The Paradox of Norval Morrisseau   170

The Consuming Fire   179

Winnipeg   180

Bad Medicine   187

At the McMichael   190

Eckankar   195

Man Changing into Thunderbird (Transmigration)   200
The Garden Party   209
Fame   218
Tom Thomson's Shack   220
Doctor Morrisseau   224
The Bear   228
An Open Embrace   229
A Bridge   236
Thunder Bay Motel   238
Fall from Grace   241
Oranges   250

IV 　◉　 NIIWIN

Born Again   257
An International Artist   265
The Shaman's Return   271
Grand Shaman Grandfather   273
In Healing Colour   277
Medicine Man with Bear (The Poisoned Bear)   280
One Last Time   281
Fortress Morrisseau   285
The National Gallery of Canada   291
Conjuring   294

About Norval Morrisseau   303
Acknowledgments   305
Index   308

Introduction

WHAT BEGAN IT ALL was Norval Morrisseau rising like his spirit name Copper Thunderbird from the alleys of Vancouver's east end and, again, making headlines. He would become the first Indigenous painter to have a solo show at the National Gallery of Canada. The year was 2005 and Greg Hill, curator and head of Indigenous art for the National Gallery, was organizing the *Norval Morrisseau, Shaman Artist* retrospective. Knowing that I am of Ojibway heritage, he asked me if I would write something about the acclaimed Ojibway painter for the accompanying catalogue. I told him that I would have to think about it. Because of Morrisseau's incredible reputation, I knew something about him—since his breakthrough solo show in 1962 he had more or less always been in the news—but frankly not very much. Although I was from northern Ontario, I never actually saw his work until I moved to Ottawa to work for the now-defunct *Native Perspective Magazine* in the late 1970s. I would later learn that in the early seventies he had participated in an educational tour of northern Ontario schools, but for some reason the "art circuit" had bypassed mine. It wasn't until 1982 that I attended an exhibition of his at the Robertson Galleries in Ottawa.

I did think about it, and I waited. Waited for something to tell me either to take on the project or let it go. What did happen, then, was a combination of dreaming and remembering. I was in bed for the night, the dark room lit only by the streetlight sliding under the drapes. I thought I heard something. I sat up and listened attentively. Footsteps. Voices. I stilled my breath and waited for a moment that seemed unending. Then a lone car passed below on the street, splashing along the wet pavement. I fell back asleep. The next morning I thought about what I had heard, or thought I heard. The voices, I realized, had come from the old flat-roof house of my childhood in the north. Perhaps from my mother and the neighbours who had dropped by for a visit, a chat, a drink. There had been lots of drinking in those days and nights. I still held the image of us kids tearing off downtown with a few coins rattling in our pockets because my mother and her friends were partying and wanted to get rid of us. Fortunately for me it didn't happen very often, but it did happen and I remember it well.

The more I thought about Morrisseau and his life, the more I realized that his experiences, while extraordinary in their own right because of his unique gifts, were fundamentally connected to something larger than himself. I realized that Morrisseau's life was representative of the profound upheaval that had taken place in the lives of Native people across the country. With their traditional economies and support systems in ruins, they were thrown into abject poverty, families literally starving to death, and it was into this milieu that Morrisseau, like my mother, was born in 1932 (which is the birth year he acknowledged in a Department of Indian Affairs cultural development application). A period that coincided with the unparalleled movement by Native peoples to cities and one-industry towns across the country to find work—shell-shocked as they were by a history of missionaries, decades of residential schooling that taught them to hate everything Indian, hate even themselves, the overt racism that made them stand at the back of the line, the total disregard and denigration of their cultures, the stereotypes that continually projected Hollywood versions of them whooping and hollering on the screen. And whoop and holler they did as many of them sought relief in forgetting. Or, on the contrary, in remembering what they could of the old ways, sought out their own kind, their community, and with what little money they had, drowned their sorrows.

The main difference of course in Morrisseau's case was his immense talent. Nevertheless, I realized that like an intricate spider's web his life was very much part and parcel of what I might call the great upheaval. The details of his life, his aesthetics, his technical achievements, his idiosyncrasies, all of it hearkened back to who he was as an "Indian" at a particular time and place in colonial Canada.

I called back a couple of days later confirming that I would write the piece, but with a few conditions. I did not want to write the standard academic essay that the National Gallery of Canada might expect. And I made it clear that I was not interested in reportage. What I wanted to do was tell a story. I wanted to employ the traditional form of acquiring knowledge that is central to Ojibway culture and to Native cultures in general. And, as much as possible, I wanted to ground my story in Anishinaabe epistemology and what we now call oral history. That would mean I would have to talk to people and learn a great many things, but then wasn't that the point? Another thing: I would write a couple of pieces and then fly out to Nanaimo and present them to Morrisseau himself. If he agreed to my approach, I would go ahead with the project.

When I finally met Norval Morrisseau I have to admit that I was intimidated by his imposing presence, even as he sat in his motorized wheelchair. Numerous journalists have spoken about it, and I'll confirm here that it's true. There was something about him that only a rare few possess. Whatever it is—call it charisma, power—Morrisseau had buckets of it, and it undoubtedly was part of the reason he was able to attract a large and continuous entourage throughout his life. I had been led into a sunlit room by his caregiver and adopted son Gabe Vadas and found myself standing awkwardly in front of the artist, glancing nervously at the spectacular paintings on the walls, while Vadas kneeled before him and spoke quietly about me. Then Vadas stood back and with a nod indicated that I should give him the book of poetry that I had brought for the occasion.

Looking up at me, emotionless, Morrisseau slowly raised his trembling hands and accepted the book.

After Gabe Vadas told him what I wanted to do and he had leafed through my book, he looked me squarely in the face and then sat silent for a moment, before posing a question that left me near speechless. He asked me, "What took you so long?" It sounded as though he had been waiting for me all along, and I was late for the appointment. I suspected that he was probably being a bit of an old trickster, and it was probably something he said to everybody. Then he turned back to my book of poetry, and it was obvious to me that he was pleased to see a poet would be writing about him. Morrisseau had no use for what he called the mechanics of the world, and I think he was intrigued by the idea of writing as an art form—and finally becoming the subject of it.

He also told me not to leave out anything. In hindsight, now that I know so much about him, I find the very notion of his request perplexing. I assume he knew that I would discover things about him that might not be flattering, but I like to think that it was his belief in art and literature that compelled him to tell me to include it all.

I ended up reading a few parts of the manuscript to him. One of the pieces about his grandfather brought tears to his eyes, and I could see from his response that I was on the right track. Move the heart and the mind will follow, as the elders say. Before I left Morrisseau whispered to me in his garbled voice that I had his "shamanic blessing." At first I thought that this might also be something he said to everyone to make them feel special, but I have come to think of it as further confirmation of his approval.

I need to say that I personally make no claim to be a historian, or an art historian for that matter; I also have to say that I make no claim to have written a definitive, let alone a standard, biography. What I have set out to do is tell a story about Norval Morrisseau's life that is indelibly tied to his art. In this regard, I like to think that my writing has been influenced by the paintings themselves. I have adhered to the facts of Morrisseau's life as I have understood them, and, yet, I have broken from everyday realism and rendered an interpretation of his life that resides in a mythic worldview. I might add that Norval Morrisseau continues to be the kind of controversial figure who elicits everything from outright condemnation to supreme praise. These diverse threads hold this story together. And I am indebted to all the good-hearted people who were willing to talk openly to me about him. After writing my initial piece for the National Gallery of Canada's *Shaman Artist* exhibition, I have taken many roads to get to this point of publication. Life has a way of interfering with the best laid plans. The process of immersing myself in Morrisseau's work has also resulted in a book of poetry, *The Thunderbird Poems,* a collection of ekphrastic poems based on the artist's paintings, which can be seen as a companion of sorts to this book. From the beginning my goal for this biography has been to pay homage to Norval Morrisseau—without intentionally leaving anything out—and I hope this is what I have done. Although I have tried to remain true to him, in reconstructing his life, I have naturally filtered everything through my own perception and imagination and I make no pretense that this is the final word. As the old stories tended to change with the teller and the telling, so too will the story of "Man Changing into Thunderbird" transform with time.

Life Scroll

Where your dreams find you in the blue lake of your mind
and vibrate to the surface like a speckled trout.

Where a long forgotten rock face turns into your face
and vision points in the direction of youth, middle age, old age.

Where gnarled fingers slide with precision along a map of birchbark
and belief and ritual hold hands.

Where there is no one but you and the echoes of ancestors
in the halls of your loneliest night.

Where all creation rests on the back of the strongest and depends
upon the grasp of the weakest, and all is related.

Where you learn the art of listening and the old words drip
into the stone bowl of your deafness.

Where you learn the art of seeing and the old signs are owl eyes
that stare into the forest of your ignorance.

Where you must learn how to love and be loved
and admit that your journey too will soon come to an end.

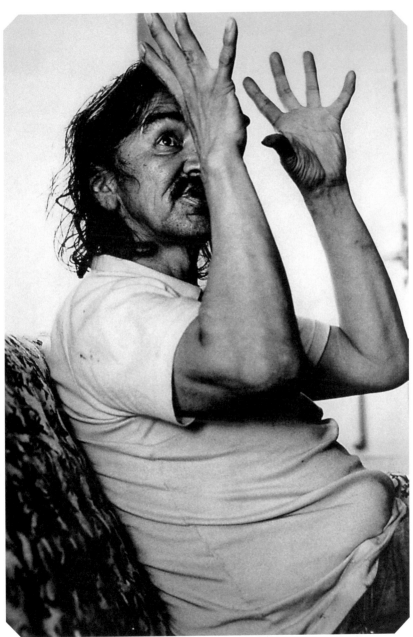

Helena Wilson took this photo of Norval Morrisseau in the summer of 1983 in his house in Thunder Bay, Ontario, during a conversation about his source of creativity and techniques. *Helena Wilson photo*

Northern Ontario—"in the eye of the thunderbird." *Armand Garnet Ruffo photo*

I ⊙ BIZHIG

Destiny

Toronto, September 12, 1962. The official opening of Norval Morrisseau's thirty-five-painting exhibition at the small Pollock Gallery on Elizabeth Street, and the press are calling it a sensation. Anyone who is anyone in "Toronto's bitchy art scene," as Jack Pollock calls the arts community, is there, and nobody has seen anything like it before. After a few introductory remarks by Pollock, Selwyn Dewdney, the London, Ontario, based artist and expert on Native pictographs, glowingly introduces the recently discovered painter, referring to Morrisseau's genius and the new kind of art he's ushering in. Dewdney says he first met Morrisseau up in Red Lake, the furthest corner of northwestern Ontario, where he was doing field research for the Royal Ontario Museum. From their first encounter he was so impressed by the young painter—the epitome of the struggling artist—he decided to help him by providing art supplies and tips on how to paint for a professional market.

Following Dewdney, Ottawa's Allister Grosart is quick to chime in. A national organizer for the Progressive Conservative Party and Morrisseau's first official patron, he goes on for what seems like an eternity about their serendipitous meeting, after a CNR trainman happened to mention the young painter was looking for support. Also on hand to congratulate Morrisseau is Alan Jarvis, former director of the National Gallery and now editor of the prestigious magazine *Canadian Art*. Gathered around Morrisseau, they are thrilled by the thought of having discovered the next great Canadian artist.

In sharp relief, Morrisseau is doing his utmost to contain himself, lest he explode, not in joy and celebration as one might expect, but in rage. The painter is uncertain about his sudden success. While believing it is his destiny, at the same time he knows there is a price to be paid. And at times a feeling of desperation settles over him like wet snow dragging him to his hands and knees. During the exhibition he finds himself cornered by June Callwood, a young reporter working for the CBC, and he masks his unease. "Shaman? Artist? Who is the real Norval Morrisseau?" she asks. "An Indian," he answers flatly. "And what about your sudden success? How do you feel about it?" "Indians aren't supposed to show emotion," he says, trying to be as evasive as possible. But try as he might this stifling of emotion doesn't last. After the camera lights are turned off, and the guests finish their last canapés, drink their last glasses of wine, he finds himself alone, staring at his paintings. Each bearing a little red sticker. And it's then that he feels that he has done something terribly wrong. Deflated, he reaches for his first drink of the evening.

To celebrate their success, Pollock invites the artist and a few guests, including Selwyn Dewdney and Senator Grosart, out to a nearby Chinese restaurant. It's there it happens. Morrisseau's six-foot-two frame explodes. "I sat there in terror," Pollock recalls. "Suddenly he unleashed his pent-up hostilities by getting gloriously drunk. Untamed rage broke up a façade of quiet reserve and, torn apart by inner contradictions and dualities, he shouts, 'The white man doesn't deserve my paintings! They should be destroyed here and now to protect the mystical culture of my forefathers.'" It is a refrain that Morrisseau's tongue lashes out again and again, each time he finds himself in the pit of doubt and despair. "The white man took everything, why should he take these!"

Maybe it is the fear of breaking the age-old taboo against reinterpreting the stories, beliefs and customs of his people that grips him. Maybe it's the paranoia of Christian brainwashing, warning him of fiery damnation, or the authority of the day warning him of arrest. Or the history of disenfranchisement and poverty—his land flooded, his people condemned to live on road allowances, town dumps. He bangs the restaurant table so hard Pollock thinks he's going to break his hand. While other patrons look on uneasily, worried, whispering about the Indian going Indian, Pollock waves frantically to the waiters that everything is under control. And so it is. Morrisseau's rage passes as quickly as it comes. He is calm and passive as he drinks himself into a complete stupor.

The day after the opening, Morrisseau and Pollock are back at the gallery reading the reviews, and the artist turns to an article in the *Toronto Daily Star*. His finger traces the line of print. "Norval Morrisseau, 31-year-old Ojibway painter from Lake Nipigon, last night had the kind of publicity launching at the Pollock Gallery that aspiring painters might dream about. Although quite unexpected, Morrisseau has managed to sell 28 of his 35 symbolic Indian-mythology paintings and has made for himself between $1,500 and $1,800."

In the quiet of the rustling of newspapers, the idea of success now makes him smile for the first time since arriving in Toronto. He feels himself soaring, true to his spirit name, Copper Thunderbird. Morrisseau is grateful to be where he is today—and ever so grateful to his spirit guides, who have made this possible. And yet, for all his gratitude, the publicity, the barrage of reporters asking every kind of question, the shock of instant fame is truly overwhelming. The smile is as fleeting as a spark of light.

Morrisseau now turns to an article in *The Globe and Mail* by art critic Pearl McCarthy. He reads: "Morrisseau's genius for unifying or breaking space in his designs is astounding, as is his sureness of line. It cannot be classified as primitive art, because both the ideas and the expression evince cultivated thought." The word *primitive* catches him like a hook, and he frowns. He wants to say something, but he can see that Pollock is engrossed in another review, busy luxuriating in their mutual success, and he probably wouldn't understand anyway.

For a moment Morrisseau thinks of the shack he lives in back in Beardmore, banged together beside the town dump. He thinks of his wife Harriet and their newborn sleeping under its leaky tin roof. The woodstove they cook on, made from an old oil drum. The windows covered in plastic to keep out the winter wind. The empty cupboards. His beloved grandfather also comes to mind. He thinks of him sleeping under a piece of canvas on the winter trapline, and then of his whole community, displaced from their traditional lands on Lake Nipigon. All of this flashes before him while he considers his own name flashing across the national press for everyone to see. Poor, yes, this he can admit, poor to the point of starvation. But primitive, no, never. As he thinks about this label, foisted on his people, the stories of his grandfather come to mind, stories about all that his people knew and all that his people had before the coming of the white man.

From the time when Morrisseau first met his Red Lake patrons, Dr. Joseph and Esther Weinstein, and decided to become a famous artist, to this sold-out exhibition in Toronto—a mere three years. Something other artists can only hope for, the press announces, attaining such heights in such a short time. Morrisseau responds that he does not believe in luck or hope. If pressed, however, he would say he is not really surprised. He is a born artist. And this place, meaning Pollock's gallery, is where the Creator has sent him. He would even elaborate that he has dreamed the whole experience, which is why it has to come to pass. His destiny is as clear as the night sky on Lake Nipigon, clear as the Milky Way that guides the dead up to the land of the ancestors. Morrisseau knows well that his path is laid out for him: his job is simple, but huge—bigger than Lake Nipigon itself. He must tell the world what his grandfather has taught him about the greatness of his Ojibway people. Despite everything that has happened during the last five hundred years, his people have survived. He has survived. To paint and dream. To dream and paint.

Binawiigo (In the Beginning)

SEVENTY-FIVE YEARS OLD and confined to a red motorized wheelchair, Morrisseau is living in Nanaimo on Vancouver Island, two thousand miles from his Ojibway homeland in northwestern Ontario. But Morrisseau can be home anywhere, and this is where he chooses to be: on the edge of the Pacific Ocean. He rolls to a stop along a cement walkway to take in the view. It is spring and he is wearing a black turtleneck sweater to ward off the chill in the air. His shock of white hair is neatly trimmed, as is his goatee, and he looks wise and serene to the people who pass by. Those who know him call him a true survivor.

As he watches the crash of the waves along the shore and contemplates their existence, his own life, he slips through a portal of time, and he is riding with the thunderbirds. Each swoop of their massive wings turns the sky electric as he looks down through the parting cloud to those he has left behind. Morrisseau is remembering. And we are remembering with him.

Together we are travelling to northern Ontario where a swift and cavernous body of water swells like a sea, enormous, monstrous, the largest lake wholly within the province pouring a torrent into the head of Lake Superior. We land softly on the shoreline, touch the smooth, unyielding veins of rock, the blood-red ochre oozing through the flesh of stone, and focus on the sequence of symbols set down by shaman-artists who have painted the cliffs with story: Nanaboozho, Windigo, Maymaygwaysiwuk, Misshipesheu, Manitous of the People.

Animbiigoong, the continuous water extending over the horizon, where birchbark canoes lie overturned on the shoreline, where wigwaman stand steadfast and the Anishinaabek who have lived here for centuries go about harvesting giingooh (fish) and manomin (wild rice), and burn the mushkeekiwenun (the sacred medicines): wiingashk (sweetgrass), asayma (tobacco), miskwaawauk (cedar), muskodaywushk (sage). This is where they prepare themselves for ceremony, for bawajigay (the vision quest), and savour the heat of the madodoswun (the sweat lodge), a place where mind and body separate in the fiery heat of the grandfathers, exhumed from the rocky shore.

A lake named and renamed by newcomers. Lac Alimibeg or Alemipigon or Alepigon to the French, or Nepigon or Nipigon to the English. We watch as Europeans arrive to document the strangeness, a world they call new but that is really old, older than human time, historical time. But it is a world that falls into that space too, as the Jesuit priest Claude Jean Allouez steps out of a birchbark canoe and onto the beach to celebrate the first Catholic mass in 1667. The French have been in North America for 133 years by then, claiming it for France, and to this end have gone about the constant business of converting the Native peoples to Christianity. Bible in hand, spreading the word of Christ, they find other words, languages, they learn to navigate like great tributaries. Words that speak of other ways of knowing.

And through it all, the collision of people and cultures, the miracle of story. A glimpse of the old way, sinking out of sight with the arrival of the newcomers, a past that tells of the mushkobewun, the great flood, that purified the world, came down in a deluge and carried everything away. Except for Nanaboozho, whose human likeness and power connected the people to Gitchi-Manitou, the Great Spirit, and who found himself floating on a giant log with a few animals, and who called upon them to bring up a piece of soil from the bottom of the great water so that the Creator might remake the world. And so the story goes. The greatest swimmers—Nigig (Otter), Amik (Beaver), and Maang (Loon)—dived into the depths of the water, tried, and failed. In the end only tiny Wazhashk (Muskrat) prevailed, floating to the surface with a speck of soil in its paw. And Nanaboozho placed it on the back of Mikkinnuk (Turtle), and preordained as it was, the winds began to blow and howl in fury, and from the four directions they converged on Mikkinnuk's back, the soil spinning around and around to create the world as we know it today. Nanaboozho laughing all the while.

These and a myriad of other stories, not solely of the past but of the present and future, bring Morrisseau to a place of beginnings. He is again a boy at the knee of his beloved grandfather, Moses Potan Nanakonagos, an Ojibway shaman, who fills his ears with teachings, such as the prophecy of the Seven Sacred Grandfathers, which tells of a search for a boy, like Norval himself, who could be taught to live in harmony and peace with Creation. And how that boy was brought to the spirit world and given a glimpse inside the grandfathers' sacred bundle and saw all the wonders of the world, sights and sounds, colours radiant as the brightest rainbow, all the beauty of the world tucked inside the tiny container. As the boy set out on his journey back to earth and his people, he and Nigig (Otter) stopped seven times, and each time he learned the meaning of the grandfathers' sacred gifts: wisdom, love, respect, bravery, honesty, humility and truth. The boy also learned that he would have to be vigilant, because for each gift there was an opposite that lurked like a beast ready to pounce on whoever strayed from the path of goodness. He would have to be careful.

I Used to Draw

THIS IS THE MOMENT when Norval, at age six, pulls the wool blanket up to his neck, readies his prayers, and waits to hear his grandfather rise from bed. Though it is still dark the routine warms him as his breath meets the frigid air. Finally, he hears his grandfather greet the day. He stills his breathing and listens hard. The door of the woodstove opens with a creak. The metal bar stirs the embers with a soft swoosh. A log thumps as it goes into the stove. The teakettle scrapes as it is filled with water and pushed back into place. Only then does Norval shed his cover, sit up, and plant his feet on the floor. And there he is at that instant of dawn when morning is suspended in the midst of painting the room brightly. He watches keenly as it seeps across the ceiling and walls, into chairs, the table, every article of clothing, all the canned goods on the shelf, lifts the room out of blackness and gives it circumference, height, depth, boundaries, edges, familiarity.

And among these objects, his grandfather begins to take shape, his faint silhouette moving across the room. And then, with eyes turned and fixed to the east-facing window, Norval watches how all at once all the colours of day become compressed into a single moment. The room is aglow. And like his grandfather, who is quietly praying, thanking the Creator for the new day, he too begins to pray, as he tries to grab and hold onto the moment in the way he has been taught. The same way his grandfather was taught by his grandfather. The ceremony lasts moments. When it is complete, when his grandfather has finished his prayers, and he has finished his, and the room is bathed in morning, he quickly pulls on his pants, and reaches for his shirt in the cold room.

A loner—barely noticeable, he is so small against the vast inland ocean—Norval spends hours walking the sandy shore of Lake Nipigon. Looking out to the water, thinking about the story his grandfather has told him, he walks cautiously, wary of Misshipesheu, the lynx-like water manitou, which at any moment might spring out of the lake and snatch him away. As he searches the sky, he notices the darkening cloud, and he wonders if the thunderbirds are watching. Wonders if he is standing on the very spot where it might have happened.

He remembers every word of the story, and the dream that came with it the following night. In living colour he heard the baby's cries as Misshipesheu slithered to shore, its greedy mouth swooping up the child and impaling her on its horns, carrying her into the gloom. He saw the parents return from berry picking and notice the slimy tracks leading from the water's edge to the limb of the tree where they had hung the baby in its tikinagan, cradleboard. He saw the young mother fall to her knees, shrieking, her eyes imploring her husband to do something. Pulling her hair out from its roots. The helpless husband hurrying to collect wood for a fire, taking his wife in his arms and sitting her down. Sparking the flint, gathering the fire, burning wiingashk, he sought pity and called for his spirit ancestors to hear his plea. In an all-night vigil, a journey into the sacred, he prayed to Gitchi-Manitou, the Great Mystery, for intervention. And then, through the darkened sky, a yellow crack of lightning, and the wind picked up as the wings of a giant thunderbird could be heard swooping down onto the lake, and out on the distant horizon the sound and fury of a battle. The thunderbird had the misshipesheu in its giant claws. So bright was the sight and so loud the roar, the parents had to cover their ears and turn away their eyes. In the morning, they found their child's body cast upon the shore.

Stories such as these make Norval want to know more. Unlike other children, who spend their time playing, he chooses to spend his time with his grandfather and accompany him on his visits. Today old Potan is chatting with a fisherman from a nearby village, while Norval kneels beside his beached boat. Running his hand up the smooth wood, he reaches for the image painted on the side of the prow. What catches his eye is a white snake curled as though about to strike. Horns protruding from its red head. His grandfather has told him whoever dreams of such a snake will have the power to become a great shaman, to move through the four levels of the Midewiwin, the Grand Medicine Society. He will become a great conjurer with the ability to change the shape of things, to take knowledge outside the way of the world, all for the good of the people. In the sweat lodge he will call in the spirits of the four directions, the grandfathers and grandmothers, and have the ability to talk to them. In the Shaking Tent ceremony, the conjurer will call in Mukwa, Bear, the powerful one, the carrier of the bundle of Everlasting Life. Potan, deep in conversation with the boat's owner, doesn't notice the boy keenly eyeing the strong design. Doesn't see Norval's finger reach and trace from head to tip of the snake's tongue, slide down to the spiked tail.

Then one day, he is down at the lakeshore when the stories that his grandfather has told him unfold like a comic book before his eyes. A stick in his hand, Norval gets an idea. A simple idea. He glances cautiously over his shoulder to see if anybody is watching. And he does what children do. He begins to draw. Sketching circles and lines in the surface of the sand, he lets the stories guide him. Soon a network of images emerges from a network of stories and entwines him like a spider's web.

This early desire to record the stories, to relive them, takes such hold over Norval that he returns at every opportunity. The beach becomes his canvas, cleaned each time by the inevitable waves. This unrelenting determination to make art will later lead Morrisseau to use any material available to him. Throughout his career he will draw on sand, stone, birchbark, deer hide, moose hide, roofing paper, tar paper, kraft paper, cardboard, pressboard, millboard, plywood, woven paper, drawing paper, mill filter paper, linen, canvas. As for something to draw or paint with, at one time or another he will use stick, pencil, pen, ink, crayon, dye, lipstick, oil paint, water, orange juice, house paint, acrylic, gouache, tempera—even blood. From the time he puts a stick into the sand to make his first tentative drawings, he will spend the rest of his life recording the stories he heard as a child. He will come to say that from one story alone he can create hundreds of paintings. He will create thousands.

Veronique

> *I often wonder today what message I was trying to get across when I first started to paint. I realized at that time there was hardly anything known about the Native people. The only thing you came across is that the Indian people were a bunch of savages in need of salvation.*
>
> —NORVAL MORRISSEAU

SAND POINT RESERVE, northwestern Ontario. Grandmother Veronique loves her grandson and instructs him as she has been taught. In her eyes Jesus Christ is the redeemer, the sacrificial lamb for the all the people of the world. Around her neck hangs a black rosary, a silver crucifix dangles over her chest. She is a woman raised at the hands of the Oblates, who culled her from her family at age six and sent her hundreds of miles away to a residential school, where hundreds of children like herself were deposited. A little girl plucked up by dark birds and carried high above her geography of home, endless trees, rivers, and lakes, as she wiggled like a worm trying to fall free.

Years later, as second wife to Moses Potan Nanakonagos and adopted grandmother to his daughter's children, a shawl covers her head, reminiscent of the crows, while three skirts protect her modesty, one worn over the other. Heeding the teachings of the Grey Sisters, she associates only with women like herself. Those who have seen the Eternal Source of Light. Each evening she kneels on the wooden floor beside her bed and stares up at a small blue and white statue of the Virgin Mary. Her callused knees numbed to the pain. She clutches her rosary and recites the same prayers the nuns taught her upon entering the school.

With little Norval at her side, she is doubly vigilant. She frowns at him for fidgeting and reminds him of the agony of Our Lord on the cross. She has him repeat after her: "Behold me, O Lord, covered with confusion and filled with sorrow at the sight of my faults. I detest them before You with sincere grief for having offended a God so good, so lovable and so worthy to be loved. Was this, O my God, the gratitude that You deserved from me after having loved me so much as to shed Your Blood for me? Yes, Lord, I have carried my wickedness and ingratitude too far. I humbly ask your pardon and I implore You, O my God."

In an act of contrition Veronique asks forgiveness for the sin of her own Indianness, the wickedness the priests continually admonished her for. She hunches her shoulders as though the cane the sisters used was about to come cracking down on her, as it did the moment the devil's language stuck its tongue out of her God-offending mouth. Branded by the fear of damnation, the agony of roasting in the pit of hell for all eternity, she does all she can to kill the serpent inside her. Misshipesheu, the Ojibway water spirit, cast in the shadow of Lucifer.

And Norval, not fully understanding the language of devotion, tries his best to appease his grandmother so she won't be cross with him. Her prayers wash over him like a baptism. He imagines a beatific Christ gazing back at him, luminous and forgiving, and in that moment he too feels all the sin and sorrow of the world, as his hand clasps his grandmother's arthritic fingers.

Then one day, Veronique learns that Norval is to be sent away to school. Though she knows in her heart the school is not a good place for children, that children should not be separated from their family or their community, she finds herself nodding in agreement, the crucifix around her neck like a shiny fishing lure.

Giving up her grandson, no longer anticipating his daily visits, no longer making bannock and tea for him, forces Veronique to her well-thumbed bible, where she turns to Christ's Passion, God's Supreme Sacrifice, Our Lady of Sorrows. Her mind clicks like a box camera and she sees in stark black and white a leather whip flaying a bare back, stripping off flesh. Christ's suffering turned into the suffering of children. In the end Veronique knows she and Potan have no choice in the matter. It is the law. Norval, the oldest of four, will go whether they like it or not.

To Morrisseau, his aunt Cecile will always be a giant, click-clacking across the linoleum floor. Heavy and loud, a black dress, a white lace collar, she barges into his life when he's six and says she knows what's good for him—no backtalk allowed—and nothing is ever the same again. No more countless hours walking through the bush with his grandfather learning the old ways, trapping, trading, making do. "There was never a time when I could say I was hungry," Morrisseau would later say. "My grandfather was a good provider. We always had moose meat in the house. Also oranges, but no bananas! We survived in the old way."

For his auntie, learning the old ways is exactly the problem. She believes that in these modern times a white man's education is of the utmost importance, and it is up to her to see that her nephew receives the schooling he needs. Raised by the nuns herself, she believes that it is her duty to get the savage out of him. She also believes with all her heart that she is doing it for the boy's own good, and he will later thank her for her concern and effort and be grateful.

Morrisseau blames his aunt Cecile for being sent away, and he will blame her for the rest of his life. Derision will drip from his tongue. "My auntie, my father's sister, a white woman, she liked the finer, dainty things in life. A very nice lady with a strict Catholic holier-than-thou attitude." How does Morrisseau come to understand this white auntie? He says that his father, Abel, was part half-breed French extending back to the voyageurs, and his aunt leaned towards the French side of the family. The constant pressure of living with the Lord bent her like a willow in the French direction. So although he sees himself as an Indian through and through, calling himself a born-again pagan, Norval considers his father's sister white to the bone. Bleached by her indoctrination. She is the woman in his life who takes the word of God onto her lap and crochets it into a white cover for her bible and a pair of handcuffs for him. "Why don't you send him to school!" she exclaims to her brother, whose own life is crumbling around him as his wife, Grace, the mother of his children, flounders inside a bottle. "For goodness sakes, he can't continue to run around like a little heathen!" Cecile says with her finger jabbing in the direction of Norval. Abel and his Indian wife, Grace Nanakonagos, have a house full of little heathens, and if they won't do anything about it, then she will.

Norval's aunt convinces her brother that school is the best thing for the boy and arranges to send them to St. Joseph's Roman Catholic Residential School in Fort William. Hundreds of miles away. He isn't told how long he will be gone, but Morrisseau ends up staying at the school for four years. His apprenticeship to Potan, his grandfather, is effectively severed for these years. The tradition of passing on knowledge to the oldest child comes to an abrupt end, pulled up by its roots, when Norval is dashed into isolation and loneliness.

By this time he has been living on and off with his grandparents in their travels between the tiny villages of Grand Bay, Sand Point and Farlinger on Lake Nipigon. And he has begun his journey to becoming Anishinaabe, to becoming a human being, as he has learned to take the stories inside himself, the flower of them pressed to his heart as though between the pages of a book. Until the day he dies, he never forgets what happened to him. The language of his people and the sacred teachings replaced by dumb silence and hate. Those early years never recaptured. Even upon his return home, nothing would ever be the same.

Conversion

AT SCHOOL, Norval plays the movie of his leaving over and over in his head. His auntie arrives at the cabin door accompanied by the Catholic priest and an RCMP officer. His grandmother stuffs a few clothes into a flour sack. Then the officer grabs the boy and swings him into a motorboat. His grandparents stand by watching as it speeds away, and he looks back, too afraid to wave goodbye.

Each evening he lies like a statue in his dormitory bunk, amid rows of whimpering children, and stares up to the ceiling. Remembering what his life was like before he was taken away becomes an exercise in survival, because to forget is to die. He visualizes the smattering of squat log cabins, canoes pulled up along the shoreline, and fillets of pickerel on cedar racks, drying in the sun. He sees himself living on a diet of fresh fish in the summer, with berries and leaves brewed into strong tea, and in winter more fish and moose meat, either dried or smoked. He remembers the fear of starving if they ran out of food and didn't shoot a moose, trap a beaver, or have something to trade for flour for bannock. It could be death if spring came too soon and they couldn't walk out on the ice to fish, if the snow became too thick and heavy, and they got trapped inside their cabins. As hard as those times were, these are the memories he summons to comfort himself in the failing light. Despite everything, they are the good times.

Not like what happens when the priests take notice of him. When they lead him by the hand up the creaky stairs to the second floor and into their change room beside the chapel. Maybe it is his artistic temperament that draws them to him. His constant drawing. Maybe it's the look of him, his long legs. They are always on the lookout for pretty boys. His eyes are closed as tight as the lid of a paint jar as he hears the sound of his zipper being pulled down, feels the slobbering, the damp heat between his legs, and then before him a flushed face telling him to go.

Despite doing what he can to banish these memories, they will remain as vivid as blood from a fresh kill soaking into snow. How he eventually understands what happened is the same way he comes to understand most things. He goes back to his grandfather's stories: the Windigo is a giant beast in the form of a man or woman with a heart of ice. Towering above the trees with its pale skin stretched over its gaunt frame, its long claws and fangs for tearing and chewing, it is afflicted with an unrelenting hunger for human flesh. He remembers that Windigos are everywhere.

Sister Lorenzia

SISTER LORENZIA catches Norval drawing in his scribbler instead of praying. She grabs him by the ear and hauls him up to the front of the class, barks at him to hold out his hands. When the leather strap comes down on Norval's hands nothing comes out of his mouth. No praying. No pleading. No crying. This infuriates the nun and she strikes him harder. His hands ignite from the force of the blow. She grabs him again and shoves him into a broom closet, snaps the door lock. He spends the night curled up on the hardwood floor, clutching his shoulders for warmth, while gasping for breath in the tiny room. Discipline. Discipline. Discipline. The word rings in his head like the bell summoning the children to mass, just as the words dirty, dumb, Indian also ring in his head. It is the language the nuns and priests use to talk to the children.

At St. Joseph's the day is one long prayer. "Our Father Who Art in Heaven," pounded into the children. The children pray before going to bed, upon rising, at mass, before and after breakfast, before and after every lineup, before and after classes, before meals. It is endless. The morning is focused on academic study, consisting of spelling and arithmetic. For the rest of the day, the boys take classes in farming and animal husbandry, which means caring for the animals they raise and butcher. Learn blacksmithing and shoemaking for gainful employment. The girls spend most of their time doing housekeeping, meaning cooking, cleaning and sewing. The priests and nuns running St. Joseph's have one objective: to turn their Indian wards into productive Canadian citizens at the most basic level. And central to that basic training is punishment.

At 5:30 in the morning, Sister Lorenzia hauls Norval out of the closet. It is time to start the day. Together they pray, and she asks God to forgive the boy and to take care of him. She looks at poor little Norval and shakes her head. She too likes to draw, and it has given her a soft spot for him. If she could she would scoop him up in her arms. But this she does not let on. She cannot. It is not encouraged. Instead she straps him for his own good. Sister Lorenzia wants him to understand that his desire to draw must be tempered. She has seen many paintings of Indians in the art gallery in Montreal and the National Gallery in Ottawa, but she has never seen one painted by an Indian. She wonders if such a thing is even possible. When she snatches Norval's scribbler away and rifles through the pages, she tries not to admire the boy's natural talent and determination.

Sister Lorenzia's fondness for drawing allows for one art class a week, for one hour, and like everyone Norval is restricted to that hour. She teaches the children how to hold a pencil and mimic what they see. Religious icons are admired. Still life is tolerated. Everything else is trash. She sets up a box with a vase of daisies on it and teaches the children to draw straight lines, circles, squares. When she is feeling ambitious she will set up a picture of Mary and the Christ child to copy. And she will end up with a stack of stick figures or snowmen. Once in a while, however, a student will attract her attention. This time, the student is Norval. Although his drawings are as rudimentary as the others, she nevertheless can see from his concentration, his clenched teeth, that he believes in what he is doing. She thinks he has the sensitivity to become a priest.

Norval has no idea he will become an artist. It has never crossed his mind. No one has told him such a life is possible. That such a life exists. The birds and animals he hides away in his scribbler help him to remember, bring a surge of memory. In one moment he is standing in a creek cradling a tadpole while his grandfather explains that everything in life changes, everything is in the midst of transformation. It is while drawing that he realizes art holds the power to change reality. He discovers that drawing provides a doorway, a passage, showing him the way home. No matter how many times he gets strapped, he never stops drawing. He never abandons his single-minded goal of returning to the ones he loves.

Wonder Boy

AT AGE NINE Morrisseau is run over by a one-ton truck in the yard of St. Joseph's. The double wheels come down on his skinny body as the tires drive him into the earth and lightning pain shoots through his legs, abdomen, and pelvis. The vehicle sputters to a halt. A metal door slams. The driver scrambles out and grabs Norval's legs and slides him from under the truck. He places the boy on a sheet of plywood and carries his limp body into the church rectory. (Morrisseau will think of Michelangelo's *La Pietà* when he remembers this moment.) The priests and nuns scurry to help. They call the children to assemble. At the sound of the bell the boys and girls come running in from across the schoolyard.

Father Gallagher performs the last rites, and he gazes down at the boy with divine compassion, because to him death can be more rewarding than life. His words are like sacramental wine poured over Norval to relieve his suffering and carry him heavenward: "Oh God, welcome him in your presence, that he may rejoice in you with your saints forever. We ask this through Christ our Lord." He recites the mass with conviction dripping from his lips like divine unction. By now though Norval is so far away that the murmur of prayer for a blessed journey into the embrace of Christ is beyond his hearing.

He finds himself standing in a forest of brilliant green, light dappling through the leaves and crowning his head. Before him, down a long, narrow path, is his grandmother Veronique, making her way towards him. Her black skirt sways from side to side with each stride; her silver crucifix dangles on her bosom. She speaks, and he can now hear. She tells him not to be afraid. "Get up," she says, gesturing upward with a wave of her hand. And he does.

Norval's eyes open to the shock and puzzlement of everyone circled around him. He lets out a moan, as though shaking off whatever has occurred, and slides off the plywood and onto his feet.

For a second there is silence, and then the children cheer and giggle and lead Norval out into the playground, where he slumps down against the heavy wire fence that circumscribes the school. Within an hour he is up and running. The priests and nuns note this act of grace as God's intervention, and keep a watch on the boy who wants nothing more than to go home to his grandparents. Norval's reputation as Wonder Boy spreads throughout the parish and general district, the priests making sure to point him out to visiting clergy. While some speak of God's calling, skepticism abounds among the less devout and various theories are concocted to explain what happened. First, they question the driver's memory, wondering if he only *thought* he had run over the boy. Another explanation relies on the dampness of ground. Is it not soft and yielding? Did the weight of the truck simply push the boy down into the earth? Wasn't he caked in mud? Finally they conclude that young boys have pliable bones that mend easily, so even if he had gotten run over it couldn't have been too serious.

The incident works away at Norval like one of his grandfather's dream serpents. He is puzzled by it. And he returns to the spot where it happened. On his knees, he runs his hand over the ground as though feeling for some trace of the event, searching to understand. He touches his aching body and then looks up to the sky in wonderment.

Eventually he will associate what happened at St. Joseph's with the dogma and language of the Church. The memory of it will become soaked in alcohol like a limb floating in a jar and his explanation of it will shape-shift with the years, but he will continue to see it in the light of his destiny. In the voice of a prophet, he will say that he suffered no ill effects because "the Vessel of the Future, the Preserver of the Ojibways, must live on. No matter the obstacle until he has Accomplished the Purpose that he was Designed to carry out in his Existence." In 1966 he will paint what comes to be known as "Christ's Head," a portrait of a distinctly brown-faced Jesus, and the provocative *Portrait of the Artist as Jesus Christ*, presenting Jesus as a shaman-artist, wearing a red cloak, a medicine pouch, and crucifix around his neck. Portraits of Morrisseau himself. The earliest myth of himself rising from the muck of the schoolyard, interpreted in his earliest paintings.

After four years at St. Joseph's Residential School in Fort William, Norval officially graduates from grade two. At ten he runs away from the school, never to return. He walks from Fort William to Beardmore, where his family is now living, a distance of 120 miles. In a 1979 interview in the *Toronto Star Weekend Magazine*, he will shrug off his time at the school with a wave of his paint-splattered hands, his rainbow-hardened nails, and simply say, "It was alright." Other times he will have the sting of alcohol on his breath, turpentine in an open wound, and he will say in confidence, "The priests raped me." And later, surrounded by a legion of carved penises, attempting to dismiss it, he will say, "It was okay because I enjoyed it."

What he will remember above all about the school, above the constant praying, the solitary confinement, above even the beatings and sexual abuse, is the stench of the basement's dungeon bathrooms. It is the first thing that will come to mind. He will do his damnedest to try and forget it, but try as he might this "chemical smell" will fester in his brain for the rest of his life. When asked about it, Morrisseau will try to remember other things, and he will gaze off in the distance as if some kind of electrical switch were pulled. And sure enough, he will mention the stained glass windows of the chapel. His saving grace. A white Virgin and a golden Christ child framed in red and blue, Joseph and Mary, the light spilling through them, the hue of the colours changing with the time of day. He will remember the benevolence of Christ's touch, of all the saints in Heaven, shining on him through the stained glass, bringing him solace. It is this that he uses to turn off the stink of the disinfectant. This feeling of grace infusing him with the colour and light of the chapel, conjured for protection.

Vision Quest

So Long as I have my Visions and they are truly mine then my paintings will also be truly mine.

—Norval Morrisseau

NORVAL IS TWELVE when his grandfather takes him for his vision quest. It is time for the youth to leave childhood behind and move to the next stage of his seven cycles of life. That summer they paddle to an island not far from Sand Point. When they arrive the first thing they do is go about making a scaffold out of the few birch trees nearby. Potan chops them down with his axe and fashions them into poles, lashing them together with braids of moose hide. Norval will spend four nights with no food and as little water as possible, suspended twenty feet in the air.

Potan tells the boy that during this time a guiding spirit will come and take pity on him. This spirit will guide him for the rest of his life. But beware, his grandfather warns, when it comes, make sure not to open your eyes. If you are fortunate it will come at night when you cannot see it. It may take any shape, a thundercloud, a breeze, an eagle, an otter, anything. Norval is scared, but his absolute faith in and love for his grandfather give him courage. Seeing the boy's fear, Potan assures him he will not be too far away.

During the day, Norval lies on the scaffold overlooking the great expanse of Lake Nipigon, white-tipped waves in all directions. And on the opposite shore, the impenetrable lushness of the bush making him feel more alone than ever. As he watches, he tries not to think of his hunger rolling through his stomach and tightening it like a drum. To ease the ache, he wets his lips but does not swallow the water. Instead he sends it over the side, to the ground below.

At night, raised among the stars, the pale moon, every little sound seems to claw its way towards him. The trees alongside of him creaking in the breeze. The flutter of wings in the branches. The scamper of feet in the brush below. His whole body is wound up to the point of snapping, and he must force himself not to scramble down from his perch and flee. Exposed, vulnerable, as though set on a platter for the taking, Norval burrows himself in the blanket his grandmother gave him and focuses on the light of his grandfather's fire on the shore across the narrows. Then, exhausted from worry and fatigue, he closes his eyes and waits. On the third night, it comes.

By this time, having drifted in and out of consciousness all day, Norval is uncertain of whether he is asleep or awake when he hears it. Unlike all the sounds he has heard before, this he knows is different, and it makes him go absolutely still, sucking in what air he can and holding his breath. From down in the darkness below comes what he will later describe as a thumping sound moving across the ground, getting closer and closer. Finally, it is near him, so near that it is moving around at the bottom of the scaffold. And then, in an instant, a guttural sniffing at the end of his feet, the feel of warm breath through the blanket, moving up his legs to his hips, arms, shoulders... and, try as he might, Norval cannot hold back any longer. Despite his grandfather's warning, he opens his eyes.

And there before him is a huge bear. A gasp, and Norval is up and scrambling. Blood pounding through him, he musters what little strength he has left and climbs down the scaffold. Running to the shore, he yells for his grandfather to help him.

Potan, who has been patiently waiting for something to happen, calls back to him that he will be right there. It is only then, upon hearing his grandfather's canoe approaching, that Norval turns back to the scaffold and realizes the height of it. And wonders how such a bear could have stood next to him and, in the opening of his eyes, disappeared.

Stepping out of his canoe, the first thing his grandfather wants to know is whether or not Norval looked. Ashamed, the boy admits that he did. The old man shakes his head slowly, emphasizing that he told him not to look, but he does not shame Norval. Instead he tells him a story.

> Everything depended upon Bear.
> It was he who was to bring
> the message of everlasting life
> to the people. But the weight
> he carried from the Creator was very heavy
> and Bear had to struggle.
> Three times he tried
> to break through
> from the spirit world
> to the world of the people
> and failed.
> On the fourth try he stuck out his tongue
> and like an arrow
> he passed through
> to the other side.

With a grin, Potan also tells Norval that Bear is so powerful he owns three cities. They could be Chicago, Montreal and New York. He is one of the richest bears in the world. You could have had all the success you want. Yet, despite looking, still you will have a little. He took pity on you. He came to visit you.

Norval will always remember these words from his grandfather. And he will spend countless hours rendering his vision of Bear. *The Shaman Protected by Bear Power, Sacred Bear Quest, The Medicine Bear, Sacred Bear from Vision*—all these and more he will paint. Many years later, Norval, with his own grin, will say: "If I had not looked, I could have had much further success than what I have now, but I am not doing too badly. This is what, my people, I would like them to know."

Instruction

Every day an Ojibway elder dies and every day some of the knowledge of his ancestors dies with him. Only after he is dead is it realized how great that loss is.

—NORVAL MORRISSEAU

NORVAL HAS ALL THE BOLDNESS of a teenager when he decides he wants to make a birchbark scroll and record his dream visions, like in the olden days. To become a part of a tradition extending back beyond memory. Old Potan shakes his head and grins and Norval knows the answer is no. He is too young and has not gone through the requisite training. He doesn't fathom the degree of initiation and teachings required to understand the intricacies of the scrolls, the procedures and rituals required to find one's place in the sacred Grand Medicine Society, the power required to interpret the guardian manitous. And yet, what he does know, even at his age, is that he must act quickly, because aside from his grandfather and a handful of old men scattered across the northland in isolated pockets of poverty, surrounded by an onslaught of priests and missionaries, there are few left who can teach the old ways. His grandfather has told him that their culture is like a cup of spring water and they are at a time in their history when it is cracked and leaking back into the earth. All of it taken away if not for the few who still speak the old language and remember.

In the glow of lamplight, windows covered by blankets against prying eyes, Norval stands beside his grandfather, among the few old men who have gathered together, and watches as a sacred birch-bark scroll is unrolled before his very eyes. The unfurling bark cracks in the hushed room. A thick finger glides over the papery surface, stopping at mukwa (bear), and nigig (otter). Norval hovers over the outstretched bark and detects what he thinks are three figures in a longhouse connected to Sky people. He listens hard to the explanation. What little he knows about the scrolls tells him that each scroll consists of a vision transmitted by a Midewiwin shaman, and that the images have to do with protocol and power, the organizing and transmitting of ancient knowledge. Of the cosmos, above and below. Potan has told him they belong to a time when his people were known far and wide for their greatness, for their shamanism, their ability to conjure and change the shape of things. More than anything, this is what Norval wants. To be part of something so great and immense that it will pull his people up from their poverty and despair, the town dumps and city alleyways. To be a spokesman for his people and to bring about their return to greatness. This becomes his dream, his single-minded goal.

And so the scrolls hold him in their gaze. Once touched he is forever held, and there is no turning away. There is no going out to play with the other kids. No more going to school. What he has witnessed begins to work on his imagination, and he begins to make the connection between the teachings, the lines of power spinning out around him, and the current state of his people. He realizes these sacred teachings once supported his people like a spider web holding onto the moon.

When the community says he will have to wait until he is at least twenty to make a scroll, Norval nods in silence. He understands, but his desire grows as his dreams come alive in brilliant colour, and he turns to drawing with whatever material he can find. And for a while he keeps what he does to himself. When he finally does show off his dream sketches, the local Catholic Indians tell him to stop.

Call him bullheaded when he doesn't. They warn him that playing with the old ways will bring trouble, a swarm of ants, snakes, pestilence. They say what he is doing will turn on him just like it did for the evil shamans of old. Return to him at night in the form of a giant serpent or a misshipesheu with fangs. Norval sees fear glistening in their eyes when they tell him this, the quick way they cross themselves, punctuating every word.

For others the fear is practical. These people tell him that the Indian agent, along with the priest and the RCMP, will come and arrest him. Throw him in jail. They say that what he is doing is illegal. He should know that. Doesn't he know that the law says it is forbidden to practice such things? That he will just cause trouble for everybody. That it is best to leave it alone. And for a while he does stop. By now he has already tasted the fire of whiskey from an enamel cup, and at thirteen he substitutes a bottle for a brush. But the pull of his dream is too great. And he again turns to his grandfather for advice, who tells him that he must make his own decisions. It is a second step.

The first step for young Norval is to learn as much as he can from his grandfather, so he accompanies him and becomes his little shadow. And one day he finds himself in a room crammed with people. An assortment of bundles and boxes are stacked along the walls, packsacks hanging from hooks. The air smells of tobacco, sweetgrass, damp canvas, sweat. It is illegal to perform the Shaking Tent ceremony. The government of Canada has banned it, along with other ceremonies, and everyone in the room is afraid of going to jail. Indian Affairs officials have posted signs warning of the consequences. The RCMP have already made arrests. They announce they are doing it for people's own good. Like the Church, the government is determined to rid the people of superstition.

The talk in the room is about the war. It is finally over. The radio and newspapers announce that freedom has been won in Germany. This means that their sons will soon be returning home. Maybe now they too will be free. Maybe they will get the right to vote. The right to have schools in their own communities. Maybe now they will be allowed to practice their traditions. To live the way they want. The conversation fills the room. Some old men nod in agreement—surely the sacrifice of their sons will make the white man take notice. Others hold little hope for change as long as the treaties are disrespected.

When the conjurer tells them he is about to begin the room goes silent. Though some are skeptical, all are respectful, if not fearful. The ceremony is supposed to take place outdoors with the shaking tent staked to the ground and open to the sky so that the spirits might enter, but the law has forced the ceremony into hiding and into this room. Old Potan has taken his grandson with him to witness it. Norval remains quiet. He is curious but frightened, even though he has absolute faith in his grandfather. He also believes his totem, Mukwa, watches over him. Bear power protects him, he repeats to himself, trying to swell his confidence. He tries not to think of his grandmother's warning that the spirit interpreter Mikkinnuk (Turtle), who will sing or talk for the spirits coming into the tent— be it Bear, Bird, Fish, Thunderbird, Star, whatever—is really the devil.

At the conclusion of the ceremony, Potan admits to his grandson that he is impressed. "A powerful conjurer, that one," he says. He never thought the spirits would come and talk inside a house. Seeing holes drilled into the floor for the tent poles, Potan says that he didn't expect much to happen. Saucer-eyed, the boy is overwhelmed. "I thought the tent was gonna to blow away," he says, thinking about the way it was all puffed up, straining in every direction as though an invisible hand were yanking on it. Like his grandfather, Norval shakes his head at what they have just witnessed. For him, it is new. For his grandfather, this way of doing the ceremony indoors out of sight is also new. Together they learn that although times have changed, their people can adapt to change. To use the old ways in new ways.

Morrisseau takes this thought with him, bundles and wears it, as he thinks about what he has witnessed and seizes on the idea of becoming a shaman. His mission becomes to learn as much as he can about his people: stories of the Midewiwin—the Grand Medicine Society—the ancestral stories, stories of shaman conjurers, creation stories, stories of manitous, of Nanaboozho, Misshipesheu, Maymaygwaysiwuk, Mikkinnuk, Mukwa, Paakuk, Windigo, Nimkey Banasik, and the Thunderbird people, the stories he will one day preserve and render in his paintings. He will go on to say that because the shamans of the tribe were the artists, all his paintings and drawings are really a continuation of the shaman's scrolls.

Nanaboozho

The Ojibway have many legends and stories of a demigod named Nanaboozho. One story tells how he had ten wives, another how he pretended to have died in order to marry his older daughter, yet another how he tied himself to the mighty geese and flew with them up into the air and fell into a toilet.

—Norval Morrisseau

Sometimes when the teenage Morrisseau thinks of the stories he heard as a child he can't help but laugh out loud. He is sixteen and ready to take on the world, but they bring him to remember, and he is again the boy wrapped in a blanket lying on the cabin floor, listening to his grandfather tell how Nanaboozho turned the rocks red after sliding naked down a hill to relieve his itchy bum. Or how he carried his huge penis around looking for relief and pretended to be a dreaded Windigo so that he could frighten the women into lifting their skirts. Morrisseau rolls these and other stories over in his memory to get a closer look, turns them every which way, observing them as a way of understanding the way things are.

His laughter, however, comes to an abrupt stop when another memory intrudes: he and his brother Ronald awake to find themselves abandoned in a freezing shack. They hurry the quarter mile down the dark dirt road to their grandparents' place, a canopy of stars overhead providing the only source of light. In grade three now, Norval already knows how to fend for himself. He knows how to work the damper on the woodstove. How to stoke the stove to get the fire going. How to boil macaroni. With their father gone off on a section gang to repair track, or working in the bush, or just gone, and their mother off with another man, Norval grows up quickly. His grandparents' little cabin becomes a nest where he and his brother stay as long as they can, and where their grandfather's stories are like medicine.

And they would stay with their grandparents until their mother Grace showed up looking for them, limping to the door on her polio-shortened leg, knocking timidly. Or until their grandmother Veronique learned that their mother had returned and shooed them back home. A strict but kind woman they could always count on, Veronique allowed the boys to stay until they became too much for her. Sometimes she showed up at their place unexpectedly, as if a passage in the bible had pointed her in their direction. Her cane swinging like an axe at the front door, they would go outside and listen to her voice rattling the windows, and making the sky go as black as her coat and kerchief, as she confronted Grace. Before long, however, they were back again at their grandparents', with Veronique's reprimands having evaporated like a steaming kettle. No matter what she said, it did little good. She spoke of proper conduct, which meant that Grace should be prudent and modest and above all loyal to her husband Abel, who was good enough to marry her under God's all-seeing eye. She spoke of making do and was quick to point out that Abel provided for her and the boys and had put a roof over their heads. She spoke of shame. Shame heavier than all the fish in Lake Nipigon. Shame that spoke of past indiscretions, spoke of damnation and hell and the white man's way.

All Grace could think about was freedom, freedom from an older man who fought with her, who had been thrust upon her by her stepmother and aunt and above all the local priest, who warned her that she had no recourse. Should she choose otherwise she would find herself abandoned with no family, no money, and no place to go. A poor Indian woman with no education. Three strikes against her. When she looked at the future it was a cave. Her permanent limp a chain around her ankle, pulling her down to a place where she could never be good enough. And so she married and stayed married but endured married life, choosing instead salvation in drink and dreams distant from the life she had with a man who only wanted obedience. She dreamed so fiercely she barely glanced behind her when she closed the door on her boys time and time again, and they found themselves again staying with their grandparents.

When Grace did return—and return she did, because despite everything she loved her children as they loved her—and they were once again settled, she talked to Norval like an adult. As her oldest child he became her confidant, her only friend, and she told him things that he found difficult to understand at his age. And he loved her for it. In those days the family was constantly on the move around the Nipigon area: Grand Bay, Sand Point, Poplar Point, Farlinger. He is not sure why they moved so often, and he wishes to this day they had stayed in one place, but he knows it had to do with the mostly seasonal work: road work, rail work, bush work, labourer stuff, whatever his father could get. They finally ended up in Beardmore, living on a road allowance in a tin shack beside the dump, where they waited until nobody was around and then dived into each new load of garbage. There Norval would sit, perched like a crow on a mountain of sagging cardboard boxes, busted crates, rotting potato sacks, eating mouldy bread or stale cookies to fill his stomach, a comic book in his hand carrying him away to another world. And years later, after residential school, he was still at it. Only now he was rummaging for something special to wear, like a dress, a compact of colours, a half lipstick, a blue bottle of Midnight in Paris.

His eyes widen as he rips open a cardboard box, reaches in and touches the red velvet fabric of a gown with plastic pearls sewn into it. He cannot believe what he has found and holds it up in front of himself to see if it might fit. He is eager to try it on, and he slips it over his head. Wraps a scarf around his long hair and stuffs his big feet into a pair of women's shoes. Takes a few wobbly steps, pretending he is sashaying around town. A slim boy, he admires himself in a piece of mirror hanging in a tree like an ornament, thinking that he makes one hell of a pretty girl, a pretty in-between Agokwa, daring anyone who might see him to say otherwise. Studying himself, he grins cheek to cheek. Morrisseau considers dressing up a phase that he has to go through to understand his true nature.

He is not sure when he heard the story, but he remembers it this way. You see, Nanaboozho was so curious he was always getting himself into trouble. Not only did he want to know what it was like to be a man with a woman, he also wanted to know what it was like to be a woman with a man. He was just like that. Maybe he just wanted to experience the embraces and kisses of a man. Maybe it was in his nature to be both man and woman. He got it in his head to disguise himself as a woman by wearing a dress and attaching a waboose (rabbit) fur between his legs. In the dark village, with only a few stars overhead, he lured a young man to his wigwam and into his bed...

Norval's mother Grace giggles when she sees the sight of him in a dress. Her oldest boy never ceases to surprise her. She asks him why. He shrugs. How can he possibly talk to her about finding himself? He doesn't realize at his age that she has been trying to be someone else nearly all her life. Shaking her head, Grace doesn't question him further. It is the extent of her comment, and he is free to do as he pleases. Nobody knows where he goes, and he does not tell anyone. As far as he is concerned, like Nanaboozho, he too has the ability to transform himself into something else. And he does. He slips into Beardmore, where lumberjacks and miners come in from their surrounding camps and pile into the hotels and bars and drink like it is their last night on earth. As though giant pines or rock walls might fall on them at any moment and crush them like ants. And among them is young Norval, who even in the midst of poverty is looking for something extraordinary, not mere money, or shiny trinkets, but something more akin to knowledge, experience. Norval spends his time around back, or in one of the many booze-can shacks snaking around the village, where hard men with money drink, play cards and go soft for whoever is available. "Just like the wild west," the youth says with a lipsticked grin, extending a hand in greeting, "Indians and all."

Copper Thunderbird

Spring, Zaagibagaa-giizis (Budding Moon), a time for the earth to renew herself, and Morrisseau, at nineteen, is deathly sick. He falls into a rheumatic fever for four days and becomes delirious, beyond recognizing anyone. Burning up like a Jesuit martyr at the stake, he rises to the point of muttering to the woodstove, which now wears a black cloak and speaks back to him. Grace is worried sick and seeks advice from her father, Potan, and her stepmother, Veronique, who tells her that Norval needs to see a doctor. She believes in white man ways to cure white man's sickness. This sends Grace limping down the road to town to fetch the local doctor. After examining the young man and taking his temperature, the doctor moves into action and applies rubbing alcohol to his body to cool him off. When Norval's temperature refuses to come down, the doctor hurries off to a local tourist outfitter and returns with a couple blocks of ice, cut out of the lake in the January freeze and stored in a sawdust cellar for the summer. He lays the young man in a tin bathtub filled with chunks of the ice. Norval's steaming skin melts it upon contact, the steam rising around the tub like the fog of winter.

The ice does little to break Norval's fever, and the doctor packs up his bag and concedes that all they can do is wait and pray for his temperature to come down by itself. Frightened for Norval's life, both Grace and Veronique kneel beside the delirious youth and recite the rosary, their hands clenched to a string of black beads, but Norval's fever refuses to abate. Finally, the women praying help-lessly for forgiveness and intercession swallow their Catholic fear and consider Potan's initial suggestion. They should go get the medicine woman called Agnes from Ignace, a tiny community 250 miles west of Beardmore. Among their people, word of her healing power has spread across the northland like fire. Like the fire they are now trying to extinguish in Norval. Her name is whispered even among the Christian Indians who no longer believe in the old ways. Amongst those who fear her and what she represents.

A couple of days later, the tiny woman arrives dressed in a long plaid skirt and a patched brown sweater. Her grey hair braided in one long plait down her back. Except for the tiny bundle of leather hanging around her neck in place of a crucifix, there is nothing special about her. She looks no different than any other old Indian getting off a train. And yet, there is something about her. Her actions are sure of themselves. Her head is straight, not bent in subservience. Her pride is still intact. Like Potan Nanakonagos, Norval's grandfather, she has not gone to residential school, her parents having long ago secured her a life in the bush to conceal her from the authorities.

Upon looking at Norval, sweating on a mat on the floor, Agnes opens her canvas bag and lays out an eagle feather, her tools, her medicines, tobacco, sweetgrass, sage, cedar, a selection of herbs which she crushes into a cup. The procedure is simple. She has done this healing since she was a little girl helping her mother, who helped her mother. It is in her lineage. Her gift. She will give Norval the drink and then use the flute-like bear bones to suck out his sick-ness. She will pray for him in the old language, Anishinaabemowin, calling upon her ancestors for the blessing of power. She will then enter Norval's dream state to intercede on his behalf and petition the other-than-humans to fix what is wrong. To do so she must consciously navigate the world of the unconscious. She warns the family that if this does not work, the youth will probably die. She begins with a healing song.

When she finally opens her eyes in her place on the floor beside Norval, his fever has broken and he is smiling weakly. His mother is on her knees beside him, wiping his brow, Veronique and Potan beside her. Agnes has had a manitou dream, she tells them. In her healing, she has travelled many times to the spirit world, but never before has she encountered the Thunderbird people. Never has she heard such sound. Never has she seen such light. Never has she been touched by such power.

Agnes tells them that it means great things for the young man. But with great power comes great responsibility. If it is not handled carefully, she warns, it will wrap itself around him like the white man's electricity and harm him. "He will go through much hardship," she says, "but accomplish a great many things for his people. And from this day forward call him by his spirit name, Miskwaabik Animiiki, Copper Thunderbird."

Morrisseau will speak often about how he came to be named Copper Thunderbird and incorporate his spirit name into the ever-growing mythology of himself. His future wife, Harriet Kakegamic, will teach him how to write Miskwaabik Animiiki in syllabics, which he will incorporate into the signature style of his paintings. As early as 1965, he will write about the benefit and burden of such a name: "one Ojibway woman of the Red Lake area came up to me in the street... she thought she would frighten me... She said, 'I have heard about your sorcery and medicine knowledge'... I asked, 'What did you hear?' She said that my name was Copper Thunderbird, a very strong name for an Indian to have unless he was powerful... Indeed, you are a man with great knowledge of the ways of our ancestors." When asked when the naming event took place, Morrisseau will answer, "When Prince Charles was a baby." He will relate the telling of time to an occurrence, an event, much like his ancestors related it to the phases of the moon, rather than to the clock or the calendar. As Morrisseau moves into the realm of thunderbirds and thunderbird power, the everyday of here and now will have little meaning to him.

Harriet

TWENTY-FOUR, sinewy, six-foot-two, Morrisseau is as strong as a bull moose, ready to charge and crack open the world. In the north the air is clean, the water pure, and it fuels his young life as he goes about learning the lore of his people, studying the sacred scrolls, paddling past the pictographs, taking in every word his grandfather tells him, accompanying him to visit other elders. Ritual and story become his daily bread. Trapping with his grandfather in the winter, hunting in the fall, fishing in the spring and summer, guiding tourists, working for the Department of Lands and Forests clearing brush or planting trees, he does what he can to earn enough money to buy a few potatoes, apples, flour, salt—and as many bottles of Catawba sherry or Five Star whiskey as he can. He has been drinking since he was thirteen, and this too fuels his young life.

Father Gallagher, Sister Lorenzia, and the rest of the priests and nuns at St. Joseph's branded into his memory, Morrisseau now has only one desire: to learn as much as he can from his grandfather about the old glories of the people he calls "The Great Ojibway." What they tried to take away from him at school, he now listens for in the soft voices of elders sitting on a lakeshore, or on a stump beside a cabin, or in some rundown beer parlour. And he holds what he finds like a robin's egg and cradles it with the utmost care. What direction this learning will take him, he has no idea, though his vision quest has taught him that the power of belief shapes reality. And so he believes he is a shaman-artist in training, despite a litany of voices nagging at him, warning him that his sinful ways will kill his soul and bring damnation for all eternity.

Life is routine for Norval—pencil and bottle, bottle and pencil—until the day he begins to cough up blood. Too sick to protest, he is sent back to Fort William, the town he walked 120 miles to get away from. When he wakes he finds himself shut away inside a tuberculosis sanatorium, and he calls out in panic, thinking he is back at St. Joseph's Residential School, but his consciousness is fleeting, and he moves beyond walls and windows. For the next week he drifts the dream world.

The doctors think they might lose him, but Norval Morrisseau is alive to another kind of life. The vision that comes he will later describe in a CBC interview: "Behind me is a grizzly bear. In front of me, two water gods, chewing on bones. Something stronger than myself is protecting me from them. Like a shadow. The shadow starts moving. The bear shows his claws. The water gods are coming towards me. I know fear. I run after the shadow. 'Great Spirit! Help me! I am much afraid!' It says, 'I'm the Great Manitou. I'm testing you. Now, here's a charm for you.' And he throws down two pieces of silk, like flags, yes. Light blue and dark blue. Day sky and night sky. 'These will protect you. Go ahead and do these things. Never fear. I will help you.' I woke up."

When Norval finally awakes in the hospital, he is no longer afraid of exposing his culture to the eyes of outsiders. The fear associated with expressing himself has been lifted. The power to create is confirmed. And he comes away with a deeper understanding of himself and his role in the grand shape of things than he could have ever imagined. Without supplies to do his art he uses whatever is at hand, and he begins to do embroidery in the common room with the female patients, sitting among them in his hospital gown. Unlike them, however, he does not use the paper patterns the hospital supplies, but instead creates his own designs.

From this moment on the process of painting himself into existence begins. He strives to return his people to the greatness his grandfather has spoken about by combining the way of the old shaman with the way of the modern artist. When he finally asks for paper and coloured pencils, a sympathetic nurse brings them to him from the children's cabinet, much to the amusement of those around him. His fear of reprimand is gone, and he begins to draw what he knows, the Native vision of the world: thunderbird men and giant snakes battling in the old stories, like the comic book heroes and villains he has reimagined in his own likeness.

And again life is routine for Morrisseau, until the day he sees Harriet Kakegamic. One afternoon he decides to do some drawing and heads for the common room because of its big windows. And there, while deep into his work, he looks up for a moment and comes face to face with another piece of his future. This time it is in the form of a tall young woman wearing a white blouse buttoned to her chin and an ankle-length black skirt. Morrisseau immediately wants to know who she is. She gives him a shy smile and then turns back to the grey-haired man sitting beside her, but he can tell she is curious about the paper and pencil in his hand. He can tell she wants to know what he is doing. He has spoken briefly to the man beside her, a Cree from up north who also has tuberculosis, and he figures the young woman must be his daughter. And so with brashness he holds up the sheet of paper and jabs his finger at the drawing on it. For a moment there is silence as the young woman and the older man inspect a drawing of what looks like a thunderbird. Their eyes shift to the young man. Nobody shows an interest in the old ways these days. They are both speechless. They are taken aback by the young man's bold manner and even more so by his drawing. Neither daughter nor father has ever met an Indian like him before.

It turns out that Harriet Kakegamic visits her father regularly. Morrisseau makes a point of talking to her at every opportunity, and she soon begins to visit with him as much as her father. And Morrisseau comes to expect it. While opening his life to her, he returns to the Catholicism that has been pounded into him for reference, and he comes to see Harriet as his angel, his vision of mercy. To impress her, he tells her his Ojibway name— Miskwaabik Animiiki, Copper Thunderbird—and how he got it, and says he comes from a long line of shamans and has the same power inside of him. He punctuates his statement by tapping his chest and making himself wheeze—making her laugh. She tells him that she is from Sandy Lake Reserve, a fly-in reserve northeast of Red Lake. He has never been that far north and asks if there is any work up there. Her father, David Kakegamic, tells him there is a gold mine in Red Lake. "Half of our reserve works there," he says. "City living compared to Beardmore or Sandy Lake." Morrisseau nods, knowing he will join Harriet up there. Knowing she knows.

In the meantime, to impress his new love, he summons an image from his imagination that makes her marvel in disbelief as it unfolds before her eyes. Without any prior planning, he takes up a piece of paper and draws two bull moose challenging one another over a female. Showing off his budding genius, he winks at Harriet, who blushes and looks away, while he executes the drawing of the moose with their heads bent, their backs arched, their noses touching, steam rising in the heat of their passion. In a few minutes he hands her the sketch, shrugging it off, suggesting that it's really not difficult, and he can do far greater things. No sooner does he hand it to her, he is on to something else, a sketch that will become a giant Misshipesheu swooping fish up in its claws, a greedy Windigo devouring a teepee full of people, creatures and scenarios that both amaze and frighten Harriet.

On the day that Morrisseau proposes to her, he borrows scissors from one of the nurses and cuts a heart-shaped pattern from a strip of paper. Fastening the paper to his head so that it sits like a headdress or crown, he presents himself as a shaman apprentice who will eventually evolve into a full-fledged shaman and one day a grand shaman. By now he is beginning to see his drawings as visions of his inner life, and drawing daily, he comes to believe that whatever shamanist power he holds is tied to these visions. It is a belief that he will cultivate throughout his life. But for now the sight of his antics makes Harriet laugh, which makes him laugh, and she says yes to his proposal. And they begin their time together. The blessed good times mixed and shaken well, followed with a strong dose of heartache and suffering.

Archaeologist of the White Man

AUGUST. 9:15 A.M. Forecast: tinderbox trees stretching for rain. Cloudless sun blasting empty bottles into molten glass. Breeze, none. The shrill of cicadas erupting in the spiky grass and weeds around the shack.

Morrisseau wakes up so hungover he has to pry his tongue off the kitchen floor. He can't remember passing out, can't remember much of anything, because at this point in his life he is already perfecting the art of forgetting. He looks over to his wife Harriet asleep in the one bedroom, the ceiling above her head looking like it's about to cave in. He thinks that soon they will move to a better place. On all fours he crawls over to a tin bucket, sticks his head into it, and begins to lap up the water. His tongue shrinks back inside his head, the lake water almost but not quite quenching his thirsty craving, the parched need that will plague him to his dying day.

Still dressed from yesterday he has only to shove his bare feet into a pair of black rubber boots—the only footwear he has at the moment—to prepare for his escape. He grabs the empty bucket, and in a minute he is out the door and a few yards into a clearing of grass and dandelion where he finds himself standing on the edge of the garbage dump. His shack, banged together out of the remnants of his parents' old place and an assortment of discarded lumber and old tin signs, is erected on a Department of Highways right-of-way. Land designated not fit to use because it is too close to the town's dump. Located in the near middle of what Morrisseau has come to call the archaeological zone.

The first thing he does is look around so he doesn't end up face to face with a hungry black bear. It has happened before. One day picking through the refuse he suddenly heard a sniffing sound and looked up, and a few feet away from him was a huge male bear. It reared up, poking its black nose into the air to take in his scent. Knowing he couldn't outrun it, Morrisseau chose a tactic his grandfather had taught him. He filled his lungs to the point of exploding and let out a burst of "get-the-hell-out-of-here." And then in his own language: "Maadja!" He swept his arms in the air as though brushing the bear away. And it worked—the brute scurried off. Morrisseau continued on with his business.

What he does see today is a new load of boxes, and he drops the bucket and stumbles towards them. Stepping over a heap of twisted metal and rotting vegetables, ignoring the stench, he reaches his newfound booty. Someone has thrown away a few small sheets of plywood, which he puts aside. He will use these to paint on. He then rips open a cardboard box and to his delight sees that it contains half a dozen comic books. A precious find unearthed. Remnants of an ancient civilization where ordinary people had the ability to transform themselves into superheroes, Superman, Batman, Wonder Woman, wearing colourful costumes, capes and crowns, flying above the crowds, swinging from buildings. It is something that catches Morrisseau's imagination. The world white people have created for themselves never stops amazing him. Plunking himself down on one of the sheets of salvaged wood, he begins leafing through the pages, his lips mouthing the balloon words of the story, his finger tracing the colourful images. The everyday world around him for a moment forgotten.

An archaeologist of the white man eager to share his findings with his wife, he marches back to the house with the comic books under his arm. By now Harriet is boiling a pot of blueberries over an open fire and looks up when she hears him and doesn't know whether to smile, frown or weep. Blankness falls across her face. Norval can see the disappointment in her eyes, not because of the slightness of the gift, but because of where he has brought her to live. Beside a dump. And so far from her own people in Sandy Lake. To cheer her up he will lie beside her later that evening and open a page to a world of magic. And together they will read. Then, when the last light is gone and it is too dark to read, he will tell her his stories that go back to his grandfather's grandfather. He will prove to her that they are equally as fantastic and magical.

In the middle of telling Harriet a story about the Maymaygway-siwuk, the little people who dwell inside the cliffs of mammoth lakes like Nipigon, an idea comes to him. One day he will write a book himself and draw pictures in it, and it will show the white man that his people have a great ancestral culture too. Staring up at the ceiling as though it were a large blank page, he can already imagine what it will look like: an ink drawing of a demigod adorning the cover, a dozen full-page illustrations inside. In a voice brimming with confidence, as though the book were already printed and published, he tells Harriet that it will be a tribute to his grandfather Potan, for keeping the stories alive and passing them down to him. Harriet smiles to herself, listening to her man go on about all the things he is planning to do, his enthusiasm making him nearly levitate off the floor. She considers his tall boyish frame for a moment, and she thinks that her husband has so many things going around in his head that he is like a gust of wind twirling in the four directions. Then, almost immediately, her mind turns to worrying about what they will eat tomorrow.

Morrisseau too is worried, but not for himself. Doing without, living from one day to the next without knowing where his next meal was coming from, is an art he mastered long ago. Now it is different. He is not alone. He has a wife, and a baby on the way, and he is the husband who is supposed to provide for them. His plan was to return to his hometown to marry Harriet and be close to his grandfather, but living in a tarpaper shack with a tree growing through the roof, barely getting by, isn't enough. It is something he can see as plain as an overcast day from the look on Harriet's face. And so he decides to heed Harriet's father's advice and move to Red Lake where his brother Ronald is already working. In love like never before, Morrisseau would agree to anything for Harriet's sake, because when he snuggles up to her he is like a bear nuzzling deep down in its den.

Dusk. Harriet is asleep, and Morrisseau wants to make good use of the last light. He gets up, pulls on his pants, and sits at the rough-hewn kitchen table and holds his blunt crayon tenderly over the brown wrapping paper.

He wipes a strand of black hair from his face and looks up out the cabin window to the darkening spruce, and he is drawn into the penumbra of dying day. An owl descends on a chipmunk scurrying for its little life as the bush stirs in the receding light and a pair of bright yellow eyes stares back at him. Norval closes his own eyes and captures this world inside himself.

For now his aim is in the telling, and he doesn't think about *how* he is going to do a painting. That will come later. For now he just does it.

And there he is—calling in his spirit helpers—immersed in the sacred rites of the Midewiwin, Grand Medicine Society, in the wind-stirred voices of a Shaking Tent ceremony, in the wrenching heat of the sweat lodge. As his hand reaches for a braid of pungent sweet-grass, a gallon of screw-top wine, a bottle of Five Star whiskey, for whatever it takes to draw out *that thing* inside of him. (He will go on to say that he paints much better after a big drunk.)

His imagination carried by the same thing that drives migrating birds, or generations of butterflies, Morrisseau begins to relive a story his grandfather Potan has told him. And there before him, emerging out of Lake Nipigon, the land of *his* forefathers, is great Misshipesheu, water dripping from its scales, as Anishinaabek life fills the artist completely.

And like a loon calling the evening in, Morrisseau breaks through the surface of the blank paper. And he makes his first mark.

Thunderbird and Snake

A man rides on the wings of a thunderbird.
The man's body far below is hunger he is always hunger.
For the sweet flesh of the vine.
The man prays for repentance. It does no good.
When the sun is down he goes out of his mind with appetite.
He slides along the ground. Into anything.
He dreams for his thunderbird spirit to come in for the kill.
The man wants to destroy this body that has a mind of its own.
He begins with three dots of yellow for eyes: thunderbird. man. snake.
Begins with creation: sky world. world. underworld.

Red Lake

The RED LAKE of today is not one town but a group
of municipalities built around the mines of the area.
The total population of the group of communities—Red
Lake, Balmertown and Cochenour, McKenzie Island and
Madsen—is not large, possibly 5,100 over-all. The first
suggestion of possible mineral riches was made in 1872…
—"THE RED LAKE GOLD FIELD,"
MINISTRY OF NATURAL RESOURCES, 1969

TO GET TO RED LAKE, Morrisseau follows a rough gravel road straight
north until it comes to an end. And he arrives at the frontier. There
he finds himself at the hub of isolated mining towns and fly-in
Indian reserves spread out among endless lakes and rivers flowing to
James Bay and the Arctic Ocean. A community of miners, merchants,
prospectors, pilots, trappers, hunters and fishermen, the town of Red
Lake itself is a beehive of activity dominated by the Red Lake Inn,
the Snake Pit Lounge, the Hudson's Bay and Simpsons-Sears stores
and docks of float planes waiting like sentinels at the ready, flying out
to over sixty bush camps in the region.

Held up at the Red Lake Inn on the main street, he hears grum-
blings that the McKenzie Red Lake Gold Mine opened in 1935
on McKenzie Island is operating at half capacity. The word is it's
running out of ore and will soon be closing. The bad news means
that the company will be renting out houses. Morrisseau chocks it
up to destiny and stakes out a house on the island, a short ferry ride
from the village of Cochenour on the mainland.

Because more than half of the miners are already gone, Norval
is able to rent a small abandoned house for next to nothing. And
as soon as he and Harriet move in, he goes about painting it. After
purchasing a couple cans of paint from the hardware store in Red
Lake, hitchhiking back to Cochenour to catch the ferry, hauling the
cans up the steep gravel road to the house, he paints its two rooms

in a myriad of stylized designs: flowers, animals, birds, Anishinaabe demigods radiating power from wingtips, claws and eyes. He covers the house from floor to ceiling, as though he and Harriet were living inside a mural. A romantic dream for the newlyweds, who look up from their bed to the world swirling in a mythic cosmos.

At twenty-seven Morrisseau makes art to survive. He does what comes naturally and paints on sheets of birchbark or on baskets that he and Harriet stitch together by lamplight, carving wooden ladles and bowls, and selling them for a few dollars to tourists, dropping them off at Fergie's General Store. He would love to be successful and make a good living doing his art, but it has never once crossed his mind. The idea of being a professional artist is something beyond what he knows. It is a gift wrapped tightly, not yet opened. What he creates he does in his spare time, in the time between looking for real work and drinking.

Their dream is short-lived. Soon Morrisseau gets lost inside McKenzie Island's Gold Eagle Hotel, Red Lake's Snake Pit bar, and spends what little money they have on drink. And Harriet is left wondering when he'll come home. Left to go begging for an IOU to Fergie's General Store or McKenzie Meats, where with her head bent she promises to pay them back as soon as she gets their welfare cheque. The owners look down at her, pregnant and starting to show, and feel sorry for her. Unable to turn her away, they turn towards the shelf of canned goods while cursing Morrisseau under their breaths as a lazy, shiftless Indian who can't even support his own family.

Their resentment is so sharp that Harriet feels it like a knife going through butter. "No, that's not the way it is!" she wants to say, but instead she shrinks away. More than anything she wants to tell them her husband is trying to get a job in the mine and that he will come in with some bark paintings and baskets they can sell to tourists. But it isn't in her to say such things to white people, and she mumbles a few words of thanks and leaves quietly.

Patrons

BY THE TIME Norval Morrisseau meets Dr. Joseph Weinstein and his wife Esther, the Weinsteins have been living in the tiny village of Cochenour for four years. After moving from bustling Montreal to Paris, Weinstein, artist and humanitarian, seizes the opportunity to become head doctor at a local hospital in remote northern Ontario. The position includes serving the four gold mines in the area, the townsfolk, the local lumberjacks, and the Native reserves from Red Lake to Hudson Bay. His original plan was to practice there for maybe a year, make a contribution, gain some experience, save some money and then move on. Away from the blackflies and mosquitoes big enough to drag you away. Four years later he and his wife are still there, wondering if they will ever leave.

The day Esther sets out to buy groceries at Fergus McDougall's general store on McKenzie Island is much like any other summer day. A warm breeze is blowing off the lake under an azure sky. She hires the local boat taxi to take her across Bruce Channel, a short ride from Cochenour, allowing passengers just enough time to soak in the scenery. Harold, the boat operator, is an arthritic old man with a grey unshaven face who complains constantly about the immoral behaviour of various locals, especially the Indians. When they arrive he waits for her at the dock.

As Esther manoeuvres her way through the narrow aisles laden with everything from wool socks to canned goods, she spots what appears to be a roll of painted birchbark on the floor next to a box of wilted lettuce. Like her husband, who studied art at the School of the Art Association of Montreal and later at the Académie de la Grande Chaumière in Montparnasse and the École des Beaux-Arts in Paris, Esther is committed to the principles of modernism, with its appreciation of world art traditions. She has also studied the archaeology and languages of ancient cultures at the Sorbonne, so her curiosity is piqued the moment she sees the rolled-up painting. She picks it up, unfurls the curled sheet of bark and holds it up to the window. Strange mystical creatures stare back at her. Taking her time, she examines the bold images, and can barely contain her excitement. She buys the painting on the spot. There is no doubt in her mind that it's a magnificent work of art by a very talented artist. McDougall charges her five dollars and waits for her reaction. She pays without attempting to barter and even goes so far as to ask him to tell the artist that she and her husband, the doctor, would like to meet him.

Even though McDougall is getting a commission on the sale, he nevertheless shakes his head and hints that she is wasting her money. At the door, she turns and calls out that if the artist returns with more pictures, put them aside for her. She will take whatever he has. McDougall shouts after her that she can have them all because nobody else wants them. Harold the boatman also dismisses the strange picture. On the ride home he questions why she would pay good money for worthless scribbling. Esther knows there is no use in trying to convince him otherwise. Instead, she smiles and holds the painting to her chest, fearful it might blow out of her hand and into the water.

Walking into the Weinsteins' home, Morrisseau notices that the wooden floors shine golden in the afternoon light. He cannot remember ever having seen floors like this before. He kicks off his black rubber boots and stands in the entrance.

The Weinsteins have been waiting to meet the artist, whom they will later describe as "a tall, spare, native Indian with a boyish figure, shiny black hair, and a brown complexion." Joseph reaches out to shake his hand. Esther stares at his bare feet.

"My name is Norval," he says. "I have brought you some art." In their various trips to town, they have heard stories about Morrisseau from the locals. Mostly they mention his drinking, and only inciden- tally his art. Today he looks sober, and under his arm is a large roll of birchbark.

Seeing Morrisseau in her house, Esther thinks back to the day she first laid eyes on his painting, and tries now to make the connection between the man and his art. She remembers thinking the image was crude, primitive, what modern painters like Picasso were using as inspiration for their own work. The perspective flat. The colours natural. Earth tones. Red. Green. Brown. Yellow. Yet the theme of Morrisseau's work was unlike anything she had ever seen before. Mesmerizing. She was astonished by the figure of a weird bird-like creature with jagged claws—a thunderbird, she would later learn—lines emanating from its body towards an odd bear-like figure. Done in what looked like a combination of wax crayon, the kind children use, and house paint. And on birchbark! Of all things. She remembers thinking she had never seen anything remotely like it, although in hindsight Paul Klee's experiments on burlap came to mind. There she was—Esther Weinstein, an educated, cultured woman, who has lived in Paris, who has dined with the Picasso family, who has collected art and artifacts from all over the world, Europe, Africa, Australia, Tibet—in a country store of all places, at the end of the earth, experiencing the shock of discovery, the shock of genius.

With a wave of his hand, Joseph Weinstein beckons Morrisseau to follow them in. They enter a large sunny room dominated by art and shelves of art books. Morrisseau stands for a moment in awe, his head shifting from side to side, taking it all in. Stunned by the display, by the welcome, he looks to his hosts, the stocky man in a tweed jacket, and the lovely, well-dressed woman beside him. He has entered the inner sanctum of the white man, a place he has never been invited into before, and he sees that these white people are unlike any other he knows. He sees they understand and appreciate culture, his culture.

For there before him, hanging in the centre of the living room, is his own painting. His eyes fasten on it for a moment as his hosts stand aside and watch for his reaction. A quick smile opens his face. He then turns back to the Weinsteins without a word, as though studying their peculiarity, and hands Esther the painting he has brought with him. As she and her husband unroll it, his mind briefly goes to the local townsfolk, like Harold, the boat-taxi operator, whose belief in the superiority of the white man is shown in his disdain for Norval's people. He wipes away the thought and now takes in the room and notices a collection of African masks, Tibetan thangkas, ancient Egyptian bas-reliefs. It dawns on him that they have hung his painting proudly among them. The art of great civilizations.

From that first encounter Morrisseau returns often to the Weinstein home, to sell his paintings and to sit and read from their extensive library, the beloved books they have lugged with them deep into the northern bush, the subscriptions to contemporary art magazines. With the turn of each page, the world opens for him, and he finds himself basking in the tropical Africa of Benin bronzes, the windswept tundra of Inuit sculpture, the rainforest of Haida Gwaii totems, the sights of Picasso's modern Paris. And it comes to him that what his grandfather has taught him rings truer than the toll of any church bell, the truth of it sinking to the bottom of his soul like a plumb line dropping to the source, and he reaffirms to himself that he too belongs to a great culture. His mission becomes clearer than ever: he will bring the great Ojibway back into the light.

Although Joseph Weinstein has exhibited his own paintings in Paris, he never once tells Morrisseau what or how to paint. As far as he is concerned, Morrisseau is already a talented and creative artist in the process of developing his own unique style. Only once, when Morrisseau shows up unexpectedly with a few drawings that he has obviously whipped up to sell for a bottle, does he reprimand him. Morrisseau responds by standing quietly with his head bowed, in shame, while Weinstein assures him that he is prepared to help him and his family. But the moment Weinstein finishes speaking, Morrisseau reacts like he has just woken up and reaches with both hands and grasps the few dollars Weinstein holds out for him. After a moment of hesitation, as if he might acknowledge the gift, he instead turns and leaves without looking back. From these first visits Weinstein becomes aware that the expected rules of behaviour, the protocols and social graces one would expect, do not apply to

Morrisseau. He also knows that they can never become intimate friends, though friends they will remain.

Like his wife Esther, Joseph Weinstein recognizes that what Morrisseau has to offer is unique, a one-of-a-kind talent. But he brings another perspective to their encounters: that of a doctor. Having now worked in the north for years, he has been witness to what he calls a people in the midst of self-destruction: the drunken brawls, the knife and gunshot wounds he is called to mend at all hours of the day and night. He has seen firsthand the results of the swarm of missionaries descending upon the first inhabitants and stripping them of their culture and traditions. The inhospitable land of spruce and shield a fertile ground for missionaries of every conceivable denomination. And the result: a people who lived for centuries by the four cardinal directions now without direction, floundering like a moose caught in a bog, sinking hopelessly in a mire of confusion and chaos.

But Weinstein also sees that a few have held on to whatever remains. To whatever they have managed to salvage and conceal of their oral traditions, their religious customs. Norval Morrisseau is one such person. Although he too is clearly not unscathed, and is more often than not at odds with himself, balancing precariously on a high-wire between traditional and Christian beliefs. At least that is how Weinstein sees it.

Outsiders themselves, the Weinsteins firmly believe that primitivism has its own intrinsic value—as the great Picasso, himself, discovered—and it is this belief that is the foundation of their relationship to Morrisseau's art. Likewise they both believe that Morrisseau's day will come, and after buying another painting during that first visit, they make it clear to him that they will support his work and purchase it. They will become his patrons. Joseph Weinstein will pay five dollars apiece for whatever painting catches his or Esther's fancy. He will also acknowledge what he calls their "unusual friendship" by giving Morrisseau art supplies and access to their library. Morrisseau will visit frequently and will bring toys he makes out of birchbark for their children. Joseph Weinstein can see this relationship is good for both of them. He also likes the young man, and considering what he has witnessed as a doctor in the community, he feels it is the least he can do.

Grandfather Stories

MORRISSEAU STANDS ON THE DECK of the ferry taking him across the channel back to McKenzie Island. He flicks his cigarette into the water and looks out to the few lights dotting the island, the evening wind blowing straight through him. He is thinking about the Weinsteins' offer, and anticipating the look on Harriet's face when he tells her the good news. He also realizes that he will have to go to Beardmore to see his grandfather. As he explained to the Weinsteins, "All the pictures that you bought from me are taken from the dreams of my grandfather." He knows many stories by memory, and has even begun to write them down, but to continue to produce he will need more. Later, he will learn to extract many interpretations from one story, from which will come many paintings, but for now he is dependent upon his grandfather. And as there is a price for nearly everything, there is a price for each story: a bottle of whiskey, a package of cigarettes, a roast of moose meat, a fresh fish—whatever it takes he will have to supply it.

In spite of poverty and four years spent in residential school, Norval Morrisseau has good fortune on his side. Though if asked he would say that he does not believe in luck. It is not part of the Ojibway belief system. Whatever good fortune he has he credits to his grandfather, Potan, the man who raised him in a world of manitous and demigods. Old Potan will simply shrug when his grandson later points to him. He has done his best to ignore the influx of Christian missionaries and all that has come with them since the area first opened to the fur trade a century ago, and later to mineral exploration. By taking a young Morrisseau out on the land, by making sure he did not forget his Ojibway language, and by following the old ways, Potan has managed to give his grandson the tools he needs to become a shaman, an artist.

The relationship between Morrisseau and his grandfather is therefore as close as ever, and he travels frequently between Red Lake and Beardmore. In Beardmore, he is nothing less than a dutiful grandson, and he is happy to pay the old man for his stories. Sometimes when he visits he brings over a bottle, and they drink together. Occasionally Morrisseau will become unruly and Potan has to throw him out, telling him to sleep it off in the woodshed. Morrisseau's violence is never directed at the old man and rarely at his own people—it is most always at the white man. What others think, he verbalizes. More than once during a bout of drinking he has ripped up a painting, scattering it in a fury. "The white man don't deserve them. Don't even deserve to see them!" he often exclaims. The next day, contrite, head lowered, he is back selling them for whatever he can get.

Sometimes when he prods his grandfather for a story, uncapped bottle in hand, Potan surprises him, grins, shakes his head, and says, "No more." The old man will then go and sit in the shade of a big jack pine. At those times he is referring both to the drink and the stories, and all Morrisseau can do is wait. When Potan decides to stop talking and screws on the cap, his grandson lets him go without an argument, another unspoken rule, and he takes up his black spiralled notebook and writes down what his grandfather has told him so far. The wait is a lesson in patience and humility. Potan tries to cultivate these sacred teachings in his grandson, and Morrisseau is eager to learn. For this reason he will strive to take everything in his life in stride, the good and the bad, and always see it all as his destiny, as part of the Great Mystery.

In 1968, a few years before his grandparents pass on to the spirit world, a CBC reporter interviews Morrisseau and asks him what his grandfather thinks of his paintings. Morrisseau turns to the old man who is sitting beside him on a bench and asks him in their Anishinaabemowin. After a moment he turns back to the interviewer.

"He says it's okay." Although Morrisseau has always dreamed of making art, the idea of becoming a professional artist—now that he knows such a thing exists—surprises him as much as it surprises his grandfather. While he has always believed great things were in store for him, he had no idea that selling his birchbark paintings at Fergie's General Store would lead to this.

Later when the camera is turned off he tries to explain to his grandfather that white people have places called art galleries where they display whatever you make and even sell it for you.

His grandfather raises his eyebrows, his soft face breaking out into a toothless grin. He shakes his head but says nothing. In the old days everyone wore their art, lived in it, the totem designs you inscribed on your clothes told others who you were, from headdress to moccasins, medicine bag to weapon, the wigwam that encircled you, everything was made to hold beauty, so that you might walk in beauty. Or you painted or etched it on rock, or incised it on bark, so that others might learn, take heed, know the power of a place.

Morrisseau waits to hear what his grandfather will say as he holds up a drawing of a thunderbird with lightning emanating from its claws. Coloured pencil on wrapping paper. He does not do this to seek Potan's approval, but rather to show his grandfather a concrete example of what he has decided to do with his life. Unlike his grandmother and auntie and others in the village, Potan has never tried to dissuade Norval from doing his art, has never told him that what he is doing is taboo. On the contrary, the old man is well aware that change is all around them. Indians can now vote. What next? A couple of years ago when Norval first began to dabble with paint and his auntie called him bullheaded and warned him against such devil practice, his grandfather had simply said, "Don't pay any mind. It is you who has to decide."

In fact, only once did he intervene to curb the boy's enthusiasm, the time Norval wanted to make a sacred birchbark scroll and etch his dreams into reality. Without a word he had taken the boy by the arm and shook his head, no. But that was then, and he now sees that his grandson will do what he has to do. He is ready to make his own scrolls, draw them in a new way, his own way. This he can see as clear as the medicine picture that Norval holds before his eyes. Who would have thought? Instead of responding directly to his grandson's picture and the idea of interpreting the old stories visually, Potan tells him the story of Beaver Blood—a story stretching far beyond his old eyesight.

With his finger pointing to the dabs of red in the painting, Potan begins: "In another time, our people of this region around Lake Nipigon told of a family of giant beavers. These beavers came out each morning to bask in the sun and feed on tender trees they would take with just one bite of their razor-sharp teeth. And yet, even though they had such great power themselves, they were always on the lookout for the hungry thunderbirds, who lived in the sky world and were the most powerful of all manitous. Even when sleeping the beavers kept one eye open. As for the thunderbirds, they'd disguised themselves as clouds and waited patiently for the giant beavers, always searching below with their powerful eyesight.

"Then one day it happened. A giant white beaver forgot to keep his eye open. The thunderbird, in the form of an angry cloud, swooped down onto the giant beaver with his great claws ready and drew him into the air. As the claws sank deep into the flesh of the beaver, out poured all this sacred blood, so sacred that the moment it fell to the ground in the Thunder Bay area, it instantly turned into red sand—what the white man calls iron oxide. This is why we have so much of it here. It's what the Indian people used to use to record their sacred visions and dreams on the rocks. This is why after all these years it still hasn't faded away. It's all beaver blood."

Morrisseau thanks his grandfather for the story. He would normally pay him for it, but this story he can see is a gift. He recognizes that it is a story his grandfather wants him to have, perhaps just for confiding in the old man. What he is about to embark on he does not do in isolation. Behind him is a long lineage of painters, storytellers, shamans, just as there will be generations to follow. In his own way, Potan knows that his grandson has a gift unlike others, and that what the white man calls opportunity has opened up like a forest path for him.

Indeed, what Potan sees in front of him is beyond the painting. It is like his grandson has used the sacred teachings to conjure a path for himself. Each person his grandson meets along the way, for now the doctor and his wife, will be a stone step to support him. And each step will lead to another until he is across a vast lake, but what he will encounter on the distant shore is yet to be determined. What Potan does know is that his grandson will not have an easy time of it. As the stories foretell, in the taking of power there is always a price to pay, just as each story demands a gift, a piece of oneself, and the price can sometimes be higher than expected.

Constable Bob

For Morrisseau, the artist's life has many beginnings: the day he paddles past a pictograph, holds a birchbark scroll, hears a story from his grandfather, sells his first painting. One such beginning is June 7, 1960, a typical blackfly-infested northern Ontario spring: the day Constable Robert Sheppard of the Ontario Provincial Police sits down at his oak desk on McKenzie Island and writes to Selwyn Dewdney, an artist and amateur anthropologist conducting field research for the Royal Ontario Museum. He tells Dewdney that there is a young Indian from Beardmore who may be of use to him. He is looking for work and oddly enough does his own artwork. Sheppard is so impressed that in promoting the young artist, he even sends Dewdney a few crayon drawings. He says that "the artist's name is Norval Morrisseau, and he has had grade school but has done plenty of reading, and he himself studies and collects Indian lore as well by way of being an artist. He has plenty of access to his material being an Indian himself."

Having met Dewdney the previous year, Sheppard is certain he will jump at the chance to meet Morrisseau, who appears to know more than most about his culture. Although Bob Sheppard has no formal training in art or anthropology himself, he nevertheless has a deep interest in Native culture, and he does what he can to facilitate Dewdney's trip to northwestern Ontario to record ancient Anishinaabe rock paintings. Sheppard helps him identify the sites and goes so far as to lend him his boat and motor when Dewdney arrives later that summer. He will also spend hours describing the Ojibway dances he has witnessed and will even try to learn a couple of the songs.

The local Ojibway have an explanation for Sheppard's openness to their culture. And they still chuckle when they tell the story. It turns out Constable Bob was a bully who was bent on making life miserable for them. Quick to throw them into a cruiser and lock them up. Didn't want to hear their troubles. Had no heart to listen. Until one day a few of them got fed up and took up a collection, raised the requisite payment, shoved all their bills and coins into a tin can and set out on a journey—to where tradition speaks of another reality. They got hold of a trustworthy boat and rode all day to a remote site out on Red Lake to see a shaman. To see if he would do something about Constable Bob.

Red Sky, who was outside mending a fishing net with his grandson, knew they had come to seek his help the moment he saw them approaching through the waves. It was the only time anybody came to see him, and even those visits were few and far between. With all the drinking and carrying on in the village, he preferred to be alone with his family anyway. Once, he had sent out word that he was going to conduct a spring ceremony and nobody showed up. Too much Jesus in everybody, he thought. The way he saw it, he had no problem accepting Christ, or at least in the idea of Christ, but he also believed that one way did not have to rule out the other.

What the locals needed to bring besides payment was something that belonged to Constable Sheppard so that the shaman would have a trace of him. One of the group had what Red Sky needed: inside the police cruiser, he had sneezed and sneezed until Sheppard grabbed a hanky from his back pocket and shoved it into the man's face. As expected, Bob waved off the hanky when it was offered back to him. Now the man unwrapped the blue cloth from a piece of paper like a precious gift. Red Sky took the hanky in his hand and held it up to his nose and frowned. There were two smells on the cloth, and he would have to distinguish between them. He sniffed the man who gave it to him. At that moment another man offered the tin can of money. He nodded, but didn't bother to glance into it. They told him about Constable Bob and said that they didn't want anything bad to happen to him—whatever the conjurer did could very well come back on them—they just wanted to soften him up. Have him understand them, or at least understand their ways.

After Red Sky heard them through, he sent them away. And soon after, Constable Bob started dealing with the local Ojibway very differently. They knew Red Sky's conjuring was responsible, but they were nonetheless bewildered by Sheppard's sudden change of attitude. Now when they see him coming they wave and accept his ride home.

And then, along comes Morrisseau. Bob Sheppard knows he is out of work and has a new wife and child to support. He also knows the young man drinks like a sturgeon from the depths of Lake Nipigon. He has stopped him more than once. Caught him staggering down the road with a bundle of his paintings under his arm. The first time Sheppard bought one of them himself and then put Morrisseau on the ferry back to McKenzie Island. Another time it was a late winter night, and he drove him to jail. Funny thing, Morrisseau didn't seem to mind; the jail was warm, and Sheppard saw to it that he was okay. And what impresses Sheppard even more than the young man's art, which he is trying to understand, is his keen intelligence and desire to record the ancient customs and beliefs for what he calls the benefit of his people. As far as Sheppard is concerned, they need all the help they can get. He prods Dewdney for a response. "What do you think the boy's chances are? He can draw and paint, grew up with the people and knows the stories by heart. It seems a shame that his talents can't be made useful and available."

Sheppard believes that Selwyn Dewdney is the ideal person in the ideal position to help Morrisseau. With his connections in Toronto, he holds the key to the young man's future. Like Sheppard himself, Dewdney will surely recognize his talent, the resource they have in him. "Let me know if you are interested in meeting him and I'll get in touch with him even if he moves. Above all, send me back the drawings and stories when you have seen and read them because he wants to keep them." In championing Morrisseau, Sheppard takes on the role of guardian and steward as though something were propelling him. Perhaps he feels Morrisseau's hold on the past, no matter how tenuous, combined with his talent and determination, can make a difference. Bob Sheppard is an oddity among hardened police officers, and his behaviour is a mystery among them.

The Amazing Morrisseau

Sunday morning we took an L&F kicker over to Mackenzie Island, and spent most of the day... interviewing the amazing Norval Morrisseau.
—SELWYN DEWDNEY, JULY 13, 1960

SELWYN DEWDNEY arranges his fieldwork plans to take him up to the Red Lake area, where he will interview Norval Morrisseau. After so many dead ends he can hardly believe that he is going to meet someone who may actually know something about the rock paintings. The day he received the package of kraft paper drawings from Robert Sheppard remains forever chiselled in his memory. The first time he held one of Morrisseau's mythological creatures in his hands, he plunked himself down on the closest chair and just stared at it. There was no denying the connection between the paintings and the pictographs he was studying. And yet, after so many false leads, travelling for hours on dirt roads to meet people who only pretended to know more than they did, his excitement is tempered by skepticism. How can a young man possibly know very much?

What Dewdney doesn't know is that Morrisseau considers himself an anthropologist of his people. Having grown up with the Ojibway language, with a grandfather who kept the old faith, and having dismissed the idea that the white man's culture is superior to his own, Morrisseau is more than ready to meet Dewdney.

When Selwyn Dewdney was a young man he wanted to be a medical missionary; he has since transformed himself into a painter, novelist, essayist, ethnologist, and outdoorsman. His love of the bush supplants Christian dogma, and he buys a cabin on an island in remote northern Ontario (a fifteen-hour drive from his home in London) and makes a yearly pilgrimage until his death in 1979. More than once he finds himself stranded alone because of fierce weather, his canoe propped against a tree for shelter, a tarp and a bedroll, instant coffee and soup, witnessing the divine in a carpet of lightning surging over a rainswept lake like a giant hand. Shedding the Christian zeal of his father, who was among the first missionaries to work among the Anishinaabe of northwestern Ontario, he now believes that the loss of Native culture through relentless intervention is nothing less than criminal.

In his search to find and decode the pictographs, Dewdney has scoured the province. Recording rock art since 1957, canoe strapped to his Volkswagen van, he has searched throughout southeastern Ontario, the Lake Nipissing region, the Quetico-Superior region, the northeastern hinterland, westward to the Lake of the Woods, northward to Lake Nipigon and the vast northwestern hinterland. By the time he meets Morrisseau he has travelled thousands of miles by land, air, and water, and has recorded over a hundred rock art sites. Trying to systematically record the rock paintings has led him to try to decipher them. It is a perplexing job because although he is somewhat conversant in Cree, he does not know enough about the pre-Christian customs and beliefs of the Anishinaabe.

In his memoirs he laments that as a student in charge of the mission at Lac Seul in northwestern Ontario, he had the rare opportunity to attend one of the last Midewiwin spring ceremonies in the area. He chose not to go and instead lay cocooned in his sleeping bag, listening to the pulse of the drums emanating from across the lake. He admits that he was overcome by the serpentine fear of the outsider, imagining he would be expected to eat the flesh of a white dog. "Fears and objections multiplied to the point of paralysis." But it is a fear he has left in the past. Dewdney is passionate about his work, and he will spend years studying the birchbark scrolls of the Midewiwin, and write about the "Grand Medicine Society" in *The Sacred Scrolls of the Southern Ojibway*.

Like Dr. Joseph Weinstein, Selwyn Dewdney arrives at precisely the right time to support Morrisseau at another stage of artistic development. Morrisseau has no doubts about meeting Dewdney. He believes it is his destiny. If asked, he would say that the spirits have aligned his human helpers so they arrive exactly when they are needed. He also believes that if he helps Dewdney, Dewdney will help him.

The day Dewdney interviews Morrisseau he discovers something that makes him shake his head in amazement. Spreading out the binder of rice-paper tracings he has made from the pictographs, he beckons the young man to approach. For a moment Morrisseau stands in front of the images in silence, surprised to see them gathered together. Then, pointing to one of the sheets of paper, the outline of a water creature, he turns to Dewdney and speaks in his Ojibway language. When he breaks into English, Dewdney discovers that Morrisseau is animating the image with story. He can hardly believe it. The rock imagery leaps off the paper, manitous and demi-gods rise from the depth of Lake Nipigon as they rise to the surface of Morrisseau's memory and he tells Dewdney story after story. He offers to tell him more. And from this point on Dewdney relies on Morrisseau to help interpret the narratives and cultural signs behind the rock paintings. Morrisseau says he has always been interested in the old ways and considers himself a student of his own people.

Sheppard, who by now is glowing with satisfaction, asks Morrisseau to show Dewdney his work. Morrisseau is happy to oblige and unfurls a roll of paintings on kraft paper and birchbark he has prepared for the occasion. If Dewdney is a true artist he will see the power in his paintings. Dewdney's face lights up. Morrisseau surprises him even more by telling him that he is planning to write a book on the beliefs and legends of the Ojibway of the Lake Nipigon area. And reiterates that his one goal is to use his paintings and writing to instill pride in the Ojibway people. Six months later Dewdney receives a wrinkled black notebook in the mail and a letter in broken English asking him for help to find a publisher.

Dewdney notes this first meeting in a letter to his wife Irene, referring to Morrisseau's "factual dignity." He writes that it was "a really weird experience the day before, meeting an Indian who (a) was filled with a deep pride of race, origin and identity, (b) was almost a stereotype of everything you would expect to find in an artist: sensitivity, a sureness of what he wanted to paint, didn't want to paint, liked and rejected, a craving for recognition, complete disinterest in money and material rewards. He is 28, married (to a woman he met in the San at Fort William, who is pregnant), tall, unmistakably Indian in features. Maybe I'm a bit rosy eyed about him but there was a quiet dignity and gentleness with strength about him that tempts me to use the word nobility." An Ojibway renaissance man, a painter, writer, collector of his people's lore, preserver of language and culture, Morrisseau far surpasses Dewdney's expectations. Unlike Joseph Weinstein, what Dewdney fails to understand is that Morrisseau is perfectly aware of what he is doing. How he is conducting himself. Dewdney's earliest response seems to be more about himself, and his hope for the future, than about his subject, Norval Morrisseau.

Dewdney has yet to see Morrisseau's dark side. And he soon learns of the drinking and erratic behaviour. But Dewdney takes it all in stride. As a former missionary he has not only witnessed the destruction of Native culture but taken part in it. It sickens him now to recall how readily he could assume what he calls "the moral arrogance of his race." Experience has taught him well. He knows there is no use trying to turn Morrisseau into something he is not: telling him what to think, how to act, who to be. When he does see other aspects of Morrisseau's personality, he continues to look the other way, beyond, to the art. Dewdney writes, "I have seen him at times torn apart and made desperate with doubt. I have also seen him serene in an upsurge of power that issues from each fresh resolution of his inner agonies. This is no ordinary man." What matters most to him is the cultural knowledge Morrisseau has managed to preserve despite everything. Like Sheppard and the Weinsteins, Dewdney wants to help, and he is eager to share his findings with the young painter to give him a fresh look at his culture. What Dewdney sees is the potential for artistic growth.

What strikes Morrisseau about Dewdney is that he genuinely appreciates Native art and culture, and it inflates him with pride. The intensity of Dewdney's interest, glancing back and forth from painting to artist as if to reassure himself that the young man standing in front of him could actually do the work, confirms to Morrisseau that no matter what he must not deviate from his mission to use his art to bring his Ojibway culture back into the light of creation.

Morrisseau turns his attention back to the tracings spread out of the table, and examines them carefully, taking his time with each image, as though breathing each one in. He finds himself outlining them with his finger, each one bringing him to remember some long-ago tale. He remembers himself as a youngster, tucked into a canoe, skimming past some of these same sacred sites with his grandfather, but he had never actually thought much about them. While unravelling the images for Dewdney, he unravels their meaning for himself. After studying Dewdney's collection, Morrisseau sits back for a moment in silence. He is quick to realize these images are the source. The thought that they will provide a template for his art is like a vein of crystal gleaming in black rock. The faint tracings flood him with possibility.

Before leaving the Red Lake area, Dewdney visits the Weinsteins in Cochenour. Sheppard tells him that if it weren't for them, Morrisseau and his wife would have likely starved long ago. Over coffee Dewdney gets the opportunity to examine even more of Morrisseau's paintings. As he listens to Joseph and Esther go on about their importance from an international perspective, his own enthusiasm is tempered by questions of authenticity and ethnology, but he nevertheless agrees that the work is remarkable. Together they decide that they should try to find Morrisseau employment while giving him time to paint. They also agree that it would be a catastrophe to turn Morrisseau loose in Toronto. The best thing would be to find work for him around Red Lake. Maybe he could run a boat for Dewdney next spring? Or maybe he could do some drawings for the museum? Joseph Weinstein says he will talk to the mine manager in Cochenour. Their concern for Morrisseau's well-being is genuine and paramount. What they fail to realize is that despite having a wife about to give birth, Morrisseau has little value for security.

Dewdney scans the Weinsteins' extensive library, but he sees nothing to indicate a source for Morrisseau's art. (Later he will acknowledge the iconography of the sacred Midewiwin scrolls.) Weinstein confirms that he has never seen anything like Morrisseau's work in any of his books. While he has given him complete access to his collection, he says he has "wisely refrained" from giving him art lessons. Again, Esther goes on about Morrisseau's genius—in the same breath, adding his name to the likes of Modigliani, Brancusi, Klee, Matisse and the master himself, Picasso, whose work epitomizes the tenets of primitivism—a term Morrisseau will pluck from the Weinsteins' library and later use in a letter to Dewdney. Referring to his painting on plywood as having a "primitive effect," he will use his new vocabulary to go about negotiating a place for his work in the contemporary art world.

Blessed by intervention, Morrisseau has once again met the right person at the right time. "The spirits have always guided me," he confirms. By the time Dewdney enters his life, he is determined to be taken seriously and have an exhibition in an art gallery, having set his sights beyond the immediate tourist market. Realizing the potential of Dewdney's research in relationship to his artistic development, he writes Dewdney and asks him to send "some Indian designs, as well as rock paintings pictures. The ones that can be put on art." By this time Morrisseau owns five or six books and continues to visit the Weinsteins' personal library regularly. But even with his widening knowledge, his exposure to other worldly influences, he will remain extraordinarily free of them. An early letter to Dewdney dated February 8, 1961, explains as much: "Someone is guiding me as I paint as if I'm inspired by a Spirit. I put down whatever I am inspired to put down. I paint what I am supposed to paint. My hand moves and I make a picture… maybe I'm crazy, eh? ha ha."

From his first meeting with Morrisseau, Dewdney takes it upon himself to promote both art and artist. Back in Toronto he shows Kenneth Kidd, the curator of ethnology at the Royal Ontario Museum, a selection of photographs he's taken of Morrisseau's paintings, for the purpose of getting the work into the museum's collection. He writes Morrisseau suggesting that he send work done on both birchbark and plywood and that he treat each one as an ethnological study: using special paper from the mining engineer's office, he is to trace each figure and object in the painting and interpret their meaning and relationship to each other. He points to the professionalism that the art-buying public expects. He sends artist's materials: oil paint, brushes, along with a list of suggestions on how to use the supplies. How to prepare and crate the paintings for shipping: "Do not drive nails through them again!" He also tells the young painter how to market himself. To be authentic. Initially it makes sense to Morrisseau to paint on birchbark and moose hide—it's what they have in the museum and it's what the tourists like to buy—but the cost and trouble of obtaining it soon becomes too much for him.

Controversy will later arise over Dewdney's influence, over

whether the information he gave Morrisseau—hide and birchbark over paper and canvas—manipulated the artist's representation and imagery by reinforcing the idea of the primitive. It is nevertheless a transitional phase. Dewdney quickly relinquishes his fixation on authenticity, as is indicated in a letter dated March 9, 1961. "Don't be afraid to mix your oil paints to get the colour you like best," he says. "It is doubtful if the early Indians ever did this. But after all you are a modern Indian looking for a way to express ancient ideas in the most appropriate possible medium."

Morrisseau responds by absorbing and experimenting, but always on his own terms. He is prepared to do what it takes to develop as a painter while making sure to stay true to his vision. The paintings he sends Dewdney to sell to the museum are indeed muted earth tones of browns and greens to suit the buyer, but Dewdney's advice becomes impractical, and Morrisseau's palette soon takes on the colours of sunrises and sunsets, rainbows and gems, spring flowers and autumn trees. Unrolling two new brushes, marvelling at their delicacy, he rereads Dewdney's accompanying letter: "These brushes must be cleaned thoroughly after each use. Rinse them out in turpentine, wipe them dry, then work soap or detergent into the bristles till it lathers. Rise with water, soap again, and again, until the brush is clean." He realizes that Dewdney has no idea how and when he works. Spontaneously, and all hours of the day and night.

Morrisseau in turn writes back to Dewdney saying that oil paint is too messy and smears easily, and when he doesn't have turpentine it won't come off. He says he's tried ordinary gas but the smell stays, and it stinks to high heaven. Besides, he likes to smoke and doesn't want to end up like the burning bush, or like one of those missionaries the Iroquois got their hands on. Even worse, when he forgets to clean the brushes they harden like rock, and he's tried everything to try and soften them. The way he sees it, the time he spends cleaning his oil brushes could be spent painting. On top of it all oil dries far too slowly for his liking. He's tried tempera, but if unprotected it flakes off. He resorts to applying a coat of shellac, a bothersome process, but Dewdney writes back saying "shellac or varnish gives a cheap appearance that is unworthy of the quality of thought and feeling that go into your paintings." It is during this period that Morrisseau discovers acrylic paint. It is relatively cheap, washes up with water, and dries quickly. Acrylic suits him perfectly, and it does not take long for Morrisseau to move past Dewdney's advice and start painting with it. Merely months after they meet in 1960, he paints one of his early masterpieces in acrylic, a 30- by 62-inch red-tipped thunderbird. And by 1962, he has all but abandoned oil and other mediums in favour of acrylic.

From providing advice to negotiating on his behalf, Dewdney supports Morrisseau in any way he can, and their encounter remains a crucial step in Morrisseau's development as a painter. Dewdney also goes on to oversee the publication of his book, *Legends of My People: The Great Ojibway*, which, after rigorous editing by Dewdney, is published in 1965. Even as Morrisseau's meteoric career attains new heights, and he falls under other influences, they remain friends and continue to correspond until Dewdney's untimely death in 1979.

Mining for Gold

ONCE UPON A TIME there were three good Samaritans named Joseph Weinstein, Selwyn Dewdney, and Robert Sheppard, who made a call to Ed Fahlgren, the vice-president and general manager of Cochenour Willans Gold Mine, on behalf of Norval Morrisseau, an intelligent and talented Indian. And before Morrisseau and Harriet know exactly what has transpired, they find themselves floating from McKenzie Island to the mainland. There they settle into a housing compound known locally as Hiawatha Drive, a stretch of dirt road with fifty company houses especially built for Native employees. Not segregation, the mine officials say, but more like a reserve so they can feel at home, feel comfortable with their own kind. At first glance Morrisseau makes a good impression, but having spent time at the tuberculosis sanatorium in Fort William, he is far from hard-rock mining material. After a few minutes of chatting, however, company officials recognize his innate intelligence and give him a thinking man's job: flotation operator, which consists of watching over and adjusting a large vat of liquid gold ore and chemicals.

For nearly two years Morrisseau does his work unfailingly. Although the only time he takes an interest in the job is when they pour the molten gold into bricks—not because of the wealth it suggests, but because of the breathtaking colour, the dazzling reflection, the liquid gold tumbling like a waterfall. During break or lunch Morrisseau sits himself in a corner of the mill, grabs a suitable scrap of paper and with cheap markers begins any number of drawings he will later finish at home in the compound. Like a hawk circling high over a field mouse, he spends every spare second attempting to remember and capture his grandfather's stories. A bear who owned the world. A child impaled by a horned serpent. A man changed into a thunderbird to be at the side of his beloved Nimkey Banasik, Thunderbird Woman. A manitou named Nanaboozho who can outsmart everything and everybody, including himself. A flesh-eating creature called Windigo, its claws like tree branches. Imagining such a pantheon of manitous and demigods makes Morrisseau want to hide away in a secluded corner and paint.

His fellow employees take a glance at his drawings but do not say much. Those who are Native and have gone to residential school are embarrassed. The white employees smirk and dismiss his drawings. They see nothing of value in anything Indian. A word synonymous with ignorant. Others call him a slacker, though he does his job like everyone else. When he continues, doggedly, some realize his art is no joke and offer him a few dollars for a piece when their wife's birthday comes up. Morrisseau gladly takes the money. (Days like that he will go home with a big grin and a bag of groceries in hand, or, just as likely, drink away the money without going home at all.) Most of the work remains rolled in the corner of the mill floor until quitting time, when he either brings it home to finish or tries to sell it around town.

Encouraged by the Weinsteins, who are readily purchasing his paintings, and Dewdney, who is constantly sending him letters of advice, Morrisseau is more determined than ever to become the great artist they see in him. Realize his potential, as they say. A dam has opened and the work gushes out of him, his genius marked by his inexhaustible creativity. Painting on any material he can get his hands on—birchbark, hide, plywood, building paper, but mostly rough mill paper—he makes a habit of hitchhiking into nearby Red Lake and going door to door to sell his paintings. It gets so that he develops a circuit, stopping off at the Red Lake Inn, the Lakeview Restaurant, the local outfitters, the Lands and Forests airbase, the bus station, the school (to hit up the teachers) and all the houses up and down the road. He also continues to keep a cache of paintings at Fergie's General Store on McKenzie Island. On a good day he might sell three or four paintings and make up to twenty dollars depending on their size.

Although completely lacking in formal training he has no inhibitions about how to paint. When someone suggests he consider art lessons, he makes it a point to tell them that he is a born artist who paints every day. Since deciding to become a professional artist he has stopped only once. After a particularly hard night of drinking, he heard an admonishing voice emerge from one of the many religious icons scattered around his cabin. He still talks about the Holy Mother of God, Our Lady of Fatima, speaking to him out of a picture on the wall. Framed by a habit of cobalt blue and titanium white, her sorrowful face of benevolent beauty suddenly changed to stern righteousness, steady eyes gazing, voice replete with warning: "Norval, you will burn if you continue as you do." He dropped his brush and swore to stop. But it didn't last and he soon returned to his art. Now when he visits Beardmore and offers to purchase one of his grandfather's stories, and his grandmother goes on about the roasting in hell's fury, he takes the old man out for a walk in the bush, where they can talk freely and later share a drink. The task to revive his culture sanctioned by Potan's easy laughter and quiet encouragement.

After one successful evening on the circuit he sells enough paintings to get plastered at the Snake Pit Lounge on Red Lake's main drag and continue with a bottle of Catawba down by the waterfront. When he wakes he is lying in the sand with the full sun beating down on him. John Richthammer is a little boy holding the hand of his mother, out for an afternoon walk. "Norval worked periodically for my parents, who operated tourist camps and a construction business," he says. "One summer's day Mom and I were walking near the Red Lake Inn. Mom became upset and asked me to close my eyes while we stepped over a man who was asleep. Of course I didn't close my eyes, and I realized the man was Norval. I kept calling out to him. Those piecing eyes opened, and I knew he recognized me. He turned his head in shame. When I looked up at Mom, she had tears in her eyes."

But the moment passes, as it does on so many others, and Morrisseau rolls over, his mouth like burnt toast and his head pounding like a steel drum of fuel being loaded onto the dock. Flat broke, he rifles through his empty pack of Player's. At times like this he wishes he could be the best husband and father in the world, but that too is a dream. As he turns to rise he gazes into the sun and likens it to looking into the source of his artistic inspiration. Whether Christian or Ojibway, it is something so bright and intense it hurts to look directly at it. Finally he hoists himself up and braces himself as he pulls off his boots and dumps the beach sand out of them. He then dips his huge hands into the lake and splashes water over his face.

An Encounter with Genius

IN HIS MEMOIR *Dear M: Letters from a Gentleman of Excess,* Jack Pollock thinks back with mixed feelings to his first encounter with Norval Morrisseau in 1962: "I'm sure that, if I were to die tomorrow, the single most important thing people would remember me for is, damn it, the discovery of Norval Morrisseau." Elsewhere in the same memoir, however, he admits that it was Morrisseau who discovered him. By this time Pollock is living abroad in the land of Jacques Cartier and Samuel de Champlain, and sick with AIDS—and knows full well that Morrisseau's art will long outlive him. It also occurs to him that he never went looking for Morrisseau. It was Morrisseau who went looking for him. Or maybe who was waiting for him—as if he had been expecting him.

Pollock describes that first meeting in his catalogue *The Art of Norval Morrisseau*, where he says the last stop on his 1962 summer teaching tour through northern Ontario was Beardmore. It is a description romantic enough to have been culled from the pages of James Fenimore Cooper. "My class had just begun when the door opened and a tall Indian with a roll of pictures under his arm walked in. My first impression was that here was a man of power, and I felt that this lean and handsome warrior of another time had the quiet majesty of someone special." Yet, in a letter written five years later, the colourful description has given way to the stark black and white of realism. Pollock's recollection is startlingly different: "Beardmore was a ghost town. It had been home to a gold mine, but the vein had run out and now most of the main street was boarded up. But some people were still clinging on there. I was teaching three classes a day in the one-room schoolhouse. The second day I was there, the door opened and in walked this tall, young Indian man, aged around thirty. He was disgusting—drunk and he had pissed his pants—and he had a roll of birch bark and paper under his arm. He had heard this white teacher was up from Toronto and he wanted to show me his paintings. This was Morrisseau."

The fact remains that in the summer of 1962 Jack Pollock meets Norval Morrisseau in Beardmore. At age thirty-two, a painter by profession with little success, Pollock has recently turned gallery owner and opened a small private space on Elizabeth Street in Toronto. To finance his venture and raise the forty-five dollars a month he needs for rent, he takes on a government job to teach painting for six weeks over the summer to a number of mining, lumber and railway towns throughout northern Ontario. Pollock is in Port Arthur when Susan Ross, a local painter specializing in portraits of Native people, insists that he meet "this Indian who paints on birchbark." (Ross herself purchases some of Morrisseau's early pieces.) The kitschy tourist market immediately comes to mind and Pollock tells her that the last thing he wants to meet is an Indian who paints on birchbark.

As for Morrisseau, locals stop him on the street and tell him that a white man is going to be teaching art classes at the school. They say he should bring his art over and let the teacher have a look at it. By this time Morrisseau firmly believes that he is a born artist and cannot learn his kind of painting from anyone—as the sacred drum arises from the earth, his paintings arise from the old stories, and he is merely the instrument of their creation, the drummer. But he nonetheless decides to go and meet this teacher when he arrives. His decision has nothing to with lessons. On the contrary, he goes to promote himself, acting in the firm belief that his talent will be recognized.

This aspect of Morrisseau's personality will sustain him throughout his career and become his nourishment. Joseph Weinstein will later go so far as to call Morrisseau "a cunning individual who is well able to look after himself." He will go even further to say that "despite our affection for one another we continued to live in our own separate worlds with distinct conceptions of right and wrong. As far as Norval Morrisseau is concerned, truth and loyalty are only pathetic sentimental notions with no real value in his way of life where ruthless opportunism is the only means of survival." Pollock too will come to share this sentiment. Others will simply ask how could anyone make so much money and yet leave his wife and children to fend for themselves.

Everybody in Beardmore knows the crazy, moody, doggedly determined Morrisseau brother who comes around to sell his paintings. The same guy they sometimes saw standing on the street in a woman's dress, his big feet squashed into high heels, tottering like he might topple over at any minute. His face so made up with lipstick and rouge you couldn't help but stare and elbow whoever was beside you to take a damn good look. Norval was at it again. In a small way he's already famous or infamous, depending on your point of view— drag queen or queen of the drag. And in addition to selling paintings throughout the region, last year he sold a few paintings at Hughes Art Gallery in London, Ontario, Selwyn Dewdney's hometown. It has all been such a boost to Morrisseau's confidence that he is beginning to sprout wings when he talks about his art. Sometimes he even manages to take flight, although it was a grounding blow when Bob Hughes went bankrupt, and he could only pay for the last eighteen paintings in art supplies and books.

But again, help appeared at just the right moment. This time it was in the guise of a blue serge suit with a Red Ensign pinned to it. Knowing at times he must give destiny a push, six months before he meets Pollock, Morrisseau takes it upon himself to write CPR train conductor Pete Robertson, a prominent Progressive Conservative Party worker in the area: "I am an artist I am well known here at Cochenour. Among the whiteman's world it is said there are some who are born artists. This in the same respect is with the Indians, I am doing some art on the ancient demigods and animals of the Ojibwa lore… I would like to devote my time for the period of six months in the Lake Nipigon area to do this Art… You might help me through your influence as a Party member… As I said I am not after no personell gain, and your help would be very appreciated."

As destiny would have it, Robertson forwarded the letter to Progressive Conservative Senator Allister Grosart, an avid collector of Canadian art who in turn responded to Morrisseau with interest. The idea of an Indian painter piqued Grosart's curiosity, and he wrote asking Morrisseau to tell him the cost of his present requirements for materials to carry on, and the estimated cost of the six months in Nipigon. "Would it be too much to ask you to send along some samples of your work, and after seeing them I will be glad to make sure that this is brought to the attention of those who might be able to assist you," asked Grosart. Morrisseau immediately wrote back a five-page letter, saying, "If I know my art would not be excepted [accepted], I would not bother to do anything about it but I guess you know yourself each day we of the Canadians are losing some great culture or art because another Indian has died. I am asking if I could get one thousand dollars. This would be enough to assist me in my work." He also sent along a few black and white ink drawings—which he trusted would give the senator a good idea of his art. Grosart responded by contacting the Royal Ontario Museum for an endorsement.

As coincidence would have it they put him in touch with Selwyn Dewdney, their resident expert on Algonquin art. Grosart's request for an appraisal made Dewdney laugh out loud. He knew full well that Morrisseau would say there is no such thing as coincidence. Of course Dewdney gave his unconditional support and wrote back: "In my summer field work for the Royal Ontario Museum I have interviewed Indians of all sorts from the Quebec boundary to the Alberta foothills, especially those conversant with the lore of their own people. Nowhere have I met a comparable person. He is not only a talented artist with roots that go deep into his own culture, he is a natural leader... In terms of practical politics it would be a shrewd move to support his work and give it wide publicity... Any assistance offered ought to be unconditional."

With such an endorsement coming from the ROM's resident expert on Native art and culture, how could Grosart not support Morrisseau? As though to confirm that Morrisseau was destined for great things, Grosart agreed to send him nine hundred dollars for living expenses and art supplies, paid out in installments—big money in an isolated northern town. Morrisseau was to spend the summer painting.

When the senator's money came through Morrisseau took a six-month leave from Cochenour Mine and moved his family back to his shack in Beardmore. And with the determination of a forest fire managed to complete enough paintings for an art show. Despite his carrying on, and even going to the bar with one of Harriet's dresses on when she hid his pants—nine hundred dollars providing for some serious drinking—he managed once again to surprise everyone. Now even the locals were beginning to take his painting seriously. They'd stopped smirking. Grosart's loan definitely upped the ante, and put Morrisseau squarely on the path to coming into contact with his next helper, and one stepping stone closer to his destiny.

Pollock is happy to have Susan Ross, an artist whom he admires, drive him into Beardmore and make the trip bearable. The gravel road is hell, endless, boring, dusty, stones flying up and cracking against the windshield. But he is thankful to have the job. For the last couple of years he's struggled to keep his little upstart gallery, and government jobs pay well. And yet, if he didn't need the money he wouldn't be there. He would much rather be back in Toronto dividing his time between doing his own style of abstract expressionism, tending to his new gallery—while trying to find artists who will make him some money—and living the life of a self-styled gay bohemian.

As far as teaching art to a group of amateurs goes—teachers, nurses, store clerks, housewives, and the like—he considers it the penance he has to do to get his business going. Arrangements have been made to set up in one of the local public spaces, a school, with invitations going out through the library and to the local art club. Nearly every community has such an organization, and the members' idea of art usually consists of landscapes reminiscent of the Group of Seven. In the little time he has, Pollock will go over the rudiments of technique, but he has mainly settled on trying to instill passion about their work into the students. When he mentions this to Susan Ross, she again goes on about the Ojibway artist from Beardmore. If anything, she is sure about his passion. It is the one thing he has by the gallons.

On the second day of Pollock's visit, after a few drinks to perk himself up, Morrisseau gathers a few of his paintings, rolls and ties them with an old bootlace, steps into his black rubber boots, and heads out the door. He tells Harriet where he is going and when he'll be back, but this is something she no longer believes. He will be home when she sees him walking through the door.

He wonders if maybe the teacher might know somebody who could arrange an exhibition for him. If not, he's thinking that at least the man might buy one of his paintings. A sale is always good. Either way, he knows he is on the right path, believes he is in the process of taking his art to great heights, where one day he will look down with the sight of a great eagle on all he has done for his people. "For my people, not now but in the future," he constantly reminds himself. What bothers him is not whether he will become a renowned artist helping to restore his broken and abused culture—this he believes wholeheartedly. It's money that concerns him. Plain and simple. He doesn't want to go back to the mine in Cochenour if he can help it, and Dewdney himself has said it sometimes takes years and years before an artist gains enough recognition to live off his work. Morrisseau cannot wait that long. He wants so badly to believe that if he has a show his art will sell. How can it be otherwise? He has his spirit helpers. Then again, he also has his wife and growing family, and he didn't actually quit his job. In the fall when the senator's money is gone, he can still go back to the mine.

Buoyed by alcohol, Morrisseau is keen to make the most of the opportunity and feels not the least bit of trepidation as he approaches the school, rapping firmly on the door. Upon seeing the tall Indian, the all-white class goes silent, deferring to his presence. Ignoring the students, Morrisseau marches up to the front desk and with a quick nod unfurls his paintings on a mix of birchbark and kraft paper. The students rise from their chairs and clamour around for a better look.

Pollock reaches down to the desk and takes one of them in his hands. A murmur fills the room. Not everyone knows what to make of Morrisseau's art. Everybody in the room has heard of his work but few have actually seen it. The students are in the midst of learning about colour, form, and composition. All Morrisseau's images are two-dimensional, flat. The colours of earth and sky: green, brown, red, black, blue.

Pollock is amazed by what he sees. Giant lightning-eyed birds and otherworldly beasts stare back at him. He swiftly rifles through the paintings and then looks Morrisseau squarely in the face. For the first time, the Toronto bon vivant doesn't know what to say. He glances at Susan Ross, who by the time is standing beside him. Satisfied that her every assertion is confirmed, she mouths, "I told you." Pollock catches his breath. First, he wants Morrisseau to confirm that he painted them. He can't believe it. Way up here? "Did you really paint these?" he asks. His eyes take in Morrisseau while waiting for an answer: the shabby clothes, the rubber boots.

Morrisseau is incensed by the question. "Who else?" he answers defiantly. Only then does Pollock look back down to the work scattered on the desk.

"Are there more? They're very good. Different." Not knowing what else to say, he shuffles through them again like a card shark. Morrisseau tells him that he's got a mountain of paintings at his home. Pollock boldly asks if he could go home with him to see them. "I own a gallery in Toronto," he offers, as though needing to convince the artist.

The moment Pollock springs the news that he owns a gallery, Morrisseau looks up from the table, turns to Pollock, and looks him in the eyes. Behind his stoic façade, Morrisseau is laughing like ningaabiian-nodin, the west wind, with great gusto. His face breaks into a sly grin that Pollock doesn't notice. It is as if he is saying that he knew all along the next blessing would come to him today. As far as he's concerned another helper has arrived.

The next day Pollock visits Morrisseau's home and meets his wife Harriet, his daughter Victoria and his baby son David. Pollock describes this crucial scene in his memoir, but again his descriptions are inconsistent. In the 1979 version we get a sanitized story, romantically tailored for the urban art-buying public. He tells us that Morrisseau's home "was a makeshift shack erected on the garbage dump just outside of town. Crates, logs, and old tin Coca-Cola signs had created one large room, which was half exposed to the sky. Under the tall pine tree which dominated the open space sat his daughter, Victoria, who played with a tattered doll while chipmunks scurried about her." In sharp contrast, though, Pollock's letters reveal a layer of veneer stripped away, rawness exposed. Here he says, "his house was in the middle of a garbage dump—not next to it, but in it. I shouldn't call it a house… it was a tar-paper shack, half of it had a roof and half of it didn't because there was a huge tree growing through the middle of it. A little girl was sitting under the tree, Victoria, his first child. She was filthy, dirty, covered in fly bites, and a chipmunk was playing over her knee. There was no stove, no water, no toilet, but there was a table set up under the part of the shack that had a roof."

With Pollock in *his* environment, Morrisseau flings his feigned restraint out the window and takes up his hand drum (on which he has painted a thunderbird). Holding it up high in the air he begins beating and chanting an old song of welcome that sounds like noise to Pollock's ears. But Morrisseau has more in store. He has been planning this occasion for a long time. He will show Pollock that he can create art at the drop of a hat. Anywhere. Anytime. He will later say that since all his paintings come from within, he can paint with a pipe band going by. Without warning he picks up a brush and dips it into a tin of black paint and begins dabbing a sheet of kraft paper. He drops the brush and picks up another one with brown paint, and some kind of prehistoric fish takes shape. With dabs of yellow, eyes appear, fins, a tail, more black, and he ties the form together.

Like a stained-glass window, Pollock observes, stunned by the quality and apparent ease of execution Morrisseau demonstrates. Although not a superstitious man, he is not sure what to make of what he is witnessing, whether to think he is in the presence of genius or someone possessed.

In less than an hour, the painting is completed. Pollock is so impressed—"animals and birds painted so you could see into them"—"a kind of crudeness dominating"—"a slightly brutal approach"—he never forgets that first meeting with Morrisseau. Almost without thinking he makes the decision that changes both their lives almost overnight. He scrambles to capitalize, offering Morrisseau an exhibition in his gallery, and boldly arranges the show for September, a mere three months away. And the tiny gallery on Elizabeth Street becomes the talk of Toronto's art scene. What is it that compels Pollock to see Morrisseau's art for what it is—something extraordinary—and not judge it by the Eurocentric attitudes of the day? He ponders this question and wonders if it has anything to do with having a grandmother who was Ojibway from Rama Reserve. All her life hiding her heritage, pretending to be white, a pain Pollock later confesses.

As for Morrisseau, having a solo show in Toronto confirms what he knew all along. His life as an artist began the day he was born. With an advance from Pollock he buys himself a grey suit, black shoes, a white shirt, and a navy blue tie with the emblem of a crown embossed on it (he loves anything to do with royalty) and boards a train for Toronto. And so begins Morrisseau's relationship with Jack Pollock, who will swear until his dying day that the artist is a highly sophisticated painter, and what separates his work from primitive art is his growth and development. Ever the believer, Pollock will even go so far as to call Morrisseau the most important painter Canada has ever produced.

Success

THE FIRST NATIVE PAINTER to make it into big-time Toronto. Twenty-eight pieces snatched up and bought, art buyers like fish in a feeding frenzy. Gasping at the strange images, a giant bird clutching a horned serpent, an X-ray bear adorned with mysterious symbols, a mythical merman embodying a male shaman, lines of movement representing connection, communication, and power, divided circles representing duality and balance. Morrisseau is proud of his accomplishment, and it comes across in the way he carries himself in his new suit and tie, tall and straight like royalty. He shakes hands and smiles cordially, lapping up the attention. No stoic Indian here. The photographers marvel and scribble into their notepads. A female reporter approaches Morrisseau, and he is taken aback by her charm and good looks. When she asks him about his art and what it means to him, he responds matter-of-factly, seemingly unperturbed by the camera staring into his face. "I want you to think, I am," he says. The reporter doesn't understand what he is getting at and pounces for clarification, curiously, naively. "What are you?" she asks, trying to get him to discuss his art in relation to his heritage. Morrisseau in turn answers flatly, "Well, I am an Indian." His simple response confuses her—Morrisseau both epitomizes and challenges the idea of the primitive Indian. And she is as thrilled as everyone else in the room to meet him. She knows he will make a great story.

What is clear is that at this stage Morrisseau, fresh from Red Lake via Beardmore, lacks a vocabulary to explain himself and his art. Judging from the trail of letters he will leave behind, this facility will grow like a young bird's plumage as his confidence in his art grows. Although he has a good grade school command of English and fluency in Anishinaabemowin, he is still a child when it comes to meeting the public at large and explaining himself. He takes the young reporter's questions literally, which only adds to the confusion. He is too shell-shocked by all the attention to try to reiterate and clarify himself. He is also hesitant about giving more than he is already giving to the white man. In few words he then tells her that it has to do with him uncovering his potential in the Anishinaabe way, rethinking the original sources, discovering his own image bank, following his vision of things, finding his true self.

He turns his back to the crowd, admiring his paintings—it's nice to see them framed—and he begins to talk to his grandfather. Though faint, there are rumblings in his whisper. Morrisseau's grandfather's spirit is always with him, and he talks to him regularly (as he will continue to do even when the old man trades one form of existence for another). It is his grandfather to whom Morrisseau turns in times of distress. Though any onlooker might ask: how can he be distressed at a time like this? Especially when he is attaining all that he's set out to do almost overnight. A sell-out show covered by reporters and critics, it's something that normally takes an artist nearly a lifetime to achieve, Pollock tells him. And, yet, the little red stickers Morrisseau sees on the paintings cast doubt across his face, rather than bring joy.

After his show Morrisseau finds himself the centre of attention. *Time* magazine, the *Toronto Daily Star*, *The Globe and Mail*, *The London Free Press*, CBC. Meeting expectations perfectly, he becomes a darling of the media. The primitive who "moves and speaks with the traditional dignity of the Indian," writes a critic who has never met a Native person in his life. "Morrisseau comes forth from the wilds of northern Ontario to take on the Canadian art scene." Well aware of his role, he responds to the excitement of fame by putting on a wooden face. When reporters crowd about him and ask what his sudden success feels like, he responds stoically, "I'm an Indian. I am not supposed to show any emotion." But his actions speak louder than his words, and he is quickly sucked into the social life of Toronto's bohemian 1960s art scene. Restaurants, bars, parties stretch him out of the person he knows and into someone famous. The money he makes from his first show he spends on lavish gifts that have no connection to his family's reality. He buys Harriet a set of Royal Crown Derby china so that they can drink tea like the Queen of England in a shack with no electricity, no heat, and no plumbing. When pressed, he goes on to say, "People tell me I'm famous. What does this mean?" Above all what it means for Morrisseau is the rare opportunity to drum up the confidence, support, and resources to paint full time.

Upon his return to northern Ontario, Morrisseau does two things: he throws a party in Beardmore to celebrate the sweet taste of success, and he quits his job at Cochenour Willans Gold Mine in Red Lake. His return to Beardmore is triumphant, and with his percentage of sales, which is more money than anyone in the community has ever seen at one time—three thousand dollars—he goes about sharing his new-found wealth as locals would a freshly killed moose. The community alights in alcohol. Having turned his culture into cases of liquid gold, all the skepticism and condemnation poured on him for exploiting the sacred are swallowed in gulps of Five Star and Canadian Club. Like the inverse of the prodigal son, Morrisseau returns home with the gift of forgetting.

Morrisseau's return to Red Lake, on the other hand, is a disappointment. He and Harriet and the kids move out of Hiawatha Drive, the Native housing compound in Cochenour, and relocate back to a small cabin on McKenzie Island, where he is now free to paint and make art in any way he can, sculpt, carve, even paint his daughter's shoes. But his idea of the artist's life comes crashing down around him when he drinks away his money and is unable to meet the rent. The family then moves to an even cheaper shack in Balmertown, another tiny mining town a few miles out of Red Lake—constant moving will become Morrisseau's lifestyle. He tries to provide for his wife and young family, but his heavy drinking continues to undermine his good intentions. Desperate, he calls Pollock in Toronto for money. Pollock sends him a few hundred dollars in advance but receives no paintings in return. Although he is constantly painting, whatever pieces he completes he sells locally for a few quick dollars.

In an attempt to organize Morrisseau's finances and protect him from what he sees as external influence, Pollock contacts Allister Grosart and they discuss the possibility of setting up "some form of trusteeship for Norval's funds." A committee is struck but the trustees, including Pollock and Grosart, soon realize that managing Morrisseau's income is akin to trying to stop him from drinking. The Norval Morrisseau Trust Fund is inundated with bills from Eaton's in Winnipeg, the Hudson's Bay in Thunder Bay, and everywhere in between, for whatever Morrisseau wants: paints, brushes, clothes for himself, his wife and the kids, groceries. The trustees soon learn that

Morrisseau has no concern for cost and never inquires if there is money in the fund.

Madeleine Cooper, a welfare field worker with the Department of Social Welfare, writes to solicitor and fellow trustee Douglas Rutherford saying, "In my opinion Norval's finances are in an almost hopeless state, and they seem to be getting worse all the time." A few months later Grosart writes Morrisseau to say "we are still prepared to help you, but we cannot do it unless you are prepared to cooperate." Morrisseau responds with a five-page letter that ends with his philosophical and spiritual outlook on life: "From here on Fate will decide—within the wisdom of the Great Spirit, one friend may get bored but another will be Inspired, True followers of this Movement will not abandon there fellow (Despite Earthly Mistakes) if Men should be judged by his actions those artists, composers, etc could never today give us the culture we all enjoy and are proud to call our way. Men should not be criticized or judged by his fellow men of his mistakes in one year but by a thousand years for what he has accomplished for his people—despite his faults and misunderstandings." The trust fund is dissolved soon thereafter.

Through it all though, there is transformation. Perhaps it's because of the financial support he's had. Perhaps it's because of his first sell-out show. Perhaps it's because change is an essential part of his character. But back in the Red Lake region Morrisseau is a changed man. Downy feathers are already beginning to show as he continues to grow into his namesake, Copper Thunderbird. Most do not see this. They see the same man, the same character, and use words like drunkard, crazy, wild, pain-in-the-ass, shameless, neglectful, although they always make sure to add talented, they will grant him that. What they soon come to realize, however, is that Morrisseau has adopted the title of "artist." And he uses it freely to describe himself, something he has never done before and only aspired to do after Joseph Weinstein introduced him to the concept in 1958. "I wish only one thing, to be an artist and respected as one," he wrote Selwyn Dewdney on a cold December day in 1960, his letter arriving unannounced from bleak Cochenour, where he was working in the mines. And now a mere two years later, he says matter-of-factly, first to Grosart and Pollock, and then to a reporter for the *Toronto Daily Star*, "I am a born artist." And then four months later to *The London Free Press* he elaborates, "I pray directly to the Great Manitou of the Indian and thank him for beauty and for the gift of being an artist." Man Changing into Thunderbird—Man Changing into Artist. In four years, Morrisseau's transformation has been complete.

Devil Thirsty

When I knew him he was an alcoholic who wanted to sell his paintings when he was drunk. He loved children and was a great storyteller who enjoyed shock value. I believe that art gallery people took advantage of Morrisseau. Perhaps the people in Cochenour like myself also took advantage of him. I have twenty paintings that hang in my home.

—LYNN HUTTON, COCHENOUR

Lynn Hutton brought us all together at her house in Cochenour. She had many of Norval's paintings. Lynn and I went to Norval's house to see if we could buy some. I then became one of his Red Lake patrons. His marketing strategy was to come to our houses in the early afternoon when our husbands were at work. If he needed money, we gave it to him on the basis of an IOU, which he always honoured. Eleven paintings hang on our walls.

—CYNTHIA RANCE, RED LAKE

TODAY MORRISSEAU WAKES UP SICK. So sick that if Red Lake were booze he would go down to the shore, cut a hole in the ice, get down on his hands and knees, stick his head in the freezing water, and lap it up like a dog. The sweep of arctic wind drives through the drafty little house, the loose chinking between the logs, the nearly collapsing roof. The stove burns what little oil is left. Harriet, little Victoria, and baby David are huddled together in the bedroom, and all Morrisseau can think about is his bloated tongue. He scrapes it across his dry lips and tastes salt and sweat. By now he's already checked every empty bottle in the house, dug through the garbage. There's a group of white ladies and he wonders if he could squeeze something out of one of them. His plan is the same as usual. He'll wait until their husbands are gone to work, and then he'll take whatever art he has on hand and sell it for whatever he can get.

Morrisseau never gets attached to his paintings, no matter how thrilled he is by their execution, because he knows he can always do more. His art is like air. Only death will stop him from breathing. Only death will stop him from painting. And it is not easy to die. Today he knows this only too well as he lurches for the door to retch up his empty guts. And he's not stupid. He knows the locals who don't want to pay him a fair price for his work. Who try to get it for nothing. He calls them leeches and only goes to them as a last resort. He knows everybody has heard about his show at Pollock's gallery, and although some let on as if it's of no importance, he knows what they're thinking: investment and profit. He knows that sooner or later they will double their money, resell his paintings to outsiders for hundreds of dollars. Some are already doing it. He's not stupid. At the same time he also knows that he's benefiting from selling to them. When he comes knocking, he needs the money desperately, because when he's thirsty nothing matters except the drink. Not his art, not his wife, not his kids, not even his life, nothing. When it comes to this point it doesn't matter how little they give him, as far as he's concerned a deal is a deal.

That's when he knows the devil has got him. Sin, he admits, is his greatest problem. "There's the problem of getting Christianity out of your mind," he says. And yet he knows that traditionally among his people there was no sin. "Indians don't have a devil," he reminds himself repeatedly, as if trying to rebuke his need for alcohol. There is only Manitou. God. If only he could believe it. If only God's great hand would come down and bless him, and he could stop drinking. Then he could stop telling Harriet he's going to quit tomorrow. Then he could give her the life he promised and stop telling everyone in town that the drink in his hand is his last. Not have to endure their smirk or worse, their look of pity for his family. Knowing that everything he does or doesn't do, all the pent-up guilt, burning inside him like molten rock, is his own damn fault. No one to blame but himself—and the devil. Meanwhile his paintings littered across watering holes from Red Lake to Winnipeg.

On Ne Sait Jamais

ALTHOUGH THE TASTE OF SUCCESS still lingers like a shot of crème de menthe in his mouth, the jackpot from his first show is a memory, as is the bottomless well of his trust account. Frost is on the windows, a thin coat of ice is on the water bucket, and the oil tank is empty again. Morrisseau now finds himself torn between his family's needs and his need to make art. He and Harriet now have three kids, and out of necessity she coaxes him to return to the mine.

Mine manager Ed Fahlgren, who has promised Morrisseau and Cree painter Carl Ray a workshop in which to do their art, welcomes him back to his old flotation operator job at the Cochenour Willans Gold Mine. Sleepwalking through the routine, Morrisseau is again shackled to a job that robs him of time to paint, but all the same he is initially grateful. The first thing he does is take his family to the company store and buy all the essentials they are lacking: food, clothing, shoes, blankets. The year is 1963, and he writes Selwyn Dewdney in London assuring him that he is still painting. "It went off hand into Junk," he says, "but thanks to my friends at Cochenour (Weinsteins) I was put again on the Right track." That winter he attends the Indian-Metis Conference in Winnipeg, but later writes again that he "met a lot of friends but No sale except four that mostly payed my Expenses etc." Nonetheless, he concludes that "money is no problem now… and I am glad to work for a living and on the side make a little on art." As though trying to convince himself, he adds, "I am sure you and your wife will be pleased for making this right decision."

But the return to the mine cages him like bear in a zoo and he reminds himself that he is squandering his God-given talent, the spirit power inside him. A month later he writes again: "all day today I was doing Art and tonight I work the Night Shift. I hate it but I will do it. I hope I will one day Reach my desire to be on my own." To compound his frustration, he waits patiently for the promised workshop, but it never materializes. Fahlgren gives him a drivel of excuses, such as the carpenters are too busy working on the local arena, and that for the time being they need the proposed shed for storage. By way of appeasement, he says that he can remodel a shack in Cochenour near Hiawatha Drive instead, but that won't happen until next summer at the earliest. And so Morrisseau sits at the kitchen table after his shifts, in his little company house with his small children crying, staring at the rough mill paper, trying his best under the circumstances to get something down.

And then, as before, intervention. This time it is in the form of a phone call from Jack Pollock, who wants to organize a second show in Toronto for the coming October, barely a year after the first. He reminds Morrisseau of the potential to attain even greater success, along with a good bundle of cash, and his words are barely out and Morrisseau is licking his lips in anticipation of the sales. Judging from the first show, Pollock is equally excited about the possibilities and wants Morrisseau to strive for even greater heights. He expounds on the integrity of serious work versus shameful knock-offs, goes on about materials, size, critics, publicity. He is already imagining another sold-out show, while Morrisseau is worrying about trying to get enough painting done between shifts.

To celebrate, and at the same time solve his problem about getting enough paintings completed, Morrisseau quits his job, collects his severance, and swears never to go back. Goes into town with his daughter Victoria and buys her the biggest chocolate ice cream cone available. Buys art supplies and groceries, buys everything his family needs. He then buys plane tickets to Sandy Lake, Harriet's reserve, an isolated village in the stunted spruce an hour northwest by bush plane. The plan is to spend the summer on the reserve, where she can visit her family and he can paint—which to her means dry out. Harriet is used to surprises, like him coming home with an expensive Spode teapot when there's no food in the house, or coming home in a police car, or not coming home at all, and she is happy not to have to spend so much time alone with the kids.

While preparing to leave for Sandy Lake, Morrisseau hears that Dr. Weinstein and his wife are leaving for the French Riviera and will not be returning. A week before their departure he goes over to say goodbye. They were the first to believe in his natural talent, to support his art, and he is sorry to see them go. Morrisseau and the Weinsteins spend their visit talking about his art, how far he's come in such a short time, the galleries the Weinsteins will visit in France, the master Picasso, whom Morrisseau has taken interest in since being introduced to his work through the couple's library, and their connection to his family. On his way out, Morrisseau hastily opens a small cardboard folder and presents Esther with two watercolours in appreciation, for all they've done for him, and then stands at the entrance shifting his weight from leg to leg. "He seemed to be standing before us with a bewildered air about him as if he was searching for words with which to express his sorrow at our impending departure," Joseph Weinstein recalls.

Then, at the open door with the moon brilliant against the black northern sky over his shoulder, Morrisseau tells them something that both Joseph and Esther will always remember. As Joseph recalls, "His hands were trembling when he said in a dramatic tone of voice, almost growling. 'I speak to you now as a shaman. This full moon is a very important and powerful omen for your future. I can see that in years to come long after you leave this place, you will have many occasions to travel in distant lands.' With these departing words he disappeared into the night."

On the day of the Weinsteins' departure Morrisseau unexpectedly appears again. This time he brings them a handwritten copy of *Legends of My People,* the book he is currently working on with Dewdney, and a large ink drawing of a thunderbird grasping a snake in its claws, dedicated to Picasso and to be presented to him as a personal gift—signed "from one great artist to another, Norval Morrisseau, Copper Thunderbird." A couple of months later on the French Riviera, the Weinsteins will have the occasion to present the gift to Picasso at a dinner party. And after they explain who Morrisseau is and where he comes from, the artist will examine the painting carefully and then break into a huge smile and say, "On ne sait jamais."

When Joseph Weinstein resigns his post as head doctor at the hospital and leaves Cochenour, he and Esther have some fifty Norval Morrisseau paintings in their possession and no idea what to do with them all. Then one day at a newsstand on the Riviera Joseph spots a copy of *Time* magazine with a photo of Morrisseau on the cover, and with all the excitement of their initial discovery, he purchases a copy and holds it up for Esther to see. It has happened: Norval Morrisseau is an internationally renowned artist. And nodding to himself, he turns to his wife in belief, knowing all along that such a thing was inevitable—Morrisseau's day has come.

A Fickle Public

UP IN SANDY LAKE Morrisseau does his utmost to ignore the pull of Christian dogma, the nagging complaint of his conscience as he works relentlessly like a fiend right out of Bruegel's inferno, his body hitched to a great millwheel of doubt as he plunges into the metaphysics of Indianness. Misshipesheu, the Water Lynx demigod; Maymaygwaysiwuk, the water beings; Nepii-Naba, Merman;

Mikkinnuk, Turtle. He paints them in the belief that he has no choice, that it is his destiny, even at the cost of his soul. Believing in his own greatness, as confirmed by the Weinsteins and later by his sold-out show in Toronto, and the publicity that followed, he paints the night away in isolation, up past roads and intrusions, buttressed by remoteness.

Almost disciplined, he cuts his drinking by half and is productive to the point of shipping paintings to the Canadian National Exhibition in August of 1963, and then the Kitchener–Waterloo Art Gallery, while in October he is still able to send Pollock twenty-three new paintings. Some of them far more complex than previous work, his inner articulation expanding, his visual vocabulary developing, the palette including a broader range of colours. The mysticism of his paintings deepens so that lines of communication and power become central to the disparate images of serpents and thunderbirds, and like his use of colour they provide a means of connecting images and balancing composition. He also turns to familiar subjects, such as bears, birds, and fish, and paints them in an intricate geometrical pattern, fitting them together like pieces of a puzzle.

But only three paintings sell. Pollock is shocked. He blames a fickle public. He rants and raves at the incestuous, parochial Toronto art scene. He tries to rationalize it, thinks moving the gallery from Elizabeth Street, the heart of downtown, "Our Greenwich Village," to Markham Village in the north may have had something to do with it. Not having Morrisseau there in person has meant not having the publicity of the first show, which he thinks has also contributed to weak sales. He rereads Pearl McCarthy's column in *The Globe and Mail,* where she says that "the present exhibition at the Pollock Gallery is so much superior to his earlier work as to be thrilling, because it shows that his primitive talent had capacity for growth and enlargement without loss of the native genius." He slams his hand down on his desk. He believes in Morrisseau and his work more than ever—even if the painter is temperamental, impossible to manage and a complete pain in the ass. As far as he's concerned it's a matter of the public catching up to what Morrisseau is doing, rather than a reflection of the quality of the work. And if they need a helping hand Pollock is just the man to do it.

Without the hurricane of money and publicity that followed his first show, Morrisseau finds himself crushed, flat on the ground, broke, as worthless as roadkill. He wonders what happened to the admirers, the collectors. Holding up his paint-stained hands in front of him, he broods over the nature of art and the buying and selling of it. The white man's world. Something has happened since his sell-out show that he doesn't understand. As far as he's concerned he agrees with *The Globe and Mail* that his work is even better, and he has said as much himself, commenting openly on the unity and simplicity of line in the new pieces. Although shocked, he tries to look at the situation philosophically, and tells himself what really matters is that he's a born artist, and now a professional artist.

And for a while he drinks insanely, almost killing himself with alcohol poisoning. It occurs to him that maybe he was right in the first place, and the white man doesn't deserve his work. But having no intention of returning to the mine, and with money running through his hands like water, he knows full well that somehow, anyhow, he has to sell his work. He has no choice. Again, it has come to this. He has spent the last of his severance, including an advance from Pollock, and has returned to living on credit to feed and clothe his family. He picks up a paintbrush and dabs it in the little paint he has left in the bottom of a jar.

What Pollock doesn't know is that in spite of the disappointment, Morrisseau's reputation is growing to the extent that he is developing a circle of ever-expanding contacts, each painting like a stone thrown into water, the power to attract interest pushing outward. From roaming the dirt roads around Red Lake, Morrisseau expands his circle and ventures afar. And he is unrelenting, inexhaustible, day or night, he is always on the move, a roll of paintings under his arm wrapped in plastic, hitching rides or travelling by train, bus, even taxis when he can afford it. From community to community, gallery to gallery, house to house, he goes anywhere he thinks he might make a sale. During this time he ends up in the town of Nipigon and strides boldly into the office of the Northland Hotel and introduces himself. Unrolling an armload of paintings, he asks the owners if they would stage an art show for him in the dining room. He can see they are foreigners, Mr. and Mrs. German and Ukrainian—outsiders like him—who might be sympathetic. They look at his art and wrinkle their brows, not knowing what to make of it, but agree to do it anyway. They like the idea of an Indian taking initiative.

Victoria Day, Canada Day, craft fair or conference festivities, and Morrisseau is bound to be there, travelling to Beardmore, Geraldton, Nipigon, Fort William, Port Arthur, Atikokan, Fort Francis, Dryden, Kenora, Winnipeg—four paintings sold at a conference, enough to buy a bottle for the night, and then onward. This becomes Morrisseau's lifestyle, and he is in the midst of it when Pollock calls and tells him to start preparing for a third exhibition.

Culture Shock

HAVING WRITTEN SELWYN DEWDNEY that he hopes to visit him someday, a couple months later Morrisseau is smoking one of his Player's Plains on the front steps of Dewdney's house on Erie Street in London. Anishinaabe, Spontaneous Beings, a way to describe a people of light and lightning, and Morrisseau unable to operate any other way. Travelling to Toronto for his third show at Pollock Gallery in three years, he decides to make a detour and shows up on Dewdney's doorstep, happy as a bumblebee to visit Selwyn and his family. Morrisseau is travelling with Harriet and two of their children, and they are shell-shocked to find themselves in southern Ontario, all of them looking like they have just stepped out of the bush, which they have.

Dewdney is used to life in the north and takes it all in stride. His wife Irene, although well travelled, is less acclimatized. Irene can see from the moment they arrive that it's going to be a classic case of culture shock—for everyone. And as if to confirm her thoughts, little Victoria walks into the living room with an orange the size of a grapefruit, and proceeds to chew and spit out the peelings onto the floor, the chesterfield, and the rest of the furniture. The next morning Morrisseau insists that for breakfast his family cannot eat cereal or eggs, and that they can eat only baloney with pork and beans. Dewdney jumps in his car and drives Morrisseau to the grocery store while his wife is thrown into a panic. She asks herself, "Oh God, is this what it is going to be like?" and braces herself for more.

With their own four kids at home, the Dewdneys find themselves short of beds. Selwyn wants to give their guests the master bedroom, but Irene will not have it. She is worried because there is no telling when Morrisseau will leave. It could be a couple of days, it could be week, or even a month. She knows from Selwyn that in the north it is customary for relatives and friends to drop in at any time and leave only when they are ready. Although Morrisseau has an art show to attend, she knows he could very well change his mind in a flash and decide not to go. So they gather whatever sleeping bags, duvets, and blankets they have and make a bed for their guests on the carpet in the living room. They've been on the train for three days and have arrived with all the grime and fatigue of travel, so Irene offers them baths. Morrisseau uses the opportunity to find the nearest bar. Irene cannot believe it: he brings Harriet all the way to southern Ontario where she is completely out of her element and then dumps her first chance he gets. Yes, she thinks, this is what it's going to be like.

Morrisseau does his share of drinking down at the local beer parlour during his visit and tries to get to know the Indians there, but they seem to have nothing in common. He can't relate to them, and they can't relate to him. They find his mysticism obscure, downright weird, and he finds them narrow-minded, downright boring. When he tries to talk to them about the spirit world they turn away, and soon enough, when they see him coming they close ranks and turn their backs to him. He thinks it's because they're Oneida and he's Ojibway. They speak different languages. Have different traditions. But it's not really that at all. Even his own people consider Morrisseau strange, the way he carries on, constantly in conversation with the spirit world. Later, he returns half-loaded to the Dewdneys while everybody is asleep and ends up sitting at the dining room table talking to himself in Ojibway.

One evening Selwyn and Irene talk about their canoe trips up to northern Ontario, to Algoma Country and beyond, gliding through glades of bulrushes and white water lilies as far as the eye can see. That's when Irene mentions that above all she misses the loons and how much they mean to her. "Well I'll just go upstairs and paint you one," Morrisseau says, jumping up from the sofa. He has yet to paint a loon but doesn't think twice about it. Taking one of Dewdney's sheets of watercolour paper, and some India ink and red paint, he goes up to their son's bedroom and sits down at a small table beside the bed. And before they know it, he's back downstairs with a family of loons, looking like they might swim off the paper. Irene is flabbergasted. It is then that she too witnesses the incongruity between Morrisseau, the man, and Morrisseau, the artist, realizing that he must have had the design laid out in his head. It is the only way he could have completed the painting so quickly. He is one of those rare artists who does not need a preliminary sketch. With great ease he can put something down on paper without working it out first. She will always remember the moment when Morrisseau, all smiles, hands her the painting, with its impeccable design and balance. All done in fifteen minutes.

The art scene in London is small. Two of the best young artists in the city, Greg Curnoe and Jack Chambers, are Dewdney's former students. Dewdney decides to take Morrisseau to meet them. Not because he thinks Morrisseau might learn something from them. The visit is purely social, and the purpose is simply to expose Morrisseau to the contemporary current of Canadian art. It is about artists connecting with each other and sharing conversation and ideas.

As Dewdney should have expected, the visit is a disaster. If Morrisseau cannot connect with the Oneidas around London, he has even less in common with the young white painters. While these artists focus on the material culture around them, urban landscapes and objects like boxes and bicycles, Morrisseau draws on the shamanic tradition of seer for inspiration—his work grounded in the realm of the spirits. Visiting each of their studios, looking over their work, all he can do is shrug, because he has no interest in it whatsoever. Though he doesn't say it, he would rather be gazing upon the Christian imagery of Bernini, Botticelli, or Michelangelo, considering the languor of ecstasy, the splendour of the nude, the eroticism of suffering. This is what interests him in Western art.

After three intense days, Irene feels invaded. Victoria swinging a dirty diaper around the bathroom is the last straw. Like Irene, Harriet tries to make the bad situation tolerable. She too knows she doesn't belong in white, middle-class London, but there is little she can do either. Morrisseau's solution is to purchase some pretty blue brocade material for Harriet and a fifty-dollar teapot for himself at the London China Shop. Irene is happy that he is at least thinking of his wife, but she cannot understand the expensive teapot. Morrisseau shrugs it off. He tells her that he has a whole closet full of teapots that he has never even used. He then asks if he can bum a smoke. It turns out he has spent all his money and has no idea how they will get home, let alone to Toronto for his exhibition. It also seems like he couldn't care less. Dewdney tries to talk to him about the value of opening a bank account for a rainy day, but he can see that Morrisseau only thinks about sunny days. He knows Morrisseau is a passionate artist, but it has never occurred to him until now that his passions rule his life.

Three o'clock in the morning and everyone is in bed, when Morrisseau suddenly decides he has to leave. Immediately. Agitated, moving around the living room like a trapped bear, he wakes up Harriet and the kids, then goes upstairs and knocks on the Dewdneys' door. He asks Selwyn to take them to the bus station.

He's divined a spiritual message out of a shaman's dream that says he has to be in Toronto. And he will not listen to reason. By this time Irene has had enough. "Living with Morrisseau is like trying to catch a hot fry pan," she will say. Unable to calm him down, Dewdney calls the bus station and finds out when the next bus in leaving. He gives the painter enough money for passage and drives them over, and a few hours later Morrisseau and his family are on their way to Toronto. Never quite knowing what Norval will do next, Irene is not sorry to see him go. She's sorry, though, for Harriet and the children.

Big as Christmas

LEARNING FROM THE DISMAL SALES of the second exhibition, Jack Pollock makes sure that Morrisseau and his family attend the third, and he tells the press that they should take advantage of their visit to Toronto, as if it were a coincidence. He offers the family to photographers, and Morrisseau proudly shows off his moose-hide jacket, a laughing Victoria in his arms, while a pleased Harriet balances her new baby Eugene in a beaded floral tikinagan, the picture of a happy Indian family. Pollock sends reporters personal invitations, and in *The Globe and Mail* on Saturday, March 21, 1964, Pearl McCarthy writes an article entitled the "Metaphysics of Indian Art," in which she emphasizes Morrisseau's "high intelligence within the framework of Indian metaphysics." She notes that "Morrisseau's second exhibition in Toronto was recognized as much superior to his first but, probably because the novelty of his unusual approach had worn off, it drew less attention."

Comparatively, the third exhibition is a success. With Morrisseau and Harriet in attendance, it pulls in a far better crowd than the previous exhibition. Morrisseau's self-esteem is recharged, but the money he makes after expenses, including train travel and hotels, barely covers his debts, and before long he is again scratching for a living.

Then, in the middle of a furious northern Ontario winter, the breath of Keewatin screaming through the chinks in walls hand-stuffed with newspaper and rags, his family living on hope and fried baloney, a clothesline of unsold paintings stretched across the kitchen like wet laundry, a warm western chinook blows in all the way from Calgary. A letter arrives and melts away Harriet's fears of starving or freezing to death. They read that the Glenbow Museum wants to purchase Morrisseau's paintings, and in a burst of joy as big as Christmas he and Harriet are off their chairs and dancing in their coats and moccasins. The museum will pay him $2,500 for eleven paintings. Not the small change he usually settles for when he's drinking. And suddenly a warm breeze from tropical Toronto, another official-looking letter arrives from the University of Toronto's Hart House Gallery, which wants to host an exhibition. As if a warm geyser has been tapped, the Red Door Gallery in Winnipeg then comes calling.

In the midst of the good news, the family finally celebrates Christmas and leaves their tumbledown shack and moves to McMarmac, another mining village a stone's throw from Cochenour, and into a small sturdy house that holds the heat. They pay the rent four months in advance—Morrisseau knows what will happen if he falls off the wagon, and he does his best to make sure his family is taken care of. He goes over to a neighbour's to use the telephone and calls Joe Pitura's taxi, and they are soon sailing down the gravel road into Red Lake to the Simpsons-Sears store on Howey Street, where they buy everything their hearts desire. First and foremost for him, plenty of art supplies, and for everyone warm clothing, luxurious blankets, a chesterfield suite, a coffee table, a phonograph and a radio. And then they head over to the Lakeview Café, where Harriet loves the warm slices of fluffy white bread. Which taste like heaven, she says, as she spreads the butter on thick. And there is a dish of bright cherry Jell-O for Victoria and the other children. Everybody is happy, with the hard times temporarily lifted, forgotten in the room's conversation, the smell of cooking, the rattle of utensils, plates of food being set down in front of satisfied customers. And for once the Morrisseau family is among them.

Morrisseau is proud of how far he's come—not to bloat himself up like a bullfrog, but to be respected as a famous artist with a nice house where people can visit him. Writing in a letter to Selwyn Dewdney that same year, he talks about his good fortune: his own paintings framed and hung in his house, the new furniture accenting antique brass goblets, copper trays, an assortment of silver teapots, Native artifacts like Ojibway medicine bags and Iroquoian false-face masks, floral beaded pillows and draperies. Living the good life, he asks about the books he should read, the kind of music he should listen to. He recognizes his lack of education and knowledge about the Western world as a potential hindrance to his further success as he reaches beyond the circumstance of poverty and sets his sights to the stars. The same stars, he tells Mrs. Joe of Pitura Taxi, one clear winter evening, that give him ideas for paintings.

For Morrisseau everything is a matter of destiny. We are born to do something—as he is a born artist—or it is conjured for us. The newspaper reviews are good, the exhibitions regular, and early the following year as if divined, he receives a phone call from a Professor Jacques Rousseau in Montreal, who wants to organize a solo show for him in Quebec City the following summer. As Morrisseau says in a letter to Susan Ross, "all Expenses paid by the Quebec Government… so I will Have to Paint about 50–60 Pictures Lrg and Small." Then a call from a government guy in Ottawa who wants him to do a mural for Canada's 1967 centennial celebrations, or more precisely wants him to travel to Ottawa to discuss the project.

Despite the growing interest in his work, Morrisseau is bitter when it comes to Jack Pollock. Above all, Morrisseau feels that Pollock is not providing the income that he believes he should be earning through the Pollock Gallery. He also complains that Pollock is not keeping him up to date on sales. He makes sure to tell Susan Ross that the Quebec exhibition "came about through my own

Efforts and also I am a free Agent." And so in the midst of winter, in broken handwriting, Morrisseau's letters flow like spring run-off as he tries to drum up sales from both galleries and individuals.

Morrisseau knows better than most what it is like to be hungry and poor, but he says hunger gives a man wisdom, and he doesn't regret it. One evening though he looks in on his wife and four little ones asleep in the crowded bedroom. Seeing them like this, he wishes the money coming in wasn't as slow as Turtle carrying the world on its back. Wishes he could simply dump pockets of cash on the floor before them.

He also feels that he is on the verge of doing even greater things that will surely sell—if only he had some place to paint. As a professional artist he thinks it's only fitting he should have his own space. Somewhere with good light and without interruptions. Because drunk or sober, above all else, the one thing that occupies Morrisseau's mind is painting. When he's drinking he's either making deals to sell or trade his work or sourcing out materials to make more. When he's sober or half-sober he's doing it. Hungover or not. Middle of the day or middle of the night. If asked, though, he would say he prefers the quiet of night, when his family is in bed. Waking beside Harriet and the kids, slipping into his clothes, tiptoeing into the kitchen, and pulling the cord to a single light bulb over the table, folding and tearing off a sheet of rough mill paper, taking up a favourite brush from the jar of water, wiping it on his pants, dipping the brush into a tin of black and beginning. By morning, the paintings are hung on the clothesline to dry.

The invitation to come to Ottawa on his mind, the more Morrisseau thinks about it, the more he likes the idea of painting big. *Thunderbird with Serpent*, at 32 by 70 inches, is his largest piece yet, and just last year he designed a 7- by 10-foot brilliant glass and ceramic mosaic of *The Man Who Changed into a Thunderbird* for the public library in Fort William. As early as 1964, art critic Pearl McCarthy had asked him if the themes of the oral stories he interprets are suitable for larger works, such as murals, and Morrisseau answered, "Yes, I believe they are." He added, however, that "large works would require much thought to concentrate the story pictorially." But now, looking around the room, he admits to himself that he doesn't have enough space in the small house they're renting. The rooms are small and cramped, and the kids climb everywhere. It's gotten so he's taken to painting outdoors, clipping the paper onto a sheet of plywood with clothes pegs and propping the board up against a few large rocks. It works as long as the weather is mild and the blackflies and mosquitoes aren't out in full force, eating him alive. In desperation he again turns to the house itself with whatever paint he can rescue from the town dump or the neighbours' garages, a miscellany of colour turning the walls and ceiling into a continuous mural, a dazzling interconnection of sacred creatures and powerful demigods, the artist's own family, floating across the tiny house and into the realm of the sacred.

Having finished less than half a bottle he finds himself hesitating at the door of a Scandinavian neighbour he knows will tell him that he shouldn't drink so much, and likely that they don't have money to buy paintings. He works hard for what they have, the husband will say, without caring to consider the roll under Morrisseau's arm, while the wife with sad eyes will feel sorry for him, but all the same will remain silent. For this reason he much prefers to do his rounds during the day when the men are at work, and the women can dig into their grocery money.

Hearing the dim voices inside the house, his fist inches from the door, in that very instant he remembers something the Weinsteins told him before they left Cochenour, and he takes a step back and walks out to the gravel road. With the determination of a man on a mission he walks the couple miles of black spruce into Red Lake and takes his work directly to John Sweeney, the local Simpsons-Sears agent and owner of the only furniture store in town. What he remembers is the Weinsteins telling him that the Sweeneys were over for a dinner party one evening and asked about his art, which they saw framed and mounted on the walls of the living room. Joseph Weinstein had described Sweeney as being sympathetic, which Morrisseau thinks is an interesting way to describe someone. Sympathetic. He remembers Sweeney from purchasing furniture there a year ago when he was riding the crest of success. In the midst of spending, it never occurred to him to strike up a conversation with the soft-spoken Scot, who immediately took notice of the wad of cash crumpled in his hand and welcomed them into the store with open arms. Like Weinstein, Sweeney didn't appear to have any biases against Natives whatsoever. On the contrary, he appeared all business.

A local entrepreneur, John Sweeney is a quiet, wiry man known for taking advantage of whatever opportunity avails itself to him, trying his hand in everything from selling furniture to buying furs. A man who prides himself in fairness and profit, which for him means equal respect for all his paying customers, be they white or Native. He is best known for having flown the first televisions into Red Lake and setting them up on the cement steps in front of his store. The local miners' children lined up in rows on the road to watch Saturday cartoons before running home with their mutts to tell their parents all about it. The parents showing up later that evening to catch a period of *Hockey Night in Canada*.

Morrisseau happened to be in town that day, mailing paintings to Pollock for his first show, and saw the commotion, heard the chorus of cheers from the gathered crowd, and went over to have a look. There on the cement steps were five televisions connected to a web of extension cords. As with nearly everyone in the community, it was the first time he had ever seen such a thing. A box of moving pictures. His own pictures still rolled up under his arm, he stood for a moment and marvelled at the idea of it. He thought the owner was smart for bringing them into town, where gold miners with deep pockets would probably snatch them up. He too would buy one, he told himself—as soon as he had another show he would march in there and slap down the cash. A few days later when he passed by and looked in the window, there was only one television left and it had a sold sign on it.

Unlike stepping into a white man's home with his paintings in his hand like a hat, head bent, reserved to the point of silence, Morrisseau has no qualms about walking into the Sears store. For him it's like walking into any hotel or bar to sell his art. Perhaps it's because the store is a public place, or Sweeney was also a friend of the Weinsteins and, like them, appreciates art. Upon entering the store Morrisseau marches directly to the counter and unrolls his paintings, as always.

Like smoke in the air, Morrisseau's reputation precedes him, and in addition to what the Weinsteins told him, Sweeney has heard it all about town. Not only that Morrisseau is infamous around Red Lake for his drinking, but that he had a sold-out art show in Toronto a few years ago and articles have been written about him. He still commands interest.

It turns out that Sweeney has a keen interest in art and culture, in a land where such interests are rare. Art books scatter his coffee table along with magazines—*The Beaver, National Geographic, Life*—while purchases from book clubs fill his cabinets. He has also collected Native artifacts for years, and has an immense museum-quality quill and birchbark basket collection. Sweeney's eyes widen at the sight of Morrisseau's latest paintings: a thunderbird with its wings outstretched as though rising off the paper, an owl with its all-seeing eyes, a half-human water serpent demigod. He is also a man who knows a good investment when he sees it, and in all his years in the north he has never imagined having access to such unique pieces of art. And with Morrisseau asking as little as twenty dollars for a painting, he is more than eager to take advantage of the business opportunity. In Red Lake—the land of gold—an unexpected golden egg lands on his doorstep, and the irony of it is not lost on him.

Shuffling through the paintings, the normally reticent man can barely contain his composure, and he calls in his wife Doreen from the back room, who admires them as well. Unable to extricate himself from their hypnotic gaze, the limbs of the water demigod Misshipesheu already wrapped around him and carrying him into

Morrisseau's Anishinaabe world, Sweeney cannot decide what to buy. And it is beginning with this dilemma that he and Morrisseau strike up a deal.

Morrisseau's search for a buyer and a studio abruptly comes to an end. Sweeney offers to install him in one of the rooms above the store that he normally rents to single teachers. The deal gives Morrisseau a quiet place to paint with good light, art supplies ordered and purchased from the Simpsons-Sears catalogue, even his noon meal delivered upstairs if he is there over lunchtime. And no booze. Sweeney will not tolerate Morrisseau drinking in the room, which is fine by him because he is there to work anyway. In return Sweeney is to be paid in paintings. Beyond what Morrisseau owes him for the rent and expenses, all other purchases will be made in cash.

As for Morrisseau, he is happy with the arrangement. Whatever he gets from Sweeney is better than selling his paintings for a glass of beer in the bar, a few coins in the laundromat, a taxi ride home. Better than going hat in hand into the homes of the locals and being paid five dollars or less or getting stuck with a cheque that he has trouble cashing without a bank account. Above all Morrisseau likes that Sweeney can pay him instant cash. In the habit of buying what he wants when he wants it, spending whatever he has like there is no tomorrow, Morrisseau is in need of a constant supply of ready cash. The arrangement he makes with Sweeney, like with the Weinsteins before him, suits him perfectly, because when he shows up with paintings, most often unannounced, Sweeney simply writes the store a personal cheque and draws whatever he needs from the cash register.

More often than not, though, Sweeney tries to convince Morrisseau to take a combination of cash and groceries, knowing that he will likely make a beeline to the Snake Pit and drink away every cent he has, leaving his family hungry. After a sale, Sweeney and Doreen will often send their fourteen-year-old daughter Sandra running across the street to Hurmet's Grocery for an order of milk, bread, eggs, a few tins of vegetables, and a package of meat, which they will either drive over to Harriet or send by taxi.

In the four years that he spends working on and off above the store, until the Sweeneys also move away, he comes to think of the couple as friends. Not like the Weinsteins exactly—this relationship is more formalized, his visits in the store and not their home—but nonetheless friends. As with the Weinsteins, he seeks out their advice on everything from his professional career to his family life as a father. And he even goes so far as to try and curtail his drinking when he is around them.

But not always. Because invariably he will arrive at the store dishevelled with one shoe missing and drunk. He will have hitch-hiked from Cochenour or McMarmac or McKenzie Island, wherever he has moved to at the time, because he is always running out of cash and moving, with his ubiquitous roll of paintings under his arm, and he will demand that Sweeney buy them on the spot, threaten to take them elsewhere. Sweeney will convince Morrisseau to leave the paintings in the store, give him an advance from the big brass till, and tell him to return the next day when they can sort it out. If he's lucky he can convince Morrisseau that he's had enough to drink and organize a ride home for him.

What he doesn't do anymore is purchase the paintings when Morrisseau is drinking because experience has taught him that nine times out of ten the sale will result a big headache for him. He knows Morrisseau will return the next day with his tail tucked between his legs, feeling sick and remorseful for making the sale, and he will look over what he's sold lovingly, as though they were lost children, like the ones he neglects at home, and a hardened look will appear on his face—he will feel cheated. At times thoughtless, certainly foolish to the point of irresponsible, Morrisseau is nonetheless far from stupid, although many in the community see him that way. But he is well aware of those who take advantage of him and those who do not. The last thing Sweeney wants to do is breach their friendship and break the backbone of trust in their arrangement.

Given the chance to paint every day at all hours in his own space, Morrisseau soon completes more paintings than Sweeney can handle, and the Sears agent begins selling the excess ones out of the store to anyone looking for souvenirs to bring back to the city. The arrangement is much like that of a gallery. He sells new paintings on Morrisseau's behalf and gives Morrisseau whatever he is owed in cash, after taking a percentage for displaying the work. If he sells a piece he owns outright he keeps the profit for himself.

Although Sweeney's business acumen helps keep Morrisseau in cash and groceries, some days Morrisseau feels deep regret for a sale he's made. He gets what Sweeney calls seller's remorse. He will say things like "I shouldn't have sold you that one. It's one of my best paintings and I sold it too cheaply." Sometimes if he is preparing for a show, Sweeney will break down and sell him back a few pieces. But not always. If Sweeney is smitten by a painting, or recognizes its value, he will be hard-nosed, dig in his heels, and remind Morrisseau that a deal is a deal. Morrisseau in turn will never lower himself to beg or even plead his case. Rather, he will offer to trade one piece for another. Maybe even two for one. He knows that Sweeney has more of his paintings than anyone else and that he stands to make a small fortune selling them to galleries and museums, but that is not his concern. He is firm when he says, "I don't paint for money. I only need enough to get by," and so he has settled into a business arrangement he can live with, most of the time.

And so for now Morrisseau is grateful to be tucked away upstairs in the Sears store, above all the brand-spanking-new furniture, living room suites, sparkling white appliances, televisions. To have a space to paint with good light, a chance to create new work away from the distractions of family, a safe place away from his boozy self, means more to him than everything he has done to date. Because when he is submerged in the world of his work he knows without a doubt that what he has yet to do will be far greater than anything hanging downstairs. At this point as an emerging artist he knows he has much to learn, but that he is making breakthroughs. The challenge is not to repeat himself but to infuse his work with more of his Anishinaabe worldview, his beliefs about spirituality, his sense of mystery in creation, mixed and brushed on with his own personality, and what he himself has experienced as a living, breathing Indian who has survived into the twentieth century.

Sometimes at closing time when there is nobody in the store and the late-afternoon light is perfect, streaming in though the windows, he goes downstairs and walks around the showroom where Sweeney has thumbtacked his paintings to the four walls. And he sits there on one of the new couches with his arms outstretched as though taking each and every piece back inside himself, dressing himself with his art. And he knows they are all part of a story that extends back to the beginning of time and religion, and they remind him of who he is and how much work he has yet to do.

An Incredible Journey

As she is flying above Sandy Lake, Susan Ross's painter's eye notices two things from the air: an extraordinary, long boardwalk unfurled like a grey carpet from the lakeshore, where the planes dock next to the village, and a huge white mound against a backdrop of black spruce. It is upon approaching that she realizes that what she thought looked like snow from high above is actually a grave-yard of discarded washing machines on a knoll behind the village, the broken-down appliances refusing to melt back into the earth. Ross and her writer friend Sheila Burnford, famous for her book *The Incredible Journey*, have come for a visit. Three years ago, living in a hinterland and finding herself in need of artistic companionship, Ross had wanted to meet the painter everybody was talking about. She wasn't disappointed. And despite the stories of Morrisseau's extreme moodiness that travel with him like ticks on a moose, she found him quite amicable, and they have since become friends. Or at least as friendly as any white person can get with him, everyone tells her.

Upon his advice, a couple of years ago she and Burnford travelled up to Gull Lake, a Native community on the north shore of Lake Nipigon. It was her first encounter with Indians. In hindsight she found it an odd thing, being born and raised in Canada but having no idea about Indian people. From that moment she knew she had found her subject. But so ill at ease and ill equipped was she during those early forays into the bush, her writer friend described them as "two white matrons affiliated with neither the church nor government and totally out of place." She has since flown to some of the most remote communities in northwestern Ontario, to do portraits of Indians involved in their traditional lifestyle before it vanishes, which she sees as inevitable—the region being awash with a flood of bureaucrats and missionaries in the midst of damming rivers and saving souls. And so Susan Ross, the painter of a people in transition, as she calls herself, is genuinely excited to meet Morrisseau again and do some sketching in the community.

After cobbling together airfare from recent sales, Morrisseau has once again come with his family to his wife's remote community of Sandy Lake to dry out. It is where Harriet and the children are happiest, and his only hope to stay sober is by keeping away from temptation. Ross is relieved to find him sticking to his guns and not drinking. At least for the time being. In a letter she received a year earlier, dated January 6, 1964, Morrisseau announced, "I have promised to stop for six months. I know I'm being helped and I won't forget I am being helped and I Really understand now… The bottle really Destroy's me Phiscally (body) and Soul and Mind… I must Quit. I must truly and Sincerely make up my mind to Stop." The letter is from a period when their relationship was as new as his children, and there was Morrisseau already baring his soul to her. She found it odd, if not embarrassing, to hear such things from someone she hardly knew. To Morrisseau it was like he had known her forever, and with a single "auniin" he welcomes her again.

The tiny house is festooned with paintings, some tacked to the walls, some propped against the furniture. Morrisseau is working outside on an old plank table placed in a sunny spot in the yard, and his wet paintings, pegged to a clothesline strung between two trees, flap in the wind. Harriet and the children are with him, and the atmosphere is one of celebration. The family appears to have enough money coming in through sales. Everyone appears well fed and clothed. Morrisseau himself is wearing a pair of olive green pants and a blue canvas shirt, and his tanned Kodiaks also appear fairly new. The kids are gnawing on what looks like some kind of jerky.

Ross spends a good part of the afternoon asking Morrisseau about his work as he continues painting. She paints the outside of things, he remarks, the way they look to the naked eye, and he paints the inside, the soul side, the way they look to the eye of the mind. That's when he explains that in the Ojibway people's beliefs everyone has two spirits, or souls, one for the daytime and one for the nighttime. One for the awake world, and one for the dream world. She paints the awake world, while he paints the dream world. That is the nature of their conversation. Fascinated by his work, Ross and Burnford each purchase a painting before they leave. For Harriet this means more groceries. Everybody is happy.

When Morrisseau is back in Beardmore or Red Lake, Thunder Bay or Winnipeg, and peddling his art from highway to doorway, he makes a point of visiting everyone he knows who might buy something. Doctors, teachers, businessmen, lawyers, and judges are high on his list. Although Ross is an artist herself, her life is far from that of a struggling artist. Her husband is a judge and she is comfortably ensconced into upper-middle-class white society; she will fly when and where she wants to paint. Morrisseau knows this about her, and she confirms what his grandfather has told him about white people: having taken the land, they are born to privilege. While she considers him a painter of remarkable talent, and believes they share a bond forged in art, he sees her first and foremost as another person who can help him. This is not to say that he doesn't value her friendship. Morrisseau's relationships are based on friendship. If he can help her, fine, but he has no qualms about using her in any way he can. In fact, for him it is only natural. His reasoning is simple: she is his friend, and she has more than one person could possibly need.

Since meeting Ross, Morrisseau has written her regularly, confiding in her about everything from his family life to his drinking, asking her either to buy his paintings, mail them out, or collect money for them. So far she hasn't minded. "A character," she calls him, "chocked full of human frailty." At times, though, a frown falls over her face when he writes, "I am very pleased with your service." And she finds herself asking, "When will it end?"

And a few years later it does end, when Ross arrives at a point of exasperation. The demands to help him sell his art, she endures, but, like Harriet, she becomes fed up with Morrisseau's promises to stop drinking. She becomes tired of him turning up at her door in the middle of the night as if it were the middle of the afternoon, wanting her to buy one of the paintings rolled under his arm. In befriending him, she never realized the width of the river between them. On the other hand, Morrisseau realizes it profoundly and plunges headfirst into the current. To date Susan Ross has not only purchased paintings but has sold paintings on his behalf for the best possible prices, has acted as an intermediary between him and Pollock, has wrapped and shipped paintings, has purchased art supplies and sent them to him at her own expense. And without a doubt Morrisseau appreciates everything she has done for him, but, in considering her his friend, he simply expects more. When she cannot give more, or do more, she finally stops answering his letters, and he simply moves on. And never looks back.

Legends of My People

For him it will have sufficed that I cleaned out the portages along a route through Morrisseau's unfamiliar world that will bring him close to each significant feature of its landscape. Others, however, will reasonably expect some sort of

briefing, a map or at least a compass, before they venture so far from home.
—SELWYN DEWDNEY, IN THE INTRODUCTION TO
LEGENDS OF MY PEOPLE, 1965

TODAY MORRISSEAU IS RICH in dreams as big as the world. The spring publishing season sees him cracking open his new book like a cool bottle of beer. He flips a page, and below a black India-ink Misshipesheu is the title, *Legends of My People: The Great Ojibway*, and below that, his name. Morrisseau can hardly believe his book has finally arrived, and flipping another page he turns now to his bold dedication: TO MY GRANDFATHER MOSES ("POTAN") NANAKONAGOS. He then turns to his introduction and reads: "This book is written in honour of my great Ojibway Indian Ancestors who roamed the Great Lakes for centuries upon centuries and their descendants who live today all over Ontario. I am Norval Morrisseau and my Indian name is Copper Thunderbird. I am a born artist..." Morrisseau knows that many of his people do not trust the white man's words, and for this reason seeing his own words in print, having his own book in his hands, is an unexpected gift. Even though he's waited for this gift for five years—he can still remember handing Selwyn Dewdney the first of two black spiralled notebooks, a child's note-book with a child's scrawl, sentences careening out of control, thoughts broken as if hit head-on, a collision of language. His own way of swallowing and spitting out the white man's words. And now a real book is clutched in his hands. Despite the difficulty of getting the stories down on paper, long laborious nights as if trudging through spring snow, despite the worry about what others might think, he is proud to have persevered.

Painter, now author. Who would have thought? He thinks of the sheer amazement on Dewdney's face as he read his notebook, as if he had just discovered a map to lost treasure. And with only a grade-four education. It is something he now says he regrets, and makes sure to add, "I have read a lot to improve my education." With this in mind, he reads more: "I wish some of the educated Ojibway Indians would take the same interest in our history as I have always done." Morrisseau has never faltered in his pledge to build a foundation of knowledge about his people so that the myth of the savage can be buried once and forever, knowledge that others may build upon. And now that his book is finally released under his own name—Dewdney taking an editing credit—he knows that along with his art, he is laying that first stone, making the white man aware of his world, and his own people aware of the value of holding onto their traditions. "In another hundred years from today we will be mixed with our great country into the Canadian way of life. How will we benefit by knowing that way of life if we set aside our ancestral rites and beliefs?" For Morrisseau this is the pressing issue of his time, and he concludes that "We, therefore, must write down and record legends, art, songs and beliefs, not for ourselves alone but for all future Ojibway."

When the reviews come out they are mostly positive, by curious journalists travelling into his world without a compass—ranging from *The Montreal Star*'s "Intriguing Ojibway Legends" to *The London Free Press*'s "Ojibway Author Casts Rare Light on Indian," to the *Toronto Star*'s "An Outstanding Citizen." Some, however, like Edward Parsons writing in *The Globe Magazine*, find his writing "rubbish" and "wooden," much like how some would prefer Indians to remain. But Morrisseau knows those days are gone forever.

With his book lying on the table, dog-eared from having carried it in his pocket like a crumpled bill, Morrisseau is once again down and out in Red Lake. His excitement at seeing his words in print has been short-lived, and he is drinking daily. All feeling is gone, the prick of memory temporarily blunted, and he is little more than a shell of himself, a madman, someone who could lay his hand on a sizzling kitchen stove and smile. Much to Harriet's dismay. Her words fall like her tears as he waves her off, yells at her to leave him alone, as the children cry and huddle in a corner, and he staggers off into the night. His brushes and paint by now are hardened, as unyielding as the starry sky that soon comes crashing down on him.

By August of 1965 he is down on his knees wrestling with his sickness. Like the year before, his family is again on the verge of starvation, and, without any paintings for a quick sale, he has no choice but to write to the office of the Improvement District of Red Lake for welfare: "Can you help us out in given us some kind of relief only once until I get my money. Today I sent out all my art to different places which I am sure I will get money for but in the meantime I got no funds to buy food—if you could tell Hudson Bay to give us say $15.00 for Groceries and Charge it to you then I will pay you back this Amount when my money gets here... I am sure I could be trusted. I am considering given your office a picture at a later date—a gift."

Morrisseau is well aware of the serpent inside him, hypnotizing him with its yellow liquid eyes, so much so that he painted it writhing out of his orifices as early as 1964 in *Self Portrait Devoured by Demons*. At that time he wrote to his friend and mentor Selwyn Dewdney, exposing the one thing other than painting that consumes him: "I don't drink much although I feel like it at times, but I try not to give in to my wantings. I realize each day little by little that it is not good for me. If I feel like drinking I think how I will feel on a hang-over, and this helps because I really feel bad. It destroys me. My body, soul and mind. So it is no use to Drink if I feel this way, Right."

Born out of desperation, his letter maybe more than anything else reveals Morrisseau trying to convince himself that he no longer needs to drink. He is aware that it impairs him. He is aware that it is killing him. And yet his words are no less than a plea for understanding. As though directly responding to the artist himself, Dewdney answers a CBC reporter, "I have seen Morrisseau torn apart and made desperate with doubt," characterizing his behaviour as the result of "tortured efforts to reconcile the skepticism of a superior intelligence with the fantasies of his people's folklore," and grappling with "the bewildering complexities of the dominant culture." He calls Morrisseau "as contemporary as space travel," someone thrown from a world of shamanism and landing in downtown Toronto. What of course Dewdney does not know is that Morrisseau has experienced the white man and his culture since he was a child, especially in the form of the priests who visited the artist and the other children during the long nights at St. Joseph's Residential School. Who made them wish they were dead.

Celebrating Canada's 1967 Centennial

In Beardmore again, living beside the local dump, Morrisseau picks through the discarded magazines and newspapers and reads that Canada is planning its hundredth anniversary of Confederation celebrations. A centennial party that will rise in a chorus of voices singing, "ca-na-da, we love thee." Watching smoke rise from the stinking garbage, his bottle of whiskey almost empty, he sees nothing to celebrate. For him the commission to paint a panel for the Indians of Canada Pavilion simply means a paycheque and a trip to Montreal. Who knows who he might meet?

When his advance arrives, Morrisseau buys himself a new set of clothes and a train ticket. Harriet is not sure she wants him to go, but he goes anyway. She will stay behind with the kids and eventually get left behind for good. In Montreal, Morrisseau attends a series of meetings hosted by the Department of Indian Affairs and the Centennial Indian Advisory Committee. He meets other Indian painters like George Clutesi, Gerald Tailfeathers, and Alex Janvier, who are also contributing to the pavilion. For the first time he realizes he is part of a movement of Indian artists.

The struggle between the government and the Indian committee to determine the focus of the exhibit flares into shouts and accusations. Some believe the government is trying to control the representation of Native cultures and whitewash the relationship between Canada and the Native peoples. Between the colonizer and the colonized. Morrisseau attends the meetings but tunes out, choosing instead to focus on the mural he will paint for the south wall. The space he has to fill is enormous, 27 feet high by 14 feet wide. He has never before painted anything close to that size. And he is excited by the prospect that people from all over the world will see his work, see something of the culture of the Great Ojibway. While the others talk, he sketches his ideas on a napkin.

His mind on the greater purpose of his art, he adds his voice to the dissension only when it appears that the government is trying to control not only what will go inside the pavilion but also on the outside of it. When the organizers press Morrisseau for preliminary drawings so they might see his plans, he balks and speaks to them of shamanistic connection and divine inspiration. The civil servants have no idea what he is talking about and leave him alone. When they finally see the outline for his mural, sketched on the wall of the pavilion, the sight of both a baby and a bear cub suckling the breast of a sensuous Mother Earth offends their sense of decency, and they envision outrage and scandal. They do not approve the work and force Morrisseau to modify it. He responds by disappearing into the bars of Montreal, leaving his assistant, Cree painter Carl Ray (who goes unrecognized), to finish the mural.

The Indians of Canada Pavilion at Expo 67 turns out to be one of the most popular of all the pavilions—visited by Her Majesty Queen Elizabeth and Prince Philip, Duke of Edinburgh—despite the tough theme presented inside, which moves from celebrating Man the Explorer and Creator to one of exposing Man the Exploiter. While headlines across Canada announce: "Pavilion Rebukes White Man, Indians' Theme Angers Expo Visitors," both national and international guests continue to flock to the controversial site, the showcase of Indian art adorning the exterior of the pavilion pulling them in like a wave. What they witness, many will carry with them in their own bundle for the rest of their lives. Their perception of Canada forever changed.

As for Morrisseau, he knows he is part of something far larger than himself. Later, when asked, he is clearly aware of the impact of the work he has done: "One day maybe if there's another Centennial, I wouldn't like the white man to say he can trace back himself right to the cave days, but what's the Indian got, nothing! They're gonna say what the white man writes about him. It's not good. Even if they never mention my name, you cannot stop progress. I laid the first cornerstone already, whether I'm a drunkard or not, sober, or whatever kind of person I am, I led that thing. That's for the betterment of our people in the future, not today."

Without acknowledging the cultural legacy of the past, he knows there can be no future, so he dedicates his mural—as he did his book—to the one person who has had the greatest influence on him, his grandfather. On the bottom right-hand corner of his mural he inscribes his dedication:

> In honour
> of my Grandfather Potan Nanakonagos
> and to our Ancestors.

When Expo 67 is over, the teepee-like Indians of Canada Pavilion falls into neglect and disrepair, and Morrisseau's mural, along with those of his fellow artists, passes into oblivion.

Windigo and Other Tales

AT EXPO MORRISSEAU MEETS Dr. Herbert Schwarz, a British immigrant with a fascination for early French Canadian history. Both a practicing doctor at the Royal Victoria Hospital and a medical researcher at McGill University, Schwarz is a man with status and influence, successful at everything he does. As a consultant on the Quebec Pavilion, he is juggling his profession with his passion for culture and history when he comes across Morrisseau's panel of *Earth Mother with Her Children*. He is mesmerized by the warm earth tones of sandy brown and forest green, the bright sun highlighting each figure, all bound together by black lines of power connecting to white circles of balance, one for each figure.

Schwarz has previously written to Morrisseau and is now more determined than ever to meet him. Morrisseau is binge drinking at the time, and Schwarz tracks him down at a nearby bar. Morrisseau is happy to meet someone who will buy him a drink. Schwarz says he would like to exhibit his work, and makes him an offer. He has gallery contacts in France and his own Galerie Cartier has just opened in a historic residence in Montreal.

True to his word, Dr. Schwarz goes about organizing the exhibition at his Galerie Cartier. Morrisseau tells the *Winnipeg Free Press* that he is under commission for fifteen thousand dollars to produce thirty-one paintings in two months. The exhibition is a huge success: two floors of paintings and nearly all of them sold—a repeat of the sold-out show he had last year in Quebec City at the Musée du Quebec. The critics marvel at the work, calling it magical, calling "Morrisseau's pictorial language splendid, astonishing, remarkable." He reads an article about the show in *The Gazette*, his brow furrowed, studying what they are saying about him: "As you find yourself surrounded by Norval Morrisseau's hundred-shaped creatures, by his floating mermen, by demi-gods and guardians of dreams, by snake surgeons, and thunderbirds, by fire worshipers, by evil trout, by devil-turtles and protector bears—all magnificently embroidered by the artist's teaming imagination—you do not doubt for a moment that you have entered a world of viable magic and practiced ritual."

The mention of devil-turtles makes him laugh so hard he almost chokes on his drink. As far as he's concerned it's Mikkinnuk, Turtle, who helped create the world, a paw of soil spread upon his back, and the tree of life, along with all the birds and animals springing from it. "The only devil is right here," he says to himself, as he holds up his glass of rye and gives it a swirl. And God knows he has been trying to get out of the grip of this devil for years.

He goes back to the article: "It is a late gift and an unexpected privilege to be permitted to share in a fading culture's last secrets. To learn of a forgotten people's rites and dreams born from fear of the unknown, forming the hope of escape from its penetrating presence."

If Morrisseau understands correctly, he doesn't exist, or barely exists. He's a relic of a culture you have to squint to see. Like in *The Last of the Mohicans*, which he saw at the old Cabin Theatre in Red Lake after burgers at the Lakeview. He remembers holding Harriet's hand through the whole movie—that was the best thing about it. And to imply there are religions not born of fear—which one, Catholic? That's a good one! He takes another drink and wonders who comes up with this stuff.

The piece continues: "When Copper Thunderbird paints his account of a shaking tent rite we readily appreciate that he is giving us a valuable ethnological document. Morrisseau's designs always have a deeper than surface meaning. Duck and fish designed with continuation-lines between them. The shaman and his medicine bag joined by power-lines. Between buffaloes and humans span the lines of interdependence in sorcery."

He likes this section of the article and thinks they might be getting at something. Now that imagery and composition are second nature to him, he has to go deeper. When he paints the shaking tent, it is *his* ceremony. When he paints a medicine bag, it is *his* medicine. Just as when he paints a thunderbird, it is a thunderbird he has seen through *his* own visions. No more surface stuff. To paint a shaman he has to become a shaman. How to get there is the question. A question he finds himself pondering as he orders another round for his new friends.

Herbert Schwarz also has other plans for Morrisseau and proposes that they do a book together, a collection of Ojibway legends, stories, and ancestral beliefs, illustrated by Morrisseau. It is another chance to preserve more of his great culture on paper, and Morrisseau is eager to get involved. Quoting his grandfather Potan, Morrisseau responds by saying that "the time has come for us to write and to record the story of our people; not only for ourselves but also for our white brothers so that they will be able to understand and respect us." Schwarz is excited too and has it all figured out. He will collect stories from Morrisseau and other sources over the next year and edit them while Morrisseau completes the paintings, which Schwarz will purchase outright and resell in his gallery.

Back in Red Lake and living with his family again, cheques flying in from recent sales relieving him of the need to sell door-to-door, Morrisseau sends Schwarz the stories he thinks will be suitable for the book as he goes about finishing a dozen illustrations specifically for the project. Each illustration is based on a story. Each story is based on humans from history, such as his own grandfather, and those of legend: mythic manitous and demigods. He will go on to say that each story is a lesson to live by and that each story allows for hundreds of paintings. Far too many to paint in one lifetime.

When the book is finally published, Morrisseau picks up his complimentary copy at the Red Lake Post Office. He unwraps it excitedly, but then, as if slapped in the face, he just stares at it. On the cover below the title—*Windigo and Other Tales of the Ojibways*—is the name of the author, Herbert T. Schwarz. Below the cover's artwork, Morrisseau is credited as illustrator. Furthermore, the voices of Morrisseau's grandfather and the other wise old men have been eviscerated by Schwarz's sharp-as-a-knife editing. Having worked closely on *Legends of My People* with Selwyn Dewdney, Morrisseau is angry, and his first reaction is to throw the book in the garbage can next to him. But then his grandfather's warning comes back to him, that white people naturally want to take everything, and he realizes that he should have expected it. He looks at the book again, and he is happy that the first story is the one about "Grandfather Potan and the Bear." He knows that without his grandfather there would be no books and no paintings. And no Copper Thunderbird. And although he's struggled to make ends meet, he will continue to say in interview after interview, "I do not paint to make money."

Case in point: that December Morrisseau is flush with money, feeling good and in the Christmas spirit. It is one of those typical northern evenings, crystal clear, stars, the crunch of snow under every footstep, and he is walking down the main drag of Red Lake on his way home. As he is passing the Red Lake Hotel he meets about half a dozen Indians huddled on the front steps, shivering. Some of them he knows. Some of them he doesn't know. He stops to say hello and they ask him for a cigarette, for some spare change. He tells them to come with him and starts to walk away, hurrying to get out of the cold. They pull themselves up from the freezing cement and tag along behind his big strides. Maybe they think he's going to buy them a drink. Maybe they think he has a bottle stashed somewhere. Instead he takes them over to the Hudson's Bay Company store and waves them inside. There he buys each of them a Woods parka, the warmest they have in the store, and a pair of wool socks. He then continues on his way.

Victoria and the Bear

MIDDAY, HOT, the sound of cicadas and the smell of burning garbage fill the air. A camera crew from the CBC has arrived in Beardmore to interview the famous Ojibway artist. On cue the camera begins rolling and a tall, thin man, approximately thirty-seven years old (nobody knows his age for sure), with a distinctly Indian face and a brush of thick black hair, emerges from a tar-paper shack. He is wearing a white T-shirt, jeans and rubber boots—which seems rather odd, on such a hot summer day. The door is nearly falling off its hinges and slams behind him. A tree is growing through a corner of the shack's roof. This too appears rather peculiar.

It is 1968—Morrisseau's seventh child is born—and the CBC is making a documentary for the evening news on the phenomenal success of Norval Morrisseau, the Indian artist. If they were expecting the appearance of material wealth, judging from the surroundings, they were sorely mistaken. The director asks for action. He wants something to happen. With the camera eyeing him like a sniper, Morrisseau is supposed to do something, but he feels extremely self-conscious and doesn't know what to do. When he looks at the camera blankly, he is told to do anything, so he decides to head off down a path that leads into a scrub of spruce. When he gets to the end of the path, he turns around and does it over again. The crush of his boots over the gravel becomes an audible refrain.

The director plans to insert a series of interviews with people who have been central to Morrisseau's career, people like Selwyn Dewdney and Jack Pollock. The interviews are meant to highlight Morrisseau's history, and those of the Canadian Indian in general, to give some insight into the artist's personality.

Meanwhile Morrisseau is expected to talk about his rise to fame, showcase the anomaly of an impoverished Indian stuck out in the hinterland of northwestern Ontario becoming a successful artist. Talk about how he got to where he is. How his people got to where they are. Instead he tells them a story about a bear:

"My wife was here last summer, we throw garbage over there in the bush. One time there, a big bear he walk here. We sitting down here and he just walk right here. So my wife tell me, said, you should kill that bear. I said I don't like to kill that bear because I tell 'em, he's just like an Indian himself. So, my daughter with a shoe, he make 'em scared. They had to run all the way, till they run inside. Okay, I said, I grab my gun there, I walk there, I'm with a 303, bam, right on the head. You know I cry. I cry for it. You know that bear, it sounds just like a human, ahh, ahh, ahh. Just like he die. But he says, the Indian says, never go close to him when he sounds like that because he's dying. I go there, open his mouth, he's dead. Pour one whiskey to him in his mouth. I says to him, please forgive me I didn't mean to kill you. You, you great spirit over there, the bear spirit, we had to destroy you, but we didn't mean it. That's a funny thing to see an Indian pour a whiskey to his mouth, eh!"

In another part of the interview, he says angrily that the Jesuits did what they could to destroy Indian culture three hundred years ago. What Morrisseau is talking about is his determination to revive "the old Indian culture," as he calls it. When he thinks about it, he raises his voice in anger. "Look, I met a Jesuit priest a little while ago. He told me, he said, 'What would you do to revive the old Indian culture again?' Well I told him, look, you destroyed it three hundred years ago, I told him. Why should you revive it now? All the things what the Indian know, you destroyed that."

With this in mind he is well aware that he must work with what is left, what he has on hand, and create new ceremonies for a new time. On the spot he does a ceremony with what he does have on hand: whiskey, a powerful medicine or poison, depending on how you look at it. He grins at this point and says he feels better after that. The conversation turns naturally back to his art, which he considers an example of working with what is left, and again he states matter-of-factly that despite the criticism of some of his own people, he believes that what he is doing is for their benefit. Maybe not now, but hundreds years from now. For Morrisseau looking to the past is all about looking to the future. It is at this point that the filmmakers splice in a scene where he is sitting in front of his tin shack talking in Anishinaabemowin to his grandfather, as though they are sharing a secret.

Flying High

SINCE THEIR FIRST MEETING at the Quetico Conference and Training Centre in the summer of 1963, Robert Lavack has been helping out Morrisseau whenever he can, flying rolls of brown kraft paper from the Dryden Paper Mill to Sandy Lake for his use, and, like so many others, acting as a friend cum quasi-agent and selling work for him. And Morrisseau also becomes dependent on these sales to supplement the dry periods between formal exhibitions, which are prestigious and worthwhile in their own right but are not frequent enough to meet his needs. In 1968, for example, he has only one exhibition, at the Art Gallery of Newport in Rhode Island, and although the likes of Rockefeller and Firestone buy his paintings, whatever money he receives disappears quickly. And so he asks Robbie about the money owing to him.

Lavack hands him a tally: two larger paintings sold in North Bay for $70 each, two small paintings sold in Kenora for $90 total, and a smaller kraft paper painting to the anthropologist Ken Dawson at a "special price" (since Lavack knows him) of $50. He hands Morrisseau a cheque for $280 and tells him to make sure to bring it home. He normally likes to mail at least half the cheque to Harriet in case Morrisseau gets lost along the way, but Morrisseau assures him there's no problem.

After such success Morrisseau is brimming with love, and his family is first and foremost on his mind. He confides in Lavack that he is confident he can patch up his relationship with Harriet, and swears that he can turn over a new leaf. Clutching his cheque, he says that all he needs is enough money coming in to support his family. But money flows through Morrisseau's hands and out the holes in his pockets as though the material gain it offers is worthless to him. One might consider it his grand gesture of resistance: that to concern himself with money would be to concede to the white man's way of seeing the world. Meanwhile, selling Morrisseau's art over the years, Lavack witnesses firsthand the surging interest in Native art, and the fountain of money that flows from it, and it is during this time that he conceives of the idea to train other Native people so they might also tap into the growing market.

Lavack's official title is Assistant Superintendent of Education for the Government of Ontario. Part of his job requires him to fly into twenty-two isolated Ojibway and Cree communities in north-western Ontario to administer secondary school services and training programs. Like everyone who comes under Morrisseau's spell, Lavack recognizes Morrisseau's genius and can't help himself from getting involved. The education department soon sees the potential in developing an arts and crafts industry among Native people as part of their community cultural programs initiative, and in April of 1969, Lavack writes to Morrisseau asking him if he would like to participate in "a series of art enrichment programs in northern schools and communities" for the following year. Who better to demonstrate the new art than Morrisseau, the father of the movement, and his protegé Carl Ray?

The way Lavack sees it, he has been saddled with the artist since they first met some seven years ago and he is still trying to figure him out. But he knows that to try to help Morrisseau is a losing battle that even the archangel Michael himself could not win. Morrisseau and Lavack have a running joke. Morrisseau calls him the devil. It started when he noticed a bump on the Robbie's forehead and developed naturally because Morrisseau feels he runs with the devil every time he falls off the wagon. Lavack plays it up as much as possible to try and keep Morrisseau on the straight and narrow. He warns him that since they are friends he would hate to have to steal his soul. It is something Morrisseau half believes, especially when he is hungover and remorseful and feels that the eyes of Jesus and every saint in heaven are looking at him. Thinks of the tears they must shed for him.

Despite the bureaucracy, Lavack doesn't mind his job since it gets him into the air. Without a dedicated budget for travel, he figures they hired him because the government needed a cheap way to service these communities, and he arrived with his own pilot's licence. Morrisseau believes that the devil also works in mysterious ways, and when he looks at Lavack he sees someone who has sidestepped fate. When asked about his World War II exploits, surviving such a high-risk occupation when so many other pilots were killed, Lavack will say straight-faced that getting shot down was good training for carrying Norval Morrisseau around.

Up in the clouds, Morrisseau lurches awake from the dream of falling through the air, flailing through the realm of the thunderbirds, as Lake Nipigon reaches up and catches him in its clutch and pieces of the airplane come crashing down around him, showering the lake with debris. And then Misshipesheu, horned and malevolent water manitou, drags him down into the deep. It's at this moment that he realizes the pilot has been trying to get his attention over the roaring engine of the Cessna. He blinks a couple of times, unable to pull himself fully out of his stupor.

Turning in his seat now, Lavack can see as plain as the storm rolling in over the horizon that Morrisseau and Ray are still boozed-up from their previous night at the Snake Pit in Red Lake. He yells at them over the deafening engine to put out the cigarettes dangling from their lips. He gestures to the two drums of extra fuel behind their seats and asks them if they want to blow themselves out of the sky. Morrisseau quickly stomps out his cigarette. Ray ignores him. Lavack tells him again to toss the cigarette out while Morrisseau reaches over and tries to grab it out of his mouth. A scuffle ensues and Lavack yells at them to cut it out, but they are in no condition to listen. He looks for a place to land but the lake below is too shallow, with too many rocks and deadheads near the surface, so he reaches behind with his right arm and beckons for the cigarette. Instead of handing it over, Ray grabs hold of him and yanks him backward, and Lavack, stretched half out of his seat, lets go of the controls. The plane instantly noses upward and then banks to the left. Morrisseau closes his eyes and cries out that his dream is coming true—they're going to crash. Ray, equally startled, releases Lavack's arm, and the pilot deftly brings the plane under control. Contrite, Ray tosses the cigarette out the window to the lake below and then sits back and passes out, while Morrisseau crosses himself, thanking Jesus for saving his life, before falling asleep as well.

The flight is quiet for the rest of the trip, but by the time they reach Big Trout Lake the sky's ceiling is low and grey, and Lavack is eager to land. He sees that the Catholic mission dock is completely occupied by other small aircraft and he wonders what's going on. Creasing the surface of the lake he eases up on the speed and taxies towards the long main dock, which is also mostly occupied. And there to greet them unannounced is a row of priests looking like the black shadows of the storm. It turns out that it is the weekend of a synod and a dozen church officials serving the north have congregated in the small community.

Morrisseau is looking out the rear window as the priests approach and considers their reception in terms of divine intervention. Lavack cuts the engine, throws opens the cockpit door, and steps down onto the pontoon to grab a mooring line thrown to him by one of the missionaries. Morrisseau is impatient to get out and follows on Lavack's heels with the intention of leaping gingerly from the float to the dock. But the moment he steps down onto the pontoon, he loses his balance and his feet go shooting up in front of him, and like a drunken dancer, he goes flying into the lake. He comes up gasping and spurting water and is about to go under again when Lavack takes hold of one of the wing struts and reaches down and grabs him by his long hair. He manages to keep Morrisseau's head above the water and guides him to the dock. With the help of some of the missionaries, he gets Morrisseau and then Ray safely onto dry land.

The bishop, the local chief, and the band's council are among those standing on the dock waiting to welcome the two artists. They turn in unison and glare at Lavack, putting the blame on him. Morrisseau and Ray are oblivious to it all. All Lavack can do is shrug it off, and hope that his passengers will be able to teach tomorrow. After unloading the plane Lavack meets up with Simon Frogg, his contact at the Indian band's office, who walks him up over to the cabins where they are staying for the night. By now Morrisseau and Ray have disappeared. That evening, with the storm lashing down in a torrent of rain, Morrisseau shows up alone drunker than ever— somehow he's managed to find a bootlegger. And he is as wild as the weather. Soaked by the rain with his arms flailing madly, he stands on the boardwalk shouting at the top of his lungs. Lavack and Frogg run to him and together drag him into his cabin, but it is not where he wants to be. He fights them off, fuelled by homebrew and the power of his hulking frame, crashing into the furniture, sending it toppling over. Morrisseau is flying higher than the blustering wind, and Lavack tries to talk him down.

But he is not listening and starts roaring about the congregation of church officials in the community, the number of churches, the loss of his culture. The invasion, he calls it, as he grabs a chair and it explodes against the wall. He staggers back through the door, and that's when Lavack yells to Frogg that he has some rope inside one of his packs. With the wind whipping down sheets of rain, they manage to corral Morrisseau beside a huge spruce and tie him to it. Slumped on the ground with his long hair streaming water, he shouts and curses until he finally passes out. And the storm too subsides and the sky turns into a star-filled northern night. They carry Morrisseau back to his own cabin, strip him, and put him to bed. Frogg, who had been looking forward to meeting the famous artist, waves good-night and comments, "So that's the great Morrisseau?" Lavack, who does indeed believe that Morrisseau is great, sees no point in trying to explain away his behaviour. All he can do is write it off as an act of God.

The next morning Morrisseau is up and running as though nothing has happened, as though the previous night's rain has washed away any trace of a hangover, embarrassment, or regret. He has cleaned himself up, has combed his long hair back, and is wearing a fresh shirt. He and Ray, who has returned from visiting his mother, meet up with Lavack and walk over with him to the band council's office, carrying their art supplies for the workshop under their arms. Simon Frogg is there to greet them, and, like Lavack, he is thinking of the previous night and is skeptical they can pull it off. Lavack opens the presentation with a short talk about his department's developing cultural strategy and then goes on to introduce Morrisseau and Ray, who need no introduction. And before barely another word is spoken, they have everybody laughing out loud. Their introductory talk is spiced with ribald tricksterisms and self-deprecating humour, which they use to segue into a practical, hands-on workshop.

On sheets of paper taped to the walls, the two artists go about illustrating the concept of their art. In controlled and original forms, Anishinaabe demigods and spirit animals, a part of everyone in the room's heritage, take shape before their eyes. Are coloured to life. The participants know the images communally without ever having seen them before, and Morrisseau and Ray encourage everyone to try their hand at it. Any doubt that Lavack might have had about the pair's ability to share their vision, the preservation of culture, the transmission of technique, is allayed. They are the prophets, the Peter and Paul, of the new movement, he concludes. The two of them proselytizing in a community filled with Catholic clergy.

The Ojibway Art Circuit

By 1970 Morrisseau and his family are living back on McKenzie Island, renting a small clapboard house for a few dollars a month on Head Frame Street, a gravel road. From the window at the table he studies the lake, the ferry from the mainland bringing and collecting passengers, the distant boats buzzing like bees, the Norseman rising and disappearing into the sky. He finds himself trying to fit the pieces of his days together, a piece for Harriet, a piece for the children, a piece for his work, a piece for himself. The piece for himself getting larger and larger. When he is not selling or trading paintings to Red Lake locals for food, rent, and fuel oil, he spends his time and whatever little money he has at the Gold Eagle Hotel down the road, drinking in the gloom with the few hangers-on who still cling to the island.

With his metamorphosis into a professional artist complete, he sheds his chrysalis and stretches into the role. And he is overwhelmed by the response. Who would have thought a nearly unschooled Indian could write so many letters? Since his first exhibition, Morrisseau has breathed the winds of the outside world and he wants more. But like a season of bad weather, one day folds into the next and despair becomes the prevailing mood. He routinely leaves for a couple of hours to sell his art and doesn't return. Again and again, Harriet is left to fend for herself. The white neighbours raise their eyebrows, give her the sorrowful look of charity, a look she cannot stand. It gets so bad that for a while Harriet loses the children to Social and Family Services, but she manages to get them back with help from friends. And Morrisseau is gone God-only-knows-where, with the constitution of a bull, while everyone around him is shattering like glass.

In spite of any misgivings he may have about trying to work with an artist like Norval Morrisseau, Robert Lavack realizes the potential for what he comes to call "the Ojibway Art Circuit." A year after the trip to Big Trout Lake, the Ontario government approves an expanded version of the tour, which will take them from North Bay to Blind River, from Wawa to Whitby, and to points in between. The plan is to field a coordinator and a two-person art team and visit selected schools to stimulate and promote interest in Indian art and culture. The circuit will begin in late March and run six weeks, maybe longer depending on interest. The artists will receive $150 per week plus expenses. Along with Morrisseau, Carl Ray will again to be a team member.

Lavack works day and night to plan the art circuit and then finds himself thrown into the role of coordinator. It is something he had not anticipated. He thinks back to the previous tour and the time they had to hunt Morrisseau down in Red Lake after he had disappeared during a rest stop. They found him wandering around the waterfront, inflamed by alcohol madness, shouting to God and the saints, and for all the angels to have mercy on him. They borrowed an old half-ton from an adjacent airbase and tried to get him on board. "No wine, no Cochenour!" he said, digging in his heels and waving them off. In the end they got the wine and managed to load him in the truck and head home. At one point they stopped for gas and the attendant stepped back, startled when he saw him in the back collapsed on a piece of cardboard. By this time he was hugging his bottle and asking the thunderbirds to come and carry him away.

The gas attendant upon taking a closer look exclaimed, "My God, he looks in critical shape," and Lavack agreed and shrugged and carried on, bouncing along the gravel road to Cochenour. After a few miles he became worried about Morrisseau rolling around in the back, but as it turned out he never felt a thing.

After spending much of December and early January of 1971 drying out in the alcoholic ward of St. Joseph's Hospital in Thunder Bay, for the first few days vomiting bile into a bucket, Morrisseau moves back to McKenzie Island to join his family and behaves as though he has been on vacation. But by early March he is drinking heavily again and Harriet is at her wits' end watching her husband rile against the world, bounce off the walls. She writes to Lavack that, yes, she has received his cheque and, no, her husband is not well. She confides that she has tried so many times to talk some sense into him, but he won't listen to anything. Their fights send the children scattering like mice behind the furniture. The police have been called, because by now the white neighbours have started to complain. Once again she is barely scraping by, and she asks Lavack for an advance on the art. Her sorrow and frustration bleed onto the page.

By mid-March Morrisseau is feeling the aftershocks of his drinking. In the kitchen, his hands clutched to the counter to steady himself, his head numbed and sopping wet from having stuck it into a pail of spring water, he sheepishly asks Harriet and God to forgive him. He does his best to convince her and himself, again, that this is the last time, he has sworn off booze. After hearing from Harriet, Lavack writes Morrisseau in an attempt to keep him sober. "Beware," he says, "it is an evil spirit making you drink." He tells him that they now have twelve confirmed requests for the art circuit. Morrisseau responds that he is looking forward to it, and that he is off the demon wine. And on behalf of Harriet he asks if Lavack "would please pick up some used clothing for the kids, anything at all." Finally awake again, like a bear out of a hard winter slumber, he cannot help but see the threadbare clothes they wear. His neglect slapping him in the face.

Lavack arrives in Red Lake on April 3, navigating a road thick with mud from the spring run-off, and along with Carl Ray they are soon on the move together. Lavack knows that the success of the circuit depends upon keeping his artists focused on their work and for a while everything goes according to plan. *The Sudbury Star* proclaims "North American Indian Culture, Life Patterns, Depicted by Native Artists," and the reports that follow from one community to the next, Kirkland Lake, Timmins, Blind River, are all favourable. Who would have thought Indians could teach, let alone know something? And then the centre, Morrisseau, gives, and it all begins to fall apart.

In Haileybury, a stone's throw from the Quebec border, Morrisseau disappears after lunch and Lavack is left suspecting the worst. To Lavack's relief he returns in time for the class, but drink has tightened his face into a sneer. Listening to the French speakers in the bar that afternoon, Morrisseau is reminded of the Jesuits, Brébeuf and his brethren, the martyrs of old. He has read *The Jesuit Relations.* He has attended residential school. He knows all about them and their kind, and the lengths they went to in the name of Christianity and conversion.

By the time he returns to the classroom he is stewing in memories he would rather forget. He is at the front of the room standing beside his paintings, deciphering their iconography for his white audience, when suddenly he plunges into a lecture on what he calls "the transgression of the Catholic Church." In no uncertain terms he tells them what the priests and nuns did to his people. To him. His stature is imposing, and his largely Catholic audience is shocked. Morrisseau is not angry or bitter by nature, but the thing squirming inside him will not leave him alone. Some are frightened by this bear of a man growling in front of them. They sit nervously in their seats. Others grab their jackets and hurry out, flustered. The next day the organizer contacts Lavack's superior, D.A. Garvie, in Toronto, who asks Lavack to provide a full report. Lavack is used to dousing fires, and he does his best to defuse any irritation or misunderstanding. He explains that because the principal artist was under the influence of alcohol, he criticized the Catholic Church for their early Indian policy. "Although it was a mild attack, it shocked a few of the devout in the audience," he says. "By all accounts though, as we see in the press, the tour has been an outstanding success." By now Lavack is beginning to have second thoughts.

Then in North Bay it happens again. Morrisseau and Carl Ray are staying at the St. Regis Hotel on the corner of Algonquin and Main Streets, across the street from the K-Brothers Art Shop and Gallery, where Lavack has made arrangements to sell their art. The hotel is a stately old building, circa 1886, a leftover from an era when northern towns housed lumber barons and railway kings. Corinthian columns grace the entrance, rows of windows offer bright rooms for painting. There are also two bars on the ground floor. Morrisseau feels right at home in the old gem and, upon checking in, he tells Lavack that he is going up to his room to rest. Lavack lives in North Bay and goes home. The workshop is later that afternoon. Organized by the local chapter of the Imperial Order of the Daughters of the Empire, silver-haired women wearing dark dresses with ivory cameos and fur stoles, the event is to be held at the local public library as a social, with tea served in English china and sandwiches with the crusts removed, all displayed elegantly on white tablecloths.

By the time Morrisseau makes his appearance, he is again half in-the-bag with one shoe missing. But this time his mood is playful. As usual Lavack introduces the two artists and they proceed with the workshop. Morrisseau is standing to the side of the room when Nick Kay, the owner of K-Brothers, notices that the white pair of pants he is wearing must have shrunk in the wash because they will not close properly. He goes over to him and whispers that his fly is open. Unfazed, Morrisseau makes no attempt to zip his pants. Instead he looks out to the audience and then with a grin whispers back, "Ladies like that sort of thing." The class cannot help but notice Morrisseau's red underwear, and they poke one another with their elbows and clear their throats. Morrisseau, like the ever-present trickster Nanaboozho, smirks the afternoon away. And then he goes back to the hotel and continues to drink, and Lavack cannot do anything about it except wait for the inevitable phone call, which comes at two o'clock in the morning. Not from Morrisseau but from the hotel manager, who is screaming into the telephone "the hotel lobby is not main street Kenora!" Lavack is incensed by the remark, but to avoid getting kicked out he confronts Morrisseau and gives him an ultimatum.

For a while Morrisseau manages to stay on course, as witnessed by his impressive performance in Timmins. Although he looks like he hasn't sleep in days, he manages to amaze everyone with his ability to do multiple paintings at the same time. Without sketching anything beforehand, he adds a dab of colour here, a dab of colour there, a series of connecting lines, and the images of two huge owls emerge. The complexity of the composition, the balance of colour, makes everyone in the room stand to take a closer look. Then in Wawa, just when he seems to be on the path of sobriety, his old Red Lake friend John Sweeney catches up to him, and he gets lost visiting. When he finally returns, he is again a lumbering bear-man banging into doors and walls and knocking over anything that gets his way. Lavack is upset, and Morrisseau chides him and calls him the devil. Since his appearances are mostly in schools, Lavack reasons he cannot have him exposed to students in his condition, and he has no choice but to terminate Morrisseau's contract. He arranges for Carl Ray and Joshim Kakegamic, Harriet's artist brother, who has joined the circuit, to drive Morrisseau to Sault Ste. Marie, their next stop. The plan is to put him on a bus for Thunder Bay or Kenora, where he can continue on to Red Lake. Once in the Sault, Morrisseau refuses to leave. He demands his unsold paintings and hits the street.

With the money from the art circuit in his pocket, money he was supposed to bring to Harriet, he dives into the bar at the Central

Hotel, the local Indian watering hole, and sinks to the bottom. He brings a couple of new-found friends back to his room, where they hole up and party on cheap Five Star whiskey and Kentucky Fried Chicken. Two days later his pink alcoholic bliss changes to black ranting and raving and he tears the room apart, punching holes in the walls as though it is a canvas he is destroying. Stumbling off, he sells whatever work he has with him on the street and in the local bars. And then he returns to the hotel for more of the same. The next morning the cleaners enter the room and discover him sprawled on the bed naked, his mouth a garbage can of expletives. The manager gags from the smell of urine splattered over the bathroom floor, the sight of greasy chicken scraps hanging from the ceiling lamps, and calls the police.

Two days later, pending a court appearance, Morrisseau is released from jail to the local public library, where sympathetic staff who appreciate his work have offered to take care of him. He dries out, or at least stays functional, and paints fiendishly for an art show he holds in the library to cover hotel damages.

And Lavack once again intervenes on Morrisseau's behalf and hires him a lawyer. Everybody knows the infamous Morrisseau, and as usual Lavack sweetens the pot with the promise of a painting. The young Italian lawyer Frank Caputo takes on the case and gladly accepts Morrisseau's *Indian Jesus Christ*. And he also discovers the headache that Morrisseau can be when he doesn't show up for his June arraignment, and Caputo has to appear before the judge empty-handed to ask for it to be rescheduled. The judge is about to issue a bench warrant for Morrisseau's arrest but Caputo convinces the Crown prosecutor that he is incapacitated and has every intention of making an appearance.

Morrisseau is back on McKenzie Island when Lavack writes a letter imploring him to show up, warning that if he doesn't the police will be instructed to apprehend him, and he will get a much longer sentence. Morrisseau takes it to heart. He makes his June 30 appearance. And the judge, well aware of his painterly reputation, gives him a minimal $125 fine, all the while shaking his head over the waste of such a talent.

Morrisseau waves it off. He has much heavier concerns on his mind. Harriet is charging him with desertion and wants to leave and take the children. She tells him that she's found a boyfriend who wants to take care of her. Morrisseau responds by attending the Pentecostal Church in Sault Ste. Marie. He even talks to Lavack about joining Alcoholics Anonymous and goes to a couple of meetings, trying desperately to straighten out before returning home.

Lavack stays in touch with Morrisseau during this period and unfailingly sends him art supplies from North Bay via general delivery to wherever he happens to be at the time. And Morrisseau continues to send Lavack paintings, which he sells at the Nicholas Kane Gallery in North Bay, across northern Ontario, and in Toronto through an auction house. Lavack then sends Harriet cheques of various denominations, depending upon the prices and the sales. Besides soliciting, selling, promoting, packaging, and sending Morrisseau's art across the country, Lavack also pays Morrisseau's bills for him, like the one at K-Brothers, for art supplies. He also continues to act as a confidant to Morrisseau, and more than once advises him to go home to Harriet.

Lavack also writes his supervisor in Toronto that despite Morrisseau's display of drinking and debauchery and everything that goes with it, the students and teachers couldn't have been more enthusiastic. Everything is forgiven. Whatever else Morrisseau is, drunkard or not, as he himself says, he is an artist first and foremost. Moreover, an artist with a mission. When he stands in front of the class, sharing what he knows of his people's culture, there is a palpable sense of pride and satisfaction that he passes on to everyone present. He knows that the class will see that he and his people have something important and beautiful to offer. For imbued in his paintings are his grandfather's teachings, some of them five hundred or five thousand years young. He likens his visual interpretations of these stories to tendrils, a rhizome curling along a lilypad shore, sending out shoots, long and tender, and disappearing into the mind of the earth. This is Morrisseau at his best. This is the Morrisseau that Lavack believes in, and although he begins planning a second art circuit, it never takes place.

Perfection

STILL IN SAULT STE. MARIE, Morrisseau does his best to stay off the booze and takes part in a group show of northern artists in July, and his work is as popular as ever. He earns enough money to pay his fine and make his way back to North Bay to visit Lavack and sell more paintings. From there he catches a bus home to Red Lake, via Thunder Bay, a distance of about 1,000 miles. He is sitting on a bus when he reads in the *Toronto Star* that the Royal Ontario Museum has acquired eleven of his paintings for $2,500 from his old Simpsons-Sears friend John Sweeney.

Lugging his work around northwestern Ontario to sell for a few dollars, Morrisseau will hear this kind of news from time to time. Someone like Sweeney or Weinstein or Schwarz will resell his paintings to some institution or collector and it will make it into the newspapers. Or Pollock will be sure to tell him. It maddens him when Pollock continually harps about it, trying to impress upon Morrisseau that people are making money off of him, and he's getting next to nothing out of it. Morrisseau agrees that some of the money should be going back to him. He thinks this mostly when he's broke, without money for a drink, for rent, for food for his family, but all the same it is not something he dwells upon.

In truth he is resigned. These people paid good money for his paintings so it makes sense to him that they can do what they want with them. Pollock finds this attitude infuriating since he is constantly struggling to acquire Morrisseau's paintings for his gallery as well as keep the market for them buoyant. And there's Morrisseau undermining his own career, telling Pollock that he'll have something for him soon, when he's basically giving away his work by selling it outright to individuals and other dealers who write to him. Who resell as they see fit. Pollock routinely throws up his arms in despair and calls Morrisseau a litany of expletives, saying that he's caused him more grief than any other human being on the face of the earth. Morrisseau simply shrugs it off. "They're my friends," he says. "Everybody is your friend!" Pollock remarks.

Unlike Pollock, who has an Ojibway grandmother but no Ojibway culture, Morrisseau is all about culture. His mistrust of the white man, although always present, is submerged in his worldview, a philosophy that carries him to another plane of existence where he is removed from immediate worries, and adapts to each new situation as required. And then there's the alcohol, a bliss that comes crashing down on him when he looks at the stone hollowness of himself and sees that in order to save his marriage he truly has to quit drinking.

And with this thought driving him homeward, he steps off the bus in Thunder Bay with four paintings rolled under his arm, and a thirst the size of a city, and stops in the first bar he sees. He walks straight up to the bartender and announces who he is and that he has paintings to sell. He doesn't return home for another couple of weeks. Harriet has no idea what has happened to him and is worried sick, surviving as usual on social assistance, loans, and handouts. A letter from Robert Lavack in North Bay finally tells her that her husband got on a bus in Sault Ste. Marie and was headed her way. (Knowing full well her situation, he also tells her that he has more used clothing for the kids.)

They assume that Morrisseau is in Thunder Bay but they have no way of getting in touch with him. By this time he is holed up at the Princess Hotel, a dilapidated ruin on Cumberland Street, and is so unsteady that when he walks the ground slides under his feet. So unsteady he only half believes in reality. That tomorrow he will go home to Harriet and the kids and make everything better.

By now Morrisseau's reputation far precedes him. He is in the hotel for a week when Merv Farrow, an education counsellor for the Department of Indian Affairs, learns about it and decides to go to his room in the hope of acquiring a painting. He has met Morrisseau previously through a mutual acquaintance, a dark-haired stripper named Jackie Kay, and figures he can make some kind of a deal with him. And so he boldly goes up the creaking wooden stairs and down the dull hallway, holes punched into the plaster walls, the ceiling cracked and crumbling, and knocks on Morrisseau's door. After a moment it swings open, and there he is in a splattered white T-shirt, work pants, bare feet, a smoked whitefish in one hand and a paintbrush in the other. He welcomes Farrow into the room and tells him to sit down and gestures to the bed where a youngish woman lies naked except for her boots. Scattered across her arms like ants are crude self-inflicted tattoos. As though she might be modelling, her head is turned away and she appears not the least bit interested in what is going on in the room. Empty liquor and wine bottles of various shapes and colours are spread across the windowsills like ornaments. The partial painting of a bear is draped over a veneer dresser. At the end of the bed are two other unfinished paintings. Meanwhile Morrisseau is busy eating and going from one image to the other, dabbing them with red, blue, and brown, as though he too is oblivious to the situation.

Farrow tells him that he would like a painting but says he doesn't have cash and would prefer to trade him for something. Looking around the room he knows where the money would go. Morrisseau doesn't bat an eye. He says what he would really like is the Scandinavian half-apple design plate he saw up the street in a shop called The Treasure House. He says that he wants it because it is artistically perfect. Farrow agrees to buy it for him and says he'll be right back. When he returns with the plate, Morrisseau can hardly believe his eyes, and he takes it in his huge hands and just stares at it, beaming.

Morrisseau tells Farrow to return the next day and he will have a completed painting for him. He assures Farrow that it will be waiting for him. The next day they make the transaction. Morrisseau is so thrilled that Farrow kept his word that he gives him two paintings. Like many others, Farrow will befriend

Morrisseau in the late 1960s, and for a short time will become involved in the artist's life; he will once deliver a roll of paper from the Dryden Paper Mill to McKenzie Island, and even bring Morrisseau home on Christmas day while he is drying out at St. Joseph's Hospital. Farrow later admits that even under such bizarre circumstances he was in awe of Morrisseau. There was just something about him that you couldn't put your finger on. As for the artist, he will eventually return to his wife and their seven children with a present that holds all the weight of a slap in the face.

Hail Noble One

BEGINNING THE NEW YEAR with new resolve, in January 1972 Morrisseau again checks into the alcoholic ward of St. Joseph's Hospital in Thunder Bay. His plan is perfect. He will get sober and move with his family to Sandy Lake, Harriet's fly-in reserve, and away from everything he will paint for another Pollock show, eat fresh fish, drink clean water, and get healthy. Everyone will be happy. But by the end of the month he has already checked himself out of St. Joseph's and is living in a shack in Cochenour. A neighbour one day sees him running up and down the road half frozen, waving coloured pieces of cloth like flags, as if trying to keep his demons at bay. Harriet, who has been living alone with the children, charges him with desertion and Morrisseau is ordered to appear in family court on February 23 in Red Lake. When Judge Fregeau asks him if he has a job, he mentions the educational tour of the previous year. What Morrisseau neglects to mention is that the tour is long over and that the contract is non-renewable. The judge, thinking that Morrisseau has a steady income, rules that he has to pay a monthly stipend of $320 to his family in care of the Juvenile and Family Services Department in Kenora.

Morrisseau responds by writing Lavack, telling him that he has no time to worry about such things, and sends him nineteen paintings, asking him to forward the proceeds to Kenora. Lavack in turn writes the court administrator, explaining that Morrisseau is no longer employed by the department and that the court order needs to be delayed to give him time to sell his paintings. The judge agrees. By March, Lavack has managed to sell nearly all the paintings to the newly expanding Cambrian College in Sudbury, where he is currently working. He gives them a wholesale price they can't refuse—between forty and sixty dollars a painting, plus art supplies to be sent directly to Morrisseau. Then Lavack telephones Mrs. Wilson, the court administrator in Kenora, to advise her that he will soon be sending her the money for the court order. She tells him that according to a social worker in Red Lake, Morrisseau and Harriet are back living together. The court doesn't know what to do and waits to assess the situation. Once again Morrisseau has managed to confound everyone.

Harriet lets Morrisseau return home because he is her man, the father of her children, and because she knows there is another man inside the one who is constantly letting her down. There is man who works hard at his art and returns home with money from his sales so they can live well. He is the man who unexpectedly buys her a fridge and has it loaded onto the barge and sailed across the channel to McKenzie Island. He is the man full of smiles, standing beside the shiny white appliance as the barge approaches the dock, showing off his success for her and for everyone. This is the husband she wants and prays for. She also lets him come home because she is a poor Native woman, who by this time has seven children to feed and clothe, and she can barely make ends meet. Morrisseau is home for a week and everything is good, and then the moodiness sets in, silence envelops him like a storm coming on, and he says he has to go out.

Sure as her disappointment is real, he returns home with a couple of bottles of demon wine (as she calls it) that he drinks in greedy gulps, alone, irritably, pleasure having nothing to do with it. Next thing she knows he is accusing her of having a boyfriend. She denies it. He persists. She glares at him and tells him okay, she does. Someone who is not drunk all the time. He yells and slaps her across the face. The children start crying. He grabs for the closest one, while Harriet grabs at him, just as her friend knocks on the door. He happens to come over at the worst possible time. Morrisseau flings open the door and attacks him. The man fights back, a miner with big hands, struggling, knocking over furniture, he punches the drunken Morrisseau in the face twice, sending him sprawling to the floor. Harriet tells her husband to leave or she will call the police.

Spring, Moon of the Broken Showshoe, and Morrisseau's family life is broken for good, finally snapped like piece of hardwood. Robert Lavack writes to Morrisseau on McKenzie Island giving him a detailed accounting of his sales:

6 highly coloured frames	16 × 20 canvas paper	$240.00
Sacred fish	22 × 30 watercolour paper	60.00
Bear, Owls, Ojibwa	22 × 30	60.00
Serpents & Indian	22 × 30	60.00
Owls (3)	17 × 23	40.00
Ravens (4)	17 × 23	40.00
Great Owl	17 × 23	40.00
Moose	17 × 23	40.00
Owls (2)	17 × 23	40.00
Loon Totem	17 × 23	40.00
Sacred Bear	17 × 23	40.00
Sacred Owl	17 × 23	40.00
		$740.00

He tells him that he will forward the cheque to him along with more paint and paper—a 100-pound roll from Dryden Paper Mill—and of course more books. Concerned about Morrisseau's recent run-in with the courts, Lavack decides to send the cheque to Peter Joensen, the owner of McKenzie Meats. He instructs him to hold back $320, the amount due to the family court, in case Morrisseau ends up having to pay Harriet alimony after all. There is, however, a problem. Cambrian College's cheque is made out solely to Morrisseau. Joensen has no choice but to give him the cheque in total, and the next thing Lavack hears is that the painter is back in jail in Kenora. Charged with neglect of family support, he won't be released until September.

While in jail Morrisseau is admitted into the hospital for appendicitis, but he says he is fine. He is sober and painting again, "Thanks to the good graces of the Governor, who is a very good man." He jokes that he was teaching art with two black eyes. In a tone that betrays shame and sadness, he says he would like to go away for a while when he's finally let out.

Morrisseau's last letter to Lavack is addressed to him at Cambrian College, where Lavack is employed for only a short time before he leaves Canada to fly for the World Health Organization. He asks for work. Lavack responds by poking him as though with the devil's pitchfork they joke about. "Hail Noble One," writes Lavack, "To be completely truthful, any art circuit or class type work requires a high degree of dependence and, noble thunderbird, I sure can't say that we can depend on you. Regarding making money within the next two months, this should be easy if you keep off the juice (My hero!)." Lavack knows that the key to Morrisseau's success is for him to stay away from alcohol. "You could easily realize your $1000 per month after expenses," he tells him, and repeats, "The key, of course, is to keep off the booze!"

It is something Morrisseau will try to do again as it becomes part of a larger plan: "I want to woe the good Graces or should I say to start courting my sweetheart Harriet again," he writes, sounding hopeful. And then realistic, forlorn: "But the old magic is gone now."

In Lavack's last letter to Morrisseau, dated April 4, he writes that "after nine years what can I say but farewell until we meet again— don't know where, don't know when, but I've been assured this will happen in the future. Until then best of luck to you and a big hug to Harriet whom I admire and to whom I wish all the best."

Over coffee in a café in Prague, Robbie Lavack looks to a cobblestone street and reflects on the years he spent in the company of the painter. Unlike Morrisseau, who by now is slumped in a wheelchair, Lavack is fit and lively for a man in his eighties. He sits straight and tall in his chair and with his customary humour he smiles when he thinks of "the Ojibway Art Circuit," and says, "It is difficult to understand how anyone could cause such havoc in so short a time."

P&M What-Not-Shop

BY THE TIME young Paul Okanski played baseball against the St. Joseph's team in Fort William, he'd already heard about the famous Norval Morrisseau. A celebrity to all the Catholic kids, he is the Boy Wonder who was run over and disappeared into the bowels of the earth, only to be miraculously resurrected. The white kids eyed the Indian kid slyly, nobody actually talking to him. It's something Okanski will not think about until thirty years later when Morrisseau again walks into his life. As bailiff for Red Lake, Okanski has the occasional run-in with Norval Morrisseau for minor offences like drinking in a public place or causing a disturbance. Each time Okanski does his best to ease his predicament and guide him through the process from indictment to sentencing. He holds down the job for five years and then gives it up in 1966, mostly because he is fed up with a justice system that does nothing to help Native people, who more often than not can barely speak English.

The following year he and his wife, Mary, open a hobby shop called the P&M What-Not-Shop. At first Morrisseau comes into the store to purchase the few art supplies they have in stock. Then he shows up with paintings to sell to them and to hang in the shop. He begins to chat with Okanski, and they soon become the friends they never were in childhood. Like others before him, Okanski will act as both a quasi-agent and troubleshooter for Morrisseau.

Beginning in 1967 and into the mid-1970s, when Morrisseau

finally leaves Red Lake, Okanski picks up where people like Robert Lavack and businessman John Sweeney leave off. For a fee of twenty-five dollars or more, depending on the size of the painting, he agrees to sell Morrisseau's paintings in his shop. This arrangement suits Morrisseau because he finds he still earns more this way than from selling door-to-door to the locals. The initial plan is to sell to whoever happens to be passing through town, like tourists, nurses, and teachers. But it is revised to include whomever Morrisseau is dealing with at the time when he soon starts using the What-Not-Shop as his mailing address. Dealers like Gail Petteplace in Hamilton begin to contact the shop directly. Okanski is surprised by the turn of events—even Jack Pollock contacts him for paintings—and tries to fill the orders, while keeping meticulous records and doing his best to appease Morrisseau's pleas for loans and help of every kind. In August of 1972, Pollock flies in from Toronto to see Morrisseau about another exhibition and to meet Paul and Mary Okanski. He lands in Red Lake wearing a black cape with red silk lining, and his appearance is no less than dramatic at the Okanski dinner table in their modest Red Lake home.

By now the relationship between Morrisseau and Pollock is as tumultuous as a dark thunderstorm breaking into daylight. As early as 1964, in a letter to Selwyn Dewdney, Morrisseau inquires about the sales that Pollock is supposed to be making and wonders what happened to them. And although he has agreed to keep Pollock as his non-exclusive agent, he insists that all his paintings be recorded and handled by a trustee. But Pollock already feels betrayed by the artist for his lack of loyalty, his willingness to sell his art to anyone who comes his way. Despite their struggles, though, he affirms his genuine concern for Morrisseau by telling Okanski "that with all the bastards around it is good to know Norval has friends like you and your charming family."

Meanwhile Morrisseau is back to his old self, bouncing between McKenzie Island and the mainland like a bird returned from migration. And so on this particular day, he is sitting with Alice Olsen, director of recreation at the local Indian Friendship Centre, where he has been hired to paint a mural, along with Carl Ray and Harriet's brother Joshim Kakegamic. He feels comfortable with Alice, whose mother comes from remote Lac Seul, and he tells her an ancient story from beyond historical time that he thinks she will appreciate. It is one his grandfather has told him that has particular resonance, because more than anything he wants to patch up his relationship with Harriet. The story he tells has to do with making a love potion. It seems to him that this is his last resort. The love medicine is a strange concoction consisting of a strand of hair from the desired person, and a frog in the midst of mating speared and dried and then ground up with a tiny sparrow's head. All of it packed together into a small hide bag. A potent charm for love to be worn around the pursuer's neck. Sacred rites are integral to the blessing of the potion. Although he knows the general idea of the words, "Let me be loved by the woman I desire to be loved by," it is his own version and partly improvised. He is nevertheless prepared to do whatever it takes.

Truth be told he admits that his situation is not hopeful. He likens it to a medicine bag with a hole in it. Red Onaman sand pouring out of it like from a cracked hourglass. His time with Harriet is running out, and it occurs to him while telling the story that the best he can do is paint his love power into reality. And he does. For his section of the mural, he paints a shaman, holding a hand drum, lines of power and communication emanating from it, harnessing the forces of the spirit world. Regardless of Morrisseau's sales around town, Paul Okanski reminds him that Pollock's show is coming up in early November, a mere month and a half away, and that, not having received any paintings, Pollock is panicking. Okanski says this as delicately as he can, because Morrisseau has little love for Pollock at the moment, believing that he could sell more if he tried harder, believing that Pollock owes him money. Pollock, on the other hand, believes that Morrisseau is his own worst enemy. Okanski can see that their relationship is that of feuding brothers, and he does his best to humour the painter. He tells him that this exhibition could change everything.

But Morrisseau is adamant. "Whatever Pollock feels about me drinking or being in jail is of no importance to me," he says. "The main thing is that he forwards the money to us. He knows it took four years for me to respond to his request for a show, and ten more years could pass if he does not abide to his commitments to me!" Morrisseau's fury subsides as quickly as it arises, though, when he unfurls his magnificent *Shaman Rider*. And there he is, Morrisseau himself, a jewel-bedecked shaman with long, flowing hair, a jade and ruby necklace, astride a dazzling thunderbird. He grins and tells Okanski that this one should go to Pollock.

For the next six weeks, Morrisseau breathes, eats, and sleeps his art. And for this short period it seems to him that his shaman power painting has worked. He and Harriet are happy. She is the wife of his dreams and he is the young husband she married. She doesn't even mind him leaving the island because she knows at the end of the day he will return home. Now that they have seven children their home is far too cramped for him to work in, and Paul Okanski has set up a space for him in the basement of the What-Not-Shop. There he swears off alcohol and manages to not touch a drop. Each day Okanski's young daughter Marianne brings him a lunch of sandwiches and milk, and as he gets healthier his new vibrancy is translated into painting that becomes dynamic and daring. (Always generous, he gives Marianne a painting in return for the family's kindness.) Okanski's blue budgie becomes Morrisseau's companion and he calls it his thunderbird and lets it eat out of his hand. When the children come home from school, he sets them up with paper and paint and gives them art lessons, all while continuing to do his own art.

During this short period, Morrisseau paints as though he has had a new beginning—and in a way he has. It is the beginning of his magnificent 1970s period, in which he will produce some of his greatest masterpieces. As usual, when he finishes a painting he strings it up on a clothesline to dry. When Mary Okanski sees *Phallic God in Disguise,* its huge scarlet penis dominating the image, she suggests that some of them might not suitable for the children to see. Morrisseau takes it to heart. He wraps *Artist in Union with Mother Earth* as soon as it dries and takes it home. It is a special painting, and before sending it off to Pollock he wants to show it to Harriet. There before her eyes is one of the most erotic paintings he will ever do: the artist laid over his subject, reclined and entwined, at the moment of entering her. He tells Harriet the painting was done with her in mind. Harriet, modest as ever, blushes as red as the lovers in the painting and tells him he shouldn't be doing stuff like that. It is something he will always remember, and will mention years later while painting at the McMichael Gallery in Kleinburg.

By late October Morrisseau says he is finished painting, and Okanski crates up everything and ships it to Pollock in Toronto. Pollock is hopeful about the quality of the work, but he is anxious about receiving what he calls Morrisseau's "knock-offs," done for a quick buck, which have always been a bone of contention between them. Digging into the crate he knows he needs the best quality possible to re-establish Morrisseau's reputation among the critics, who are ready to dismiss his art as being repetitive. He carefully unwraps one of the paintings, *Sacred Bear,* and the striking image jumps out at him. Morrisseau has painted it so vividly Pollock can almost hear it roar. He studies it for a moment, two large divided circles emphasizing balance and harmony, the colours of direction—red, yellow, blue and black—along with the bear's teeth and claws, providing compositional unity. He then quickly unwraps another and another. Confronted with the likes of *Shaman Rider, Phallic God in Disguise,* and *Artist in Union with Mother Earth,* he stands back and howls in delight. "Brilliant" and "genius" are the two words that come out of his mouth. In Okanski's basement, bent over their large plywood table, under the harsh fluorescent lighting, Morrisseau has produced the kind of work that Pollock has always dreamed about.

It has been ten years since Pollock first encountered Morrisseau and his work, and he combines these new paintings with older ones still on hand to present a retrospective. The reaction by the public and the critics is overwhelmingly positive. "His brilliant canvases… have had quick collector reaction and approval," writes Kay Kritzwiser in *The Globe and Mail*. The reviews emphasize the Ojibway artist's clean lines and vibrant colours, and his spiritual subject matter: the conflict between Catholicism and shamanism. And on the strength of this exhibition, Norval Morrisseau, the wild, irresponsible, down-and-out alcoholic painter, is back in the spotlight. As Kritzwiser announces, "The result: Morrisseau's latest paintings will be shown in galleries in Zurich and London."

Legally Separated

WHEN MORRISSEAU'S CHEQUE arrives from Pollock for the latest exhibition—in care of Okanski, who is instructed to give one of them to Morrisseau the beginning of each month—he immediately goes to the liquor store and purchases an assortment of liquor and liqueurs of every colour and description and returns quietly to Okanski's basement. There he unscrews every cap from every bottle and proceeds to take sips from each of them in turn until he can barely stand. The money from Pollock allows him to purchase whatever catches his fancy, to indulge his passions, no matter what the cost, and he orders two brass goblets and a chalice inlaid with semi-precious stones—ruby red, emerald green, sapphire blue, onyx black—from an antique dealer in Thunder Bay. He will add them to the collection of religious icons that adorns his house. On a tear, however, he forgets the package in a taxi on his way to the Snake Pit, then becomes obsessed with the loss. He writes Okanski, who tracks it down for him while he is back in jail for public intoxication, about to be transferred to Kenora. Morrisseau gladly pays a hundred-dollar finder's fee to have the items returned and asks Okanski to cover it for him from his earnings.

The letters and notes to Okanski, on the back of cigarette packages, grocery receipts, scraps of paper of every kind, continue to flow in. Mostly they ask for loans of a few dollars. Always stating the money is not for booze, and promising to buy food and clothing. Always promising more paintings: "Paul, Loan me 15 dollars. Keep my board until tomorrow. I want to go home…" "Paul, I am going to sell you one painting for $30. You could sell it to Jack to get your money even Double your money…" "Paul, I am Very hungry, also I want to go to a movie show tonight. Give me $10. I want to buy 2 brushes and something to eat, and 1 pair of sox…" "Paul, I hate to ask you for some money. I know you've been fair…" "Paul, Loan me 12 dollars. I will not bother you again. I am sorry to ask you. I don't want to take advantage of you. Respectfully Norval."

During this period the jails of Red Lake, Thunder Bay, and Kenora are Morrisseau's revolving doors. By January of 1973, he is back in jail in Kenora, where he is again drying out. Jail becomes a refuge from his addiction, a sanctuary where all he can do is paint—if they let him—and pray. He writes Okanski again asking for his paints and some mat board: "Whatever I can afford." He confesses, "I will do something about my drinking problem for I cannot go on this way." He says a certain Dr. Torrie has advised him to take massive doses of vitamins, and he asks Okanski to phone the doctor for a prescription. He is clearly desperate. He also mentions his children— he knows they are suffering because of his neglect. Again he asks for Okanski's help: "Paul, First of all my children are going to school tomorrow. However they are short, especially my daughter Victoria, of one pair of shoes. The $20 you gave me I have used it toward my children. Could I sell you 3 paintings for 35 dollars or one or two color for $40? This would be used for shoes." In another letter, he asks Okanski to ask Father Geroux, the local priest, to look in on Harriet to make sure she is okay. Meanwhile the social workers advise Harriet to leave her husband for good. When he is released and asks to come home, she finally tells him no.

Morrisseau's cries for help are loud and clear, and he does not need anyone to tell him he has to stop drinking. "Paul, I need to go to a place to stop drinking. It will take four days. I got to buy food," he writes on another scrap of paper. More often than not Okanski simply gives him the few dollars he requests and more than once he tells him that it is the last time. Although now separated from Harriet, Morrisseau still dreams of getting back together with her: "Paul, Do you want to buy a painting to sell at your price. I will sell it at $30.00. I want to see my former wife." February 22, 1973, he is back in family court, where Harriet leaves him for good. The sentence comes down with a knock of the gavel as though it were actually striking Morrisseau. In turn he collects whatever paintings he has on hand and goes to see Okanski at the What-Not-Shop to say goodbye. He tells him, "I may not be in this area after this is over. But I do value your friendship you offer me, in both drunk or sober, and I wanted to come here and say what I wrote to you. Thank you." He asks for a tally of the paintings that Okanski has sold for him and whatever money Pollock still owes him, and instructs Okanski to use this money to pay his seller's fees.

Whatever Morrisseau has left he takes down to the Snake Pit Lounge on Howey Street to drown his sorrow. And gets eaten alive, night after night devoured by the snake inside him. During this time his pain percolates like boiling water, scalding his eyes, blistering his lips, making him oblivious to the subzero weather. Come daylight he has a bootlegged bottle in his hand, and he is staggering back to the house he's rented from Joe Pitura on Discovery Road. As he passes the Catholic school he stops and yells at the top of his lungs at the cross mounted on the wall. He tries to make a snowball to fling at it. Bends and falls over. Crawls on all fours. Cries like a child. Tries in vain with his hands flaying to swipe away the spectre of all the things that have happened to him and the ones he loves.

III ⊙ NISWI

Penance

*There was always the Church and the Church wanted me
to obey the dogma. But there was always the question, Who
am I?... So I turned to drinking and drinking and then
this crazy pot smoking until there seemed no end. Why do
you do it? You get drunk, and then the police.*

—NORVAL MORRISSEAU

AFTER CRYING FOR HIS WIFE at the bottom of a bottle for a month,
Morrisseau flees to Kenora, 100 miles west of Red Lake, where
whites drink on one side of the bar and the Indians on the other. But
Morrisseau doesn't give a shit because to him everybody is the same
colour on the inside anyway. And he would prefer to sit right in the
centre—of the universe. Swinging his arms off the table and over his
head, in a gesture of madness and vision, he tries to explain his point.
Slurred in half-Ojibway, half-English, he goes on philosophizing on
the nature of Creation and God, who on the first day exploded into
a dazzling shower of rainbow colour and entered everybody and
everything, and the beauty of seeing this miracle unfold daily before
his very eyes, the beauty of being an artist blessed with the sexual-like
desire to paint in the shadow and light of glorious Creation.

In a half-light of grey dullness, he shouts this and more to everybody in the room. White. Red. Black. Yellow. Whoever they might be.
Admonishing them with a wave of his hand to wake up and open their
eyes and see beyond their noses. Fighting off anyone who tries to say
otherwise. Then, on his willowy legs, he weaves a path out the door.

Sketching and selling, hawking his work for the price of drink,
he has mastered the art of trading like the old-time Indians, he likes
to say. For a run to the liquor store or booze can or bootlegger or
whoever will bring him what he needs. Though tonight he is sicker
than usual, one minute his body dipped into icy beer, the next
brandy hot. His reaction is to wash the sickness away with as much
Five Star whiskey as he can hold. Leaning in a dank alley, stinking

of piss and puke, around the corner from the bar (though it could be Paris, France, for all he knows or cares), he clasps the bottle to his greedy lips and after guzzling as much of the gold as he can, he collapses in the arms of a policeman.

Confident that the fine for public drunkenness and disturbing the peace will be paid with no questions asked—like it has been nearly every two or three months—Morrisseau tells the magistrate to call his art dealer in Toronto. Little does he know that this time the law is a black-robed man who has seen far too many skid-row casualties for his liking. He has heard of the famous Morrisseau, has read about him in *The Globe and Mail*, has seen his photograph in *Maclean's*, and cannot believe the bloated booze-hound in front of him is the same man. He asks Pollock not to pay bail. He tells him Morrisseau needs to dry out before he kills himself. He's been drinking daily, non-stop, for over a month, feeding off the liquor like it was food. Pollock reluctantly agrees and Morrisseau is locked up for six months. His longest confinement ever.

Later Pollock will admit that their actions reeked of paternalism, but he saw no alternative—save letting Morrisseau kill himself. He will also conclude that he had the impression the magistrate was speaking with Morrisseau's best interests at heart.

The jail is a small stone Victorian building, shrouded in gothic shadow, the cells lit by a dangling bulb. Morrisseau tosses in bed for three days sweating alcohol he can almost taste, shaking uncontrollably as though already in the throes of the disease that will later attack his body. All night he moans for the home he abandoned, his wife Harriet and the children. He thinks of his grandfather Potan, his grandmother Veronique clutching her rosary, and jerks himself up when he hears her calling his name, but it is only the voices inside his head playing with him, teasing him. He slams his fist down on his pillow and wraps it around his head to try and silence them.

A guard appears, bringing Morrisseau soup and a sandwich. The clanking of the cell door electrifies him and makes him crack his teeth together. The food lies cold and stale in the corner until it is taken away. Two more days pass before he sits up, and it is over. On the sixth he tastes his first meal: tomato and macaroni soup, bread and tea. And he now wants to paint again. He asks to speak to Warden Goss, who has already confided with the magistrate. Morrisseau writes Paul Okanski in Red Lake for supplies: cadmium yellow, brilliant purple, naphthol red, ultramarine, titanium white, hunter green, magenta, black, three brushes, beige board. Offers to trade him a couple of paintings for them. Waiting for the material, he thinks back to his grandmother and her strict Catholicism and he turns to the only book in the cell: the holy bible.

A week later the supplies arrive from Sherwin-Williams in Winnipeg. And he begins to paint furiously. Almost before he starts he is out of space. The 7 by 10 foot cell too small. After a visit from the magistrate, and more consultation, Goss offers him the empty cell beside his own to use as a studio. Morrisseau is now worlds away. Away from alcohol. Painting daily. Eating regularly. He hasn't felt this good in years. Feeling the divine rush of creativity surging from the ground through the cell floor and up into his body, he begins to do penance. With a stroke of his brush his religious series takes shape. Christian themes he has painted since the 1960s are consummated in *Portrait of Christ in Sacred Robes*, *Joseph with Christ Child and St. John the Baptist*, and *Virgin Mary with Christ Child and St. John the Baptist*. The multitude of Morrisseau's heavenly choir becoming entwined with his Ojibway culture, and alongside his visions of salvation appear such paintings as *Power Emanating from Ancient Spirit Vision*, *Warrior with Thunderbirds*, *First Son of the Ojibway Loon Totemic Clan*, and *Ojibway Shaman Receives the Sacred Fire from the Third Heaven*.

It is during this period that the Kenora District Jail becomes known as Warden Goss's hotel, because of Morrisseau's frequent incarceration. Goss continues to let Morrisseau paint, and he enters the annual Prison Arts Foundation competition sponsored by the Ontario Ministry of Correctional Services and wins first prize, two hundred dollars, for his painting *Fish Cycle,* and another hundred in the "Christmas card" category for his painting *Loon Cycle*. It is also during his time in jail that Morrisseau writes what he calls his "Biography—Life's Thoughts of Copper Thunderbird." Ecstatic, visionary, Morrisseau's diary embodies the suffering of the artist in a fit of delirium and tremor as he sweats bottles of alcohol from his body. "I am a born Artist a Shaman a Mystic and Seerer, a Priest and a Parson of Jesus Christ in my 39 years of life," he scrawls in pencil across his notebook. "I am a Vishionary my deep faith in the Great Overall the God of my Ancestors and the same Christian Godhead of my white brothern... I cannot explain the overflowing Estacy I feel for God when I know his love is upon myself. I am the Vessal of the future, the preserver of the Ojibways." For Morrisseau it is the balance between the two faiths that he strives to paint, each pulling in different directions.

Indian Jesus Christ

Once again he is the blessed child
in the midst of adoration, exaltation:
Our Father Who Art in Heaven.
As his knees grind into the wood floor
and a throbbing ache moves up his legs
and drips off his upper lip,
into his cupped hands.

Staring up to the stained-glass Christ
above the priest and altar
he tries to focus on the one ray of light
filtering through halo and flame
like the divine spirit Himself
so that he might rise up to the rafters
and beyond into cool heaven.

The prayer for salvation never comes to pass.
Christ and his legion of angels
never once lift the roof off the chapel,
carry him up in a chorus of hallelujahs.
Morrisseau is left to find his own wings
and he does, painting his own remembering,
his hands bursting into holy acrylic pain.

The Paradox of Norval Morrisseau

IN THE SUMMER OF 1973, Jack Pollock, film director Henning Jacobsen, and Seneca artist and cultural worker Tom Hill fly from Toronto to Kenora, where Morrisseau is now living. The plan is to shoot a documentary film about the artist, which will eventually be called *The Paradox of Norval Morrisseau* and be based on the artist's puzzling nature. Morrisseau will soon be released from jail and they will be there to meet him the moment the steel door clicks open. Nobody knows better than Pollock that with Morrisseau timing is everything, and for this reason Pollock wants to keep track of the paintings Morrisseau has done in jail. Over the last few months he has even flown in to check on him, his footsteps echoing down the hall to the cramped little cells, and there was Morrisseau, king of the castle, spread out in two cells, the police officers begrudgingly carrying out their orders to help him in any way they can. Pollock was surprised, but not totally.

When Jacobsen first approached Pollock with the proposal for a film, Pollock was skeptical about the whole enterprise, but in the end decided to jump at the chance. He saw it as another way to raise Morrisseau's national profile. The CBC public affairs program *The Public Eye* had produced a short black-and-white documentary in 1968, and it had gone a long way in promoting his art. The public was fascinated to see the striking young man with the brush cut sitting in front of a shack, jabbering to his grandfather in Ojibway. The authentic primitive as artist, the embodiment of a national myth. Henning Jacobsen Productions, in collaboration with Tom Hill and the National Film Board, were now proposing a full-length documentary. It was an ideal opportunity, but Pollock warned Jacobsen that getting Morrisseau to agree to do it might be a problem. And even if he did agree, there was no telling how the film might turn out. How he might behave. As Pollock puts it to Jacobsen, he knows Morrisseau better than anyone, and he still doesn't really *know* him.

In fact, he firmly believes that nobody can really know Norval Morrisseau.

In the years since Pollock first discovered the artist (or the artist discovered him), he has seen him working on five paintings at a time, no outline, no map, no nothing but himself, a dab of colour here and there, a cloistered line separating and connecting, a bank of rich images conjured onto the canvas. Relaxed and unruffled by the world in his creativity. And just as quickly he has witnessed him explode off the canvas and onto the street, or in a restaurant, with a litany of abuse for everyone and everything. His huge hulking frame threatening in its reckless unpredictability. So Pollock warns them, but Tom Hill, an expert in the fledgling field of Native art, met Morrisseau when they were part of the Indians of Canada Pavilion at Expo 67. The group of artists had immediately felt a solidarity of purpose, and he's convinced that Morrisseau will go along with the project.

Morrisseau is used to media attention, and the idea of seeing himself on film enthralls him—he agrees to take part. He has always loved the movies, and he thinks back to his childhood in Beardmore, begging his father for ten cents to go to the Roxy Theatre for a Saturday afternoon matinee. No matter how hungry or cold he was, the movies always came to his rescue. And later in Red Lake, when he and Harriet were still young and fresh, before the children, before the onslaught of accusations, abuse, charges of desertion, he remembers selling a painting and taking her to the Cabin Theatre for something romantic. After the film holding her in his arms like they saw on the screen, getting all melodramatic, and Harriet laughing shyly at his goofiness. Such memories going around and around as though on celluloid, until he turns them off with the twist of a cap.

With plans in place, Pollock and company arrive at the town jail first thing in the morning on the day of Morrisseau's scheduled release, only to find out that Robert Fox, a bureaucrat working for the Ontario government, has already signed Morrisseau's release. Morrisseau and all the paintings and drawings he amassed in jail are gone. Pollock is fuming. As he tells it, they finally find him "drunk and incoherent." With the film crew in limbo, then comes the frantic job of sobering the artist up and locating the paintings. Pollock gets the idea of buying six bottles of Baby Duck sparkling wine, six bottles of soda water and a large bottle of grape juice. They pour out the Baby Duck and refill the bottles with a mixture of soda water and grape juice. He then invites Morrisseau to his hotel room, where they sit around for four or five hours drinking what Pollock calls "that shit." In the end, he says, Morrisseau is slightly less pissed.

In the meantime Jacobsen manages to track down a large roll of paintings. Pollock then gets a tranquillizer from the script assistant and gives it to Morrisseau to knock him out, and they make arrangements to rent the hotel's pine ballroom and go about stapling the paintings to the walls of one section to replicate a studio. Lastly, Pollock runs out and purchases an easel and paints to make the illusion complete, along with some new clothes, extra large, for Morrisseau. The plan is to film Morrisseau painting in the makeshift studio.

When Morrisseau wakes up he is almost sober. He promises Pollock to stay off of the bottle during the filming. Once again, however, the artist summons whatever power he has and turns himself invisible, eludes Pollock and the film crew, and makes a run to the nearest liquor store. He then reappears back at the shoot. Pollock suspects that he might be drinking but Morrisseau assures him otherwise, waves him off and tells him not to worry, shouting to Jacobsen and the crew that he's ready for action. The filming begins well and Morrisseau follows Jacobsen's instructions, answering Pollock and Hill's questions, agreeing to give them a demonstration of his painting technique down at the beach. Reminiscent of his childhood experiences on Lake Nipigon, he takes up a stick and draws in the sand, illustrating for the camera how it all began. But after a few takes the play-acting feels unnatural to him and he tires of it.

As the day progresses Morrisseau becomes more and more

playful. When Jacobsen asks him to talk about the significance of Bear in his paintings, he tells him that Bear is sacred because he was the one that brought the secrets of medicine to the Indian people and is one of the main figures in the Grand Medicine Society. He goes on to explain that a lot of Indian people will never eat bear for the simple reason that it reminds them of a human being. "It reminds me too of a human," he says, "and I won't eat it either… unless I put mustard on it, which sort of takes away the human taste." "Cut! Cut!" Jacobsen yells, as everyone bursts into laughter, and Morrisseau grins and shouts that it is not a laughing matter! Acting upset, he says he needs to take another washroom break and stomps off into the nearby bushes. Only later does Pollock discover an empty bottle stashed beneath a tree.

Jacobsen wants to inject some drama into the film and Morrisseau is all for it, but by now he is both tired and intoxicated. The script calls for him to sit sagely on the shore of the small lake beside his house, look up to the sky, where a bolt of lightning will later be inserted into the film, and on cue exclaim in the Ojibway language, "My brother and my God!" Morrisseau wants to explain that the line doesn't make sense, but Jacobsen and the crew are busily checking the camera and sound level to make sure everything is running smoothly. By the time the shot is set up Morrisseau's head is nearly drooping into his lap. Although he goes along with the scene, by now he has no idea what he is doing or why he is doing it. Sitting on a rock, unsure of what he's supposed to do, a coaster-size beaded medallion hanging from his neck, he ends up looking like he might topple into the lake at any moment. They shoot the scene numerous times to try to get it right but each take is worse than the last.

Later, in the makeshift studio back at the hotel, they try to film Morrisseau painting a large canvas, but he can barely hold a brush. Acting as the interviewer, Pollock tries to get him to answer a few poignant questions for the camera. "What symbols are you painting?" he asks slowly, loudly, as though speaking to a child. "Crazy Indian ones. Okay?" Morrisseau responds. He is at a point where all he feels is numbed indifference. The concept for the film consists of shooting new footage and splicing it with some earlier CBC footage to illustrate Morrisseau's artistic development. But the questions that Jacobsen has prepared are only partially answered. And the answers themselves are largely incoherent and outrageous.

At the end of filming, they all concede that the project has been a disaster. Although Jacobsen has some interesting sound roll stuff and a few good scenes, much of the material is unusable. They have no alternative except to postpone the project until a later date. As for Morrisseau, he couldn't care less. With his head on the painting table, all he knows is that he's tired—tired of the fickle public, who don't appreciate him. Tired of exhibitions that go bust. Tired of Pollock's attitude about high art. Tired of barely scraping by. Tired of the whole damn thing. After six months on the wagon, dry as a bail of straw, he has only one thing on his mind. He wants cash in his hand right away. He is already imagining his head under the brass taps of the beer parlour, an arm around some new-found friend.

Five months later Selwyn Dewdney will write the artist to say that he will be passing through town and staying at the Commercial Hotel. Late one evening, he answers an unexpected knock at his door, and "there is Norval, dishevelled, blurry-eyed, with a rough-looking woman beside him. He comes in for a visit and asks to borrow ten dollars."

When he leaves Kenora, Jack Pollock takes the roll of paintings Morrisseau did in jail. The stack of sketches on green paper towel are nowhere to be found. In his memoir Pollock says that the day after arriving in Toronto, Robert Fox, the bureaucrat who had signed for Morrisseau's release, showed up at his gallery and accused him of theft, demanding Morrisseau's paintings. As he neither liked nor trusted the man, Pollock refuses to give them to him unless he receives permission to do so from a sober Morrisseau.

Fox threatens to sue, and indeed Pollock receives a summons. In March 1974, he returns to Kenora with Richard Baker, a young assistant lawyer, taking along his gallery files, letters, and accounts. He is in the witness box for three days. On the third day, Morrisseau arrives to testify. Filthy and sporting two black eyes, he takes the witness stand. But instead of condemning Pollock as the judge expects, he exclaims that he has only one agent—Jack Pollock, his friend! As proof of vindication, Pollock includes Judge L.A. McLennan's "Judgment, Verdict and Remarks" in his memoir: "I base my conclusion on my impression of Mr. Pollock in the witness box and my impression of Mr. Fox," writes Judge McLennan. "I will go this far that Mr. Pollock impressed me as being clear-cut, decisive and honest in the giving of his evidence without the slightest attempt at any time to evade or to parry a question... With respect to Mr. Fox, I was not always so satisfied. There were times when I cold not escape the conviction that he was evading a direct answer to the question asked... Although it may be of argument whether this prosecution was justified, or having been started that it was pursued. However... the trial may have done some good by focusing public attention on the serious and tragic social problem involving the life and potential of Norval Morrisseau... This man has clearly been exploited over the years, not by you [Mr. Pollock] that I can see, but by his own people and by other Canadians, perhaps even by people in authority and there is a danger that this unfortunate situation will continue."

When the judge announces the acquittal and Pollock leaves the witness box, Morrisseau hurries over to him and gives him a big tearful hug.

Back in Toronto a couple of months later, Morrisseau is once again a shining star, with an entourage of acolytes ready to latch on to his developing persona. This time Henning Jacobsen is more aware than ever that the artist is not the kind of Indian he imagined Indians to be. Let it be known, Pollock informs him, Morrisseau is his own man, and transformation is an essential part of his character. This fact is impressed upon Jacobsen when Morrisseau later walks into the gallery—trim and fit, his hair neatly slicked back, a blood-red sports jacket with a bear claw necklace adding to his mystic presence—bearing little trace of the man Jacobsen met in Kenora. The whole fiasco of the film shoot, the court case, it's all buried like a bad dream.

Pollock recommends that Jacobsen hand over the direction of his film to Duke Redbird, a young Ojibway poet and media artist living in Toronto. Pollock assures Jacobsen that Redbird is highly regarded and that if anyone can finish the film, he can. What he lacks in filmmaking experience he makes up for in talent, and by virtue of knowing Morrisseau. When Morrisseau and Harriet arrived in Toronto for the third show in 1964, Pollock asked Redbird if he wouldn't mind showing them around the city. For all his dealings with white people, Morrisseau still mistrusted them, and Pollock wanted someone the artist could relate to culturally.

In Redbird he found the perfect person, a kindred spirit, and although a City Indian, he was nonetheless both Anishinaabe and an artist. Morrisseau was absolutely fascinated by Toronto during that earlier visit—the clubs in Yorkville, on Yonge Street, the nightlife—and Redbird seemed to know everybody. He and Harriet had shown up looking like stereotypical bush Indians, Morrisseau wearing a fringed leather jacket, moccasins tucked into rubber boots, Harriet with a baby in a tikinagan slung on her back. Both of them speaking to one another in their native language. Redbird had seen this as a cultural asset rather than a liability, and had treated them with the utmost respect. Something Morrisseau never forgot.

Redbird is all for working on the film. And when Morrisseau learns that Redbird is directing, he too agrees, expecting that they'll have a good time together. He also likes the idea that Redbird is a published poet; having published his own book all those years ago, he can appreciate the power of the written word. He also likes it that Redbird is a Pisces like him. Another good omen. And Redbird has another plan that brings a nod of approval: he and his musician friend Shingoose will write a song for the film and call it "The Ballad of Norval Morrisseau." Morrisseau loves the idea. In the early

years, he used to record the songs of the elders himself, and says that
for Indians music is like breath.

Having reviewed the footage shot in Kenora, Redbird can see
that Morrisseau has been mischievous as a fox in a henhouse, playing
with the interviewers, basically telling them whatever came to mind.
As he proved during that shoot, he does whatever he damn well feels
like without regard for the consequences. To thwart any unforeseen
complications, Redbird's strategy is to keep Morrisseau involved
and give him as few lines as possible. He also includes Morrisseau in
the decision-making to keep him focused on the film, and asks him
what he thinks about particular scenes, or if he has anything to add.
Redbird will tie whatever footage is salvageable from Kenora to the
new shoot, which will also feature Shingoose singing on camera.

The shoot goes better than expected—they joke and laugh
between medium shots of Morrisseau painting in the backyard of
the Walker Gallery; extreme close-ups of his brush and fingers
dabbing rich colour onto the canvas; close-ups of the artist praying
in the gloomy solemnity of a church, bent in supplication, lighting a
candle, interspersed with the face of Christ set in sharp relief against
Morrisseau's demigods; medium shots of stained-glass windows
panelled with cloistered saints; wide shots of a crowded city street,
the Don Jail.

All goes as planned and Redbird, Jacobsen, and the NFB soon
have enough new scenes to stitch together a film. Morrisseau is
surprised to hear the narrator call him "a polarized personality riding
a roller coaster of contradictions... too complex, too ornate, too
tormented... crucified, damned by the present and tormented by the
past." Blah, blah, blah, he thinks. He is also surprised to see himself so
drunk in Kenora. What he does like about the film is that it says, "he
finds his integrity in the roots of his Ojibway culture." And he also
likes Shingoose's singing:

You've lived in their churches, and you've known their jails,
And you laughed when they said you had failed.

Your art will be living when they're all dead.
You took their green money and painted it red.
You paint your canvas with a brush of pain.
Your signed your works with an Indian name.
Norval, Norval, What's driving you?…

In a letter to Pollock at this time, Morrisseau appears to respond to the singer, but again, contradictions abound in the relationship between Christianity and his art: "And I must mention that I myself thank God for giving me such a great artistic ability, for I do believe whatever God has given, it is a God given gift and that I should not do anything to lose it. For I do believe whatever comes from God to inspire men in art is beauty and by creating beauty in art for others, we all own this art, are in unity with God. Personally, I am not thinking of myself, truthfully, in this present year. But years ahead when I am dead for the children of mine and the generations of my people, to feel proud of the art heritage of the Ojibway."

In 1968, when the CBC shot its initial footage, Morrisseau had already completed two of his most daring paintings to date: *Portrait of the Artist as Jesus Christ* and *Self Portrait Devoured by Demons,* which features a writhing serpent penis strangling the artist. Both paintings highlight intense Christian symbolism as though the artist was in the midst of confession. By the time of the new film's release in 1974, he has just completed *Indian Jesus Christ*, featuring a long-haired Christ with a crown of thorns, and *Self-Portrait, Devoured by His Own Passion*, another painting that features serpents emerging from his orifices. By the mid-1970s, Morrisseau the family man no longer exists, and dilapidated hotels, like the CN, the Princess Hotel, and the Parkmount in Thunder Bay, become his home, while everyone from hooker to lumberjack becomes temporary family. As though a mirror image of his paintings, his life is now ruled by both his pain and passion—his five senses completely consumed, a fanged jaw locking onto a powerless red heart—he becomes as daring and reckless in his sex life and consumption of drugs as he is in everything else.

The Consuming Fire

AND THEN IT IS APRIL 4, 1974, a beautiful starry ocean view in Vancouver, but Morrisseau is as far from beauty as he can be. Centennial Lodge Apartment Hotel. Ten floors up. Middle of the night. And the firewater he's been guzzling for a month explodes, meeting the tip of a cigarette dangling from Morrisseau's baked lips, sending curtains of flame up the walls and across the ceiling. Passed out on the couch in a suite that his sales to local galleries have allowed him to rent by the week, a blanket wrapped around him like a prayer, he wakes, his dulled senses now enveloped in shock. Amazed at the serpent writhing across room, its breath red and orange, the blue of a blasting furnace, as it closes in on him, sears his eyes.

For a moment Morrisseau thinks he must be dreaming, and it crosses his mind to turn over and go back to sleep, hold onto his dream, but the room is now thick with pungent smoke, and he begins to cough and hack up black phlegm of soot and whiskey as the vivid colours of the room begin to melt into grey and black. And then comes awareness that this is not a dream or vision of long ago. Not this. Not a night of stars and moon and a big lumbering beast coming upon him and sniffing him into sight. Though it too is part of the whole, but not the whole. There is more. For he knows that what has now appeared before him is a vision of mercy. Faith in the good way of life.

This is it. The end. It has come, and he greets it with longing, in the blessed presence of Him. The one and only Jesus. Dead for our Sins. Our Father who art in heaven hallowed be Thy name, pray for our guilt. The Son of God with halo of fire, floating on a cloud of smoke, arms open pointing to *him*. With a push he is suddenly standing with the fire now branding his body, peeling skin raw from his back like a piece of fruit, cooking him alive. Pain stuffing his mouth. He looks in the direction of the door, somewhere miles and miles across the room. His arms go up in front him as though to paint away the flames, his hands dipped in the heat, trying to wipe it away as he rises to stand, staggers blind. One step, then another, and he is at the stairs, then grabbed and hauled out of the burning building, a rubber mask with oxygen being pushed onto his face.

When he awakes, Morrisseau finds himself in St. Paul's Hospital and the morning light is gathered in the white uniform of a young nurse standing in front of him. Filled with tranquillizers, he can barely feel his body. His head is suspended like a balloon above his shoulders. Looking down at the nurse, he can see the soft look on her face, one of compassion, and he tries to touch her hand to know if he is still alive. He hears her say that he is very lucky. He mumbles that luck has nothing to do with it. The doctors call his case a miracle. Second- and third-degree burns all over his body. His hands and face untouched.

"I was baptized by fire," Morrisseau will later say, grinning proudly, while showing a yard of pink scar across his shoulders and chest. "I wore the same clothes out of the hospital as I wore in. They weren't even burnt. Jesus has a purpose for me. He wants me to paint." Morrisseau believes his explanation—for him it is the absolute truth. And truth, he knows, comes in many shades and variations. What happened becomes another story for him to carry, to remember, to draw upon, to laugh about, to use to show that he was meant for great things, immeasurable, despite himself. He will lift up the back of his shirt to show off more scars: "Look at the lines of fire across my back," he will say, "like the fingers of God."

Winnipeg

AFTER TEN WEEKS in the Vancouver hospital Morrisseau is thirsty. A hop, skip, and a jump on shaky legs, and he lands on East Hastings, where one drink leads to a bottle and another down at the Cecil Hotel, the Indian waterhole. From there he awakes in Winnipeg with his head on a table at the Mac, bush Indians all around him, the sweet cadence of their Cree and Ojibway tongues making him sit up and take notice. The stale smell of beer and sweat lost for a moment in the aroma of smoke-tanned hide. Morrisseau lifts his head off the table, wipes the dark hair from his eyes, and looks around the room, taking in the sight. Indians everywhere. A city much more like Thunder Bay than Toronto, Morrisseau enjoys the scene, and along with other artists who have congregated in the area, he decides to stay for a while.

Walking down Main Street he passes the Exchange District and all the businessmen running off to appointments, and he keeps going up along the river, past the Manitoba Legislative Building, and there he turns north on Memorial Avenue and walks past the Winnipeg Art Gallery, where he is tempted to go inside. He continues onto the grounds of the University of Winnipeg, where he turns west towards the Hudson's Bay Company Archives; he stops there for a moment imagining what must be locked away inside, all those dusty old papers. He finally turns east back towards Main Street, where he stops to quench his thirst. He sees the potential of a market for his art.

Morrisseau likes to walk, and for the next few weeks he gets to know the lay of the land. From the Mac, he makes his way to the Leland, and then to the Brunswick when he's feeling frisky and wants to watch the strippers, and finally over to the Ox, if he needs a change of scenery or the bar gets too rowdy with students. (Although sometimes if he is in the mood he enjoys talking to them.) On Saturday afternoons he prefers the National, where the bouncers are friendly, and it is quiet and dark and everybody minds their own business. Or he may hang around the arrivals and departures area of the bus depot checking out whoever may be getting off and then drink in the bar there.

Even with the drinking, Morrisseau is always thinking about his art. About where he will paint, about where to get materials, about where he might sell. Since arriving in Winnipeg he has arranged an exhibition at the Eaton's store's gallery and is now squirrelled away in a room off Main Street painting for it. He likes the idea of selling to shoppers. To get the exhibition he did what he normally does: he walked into the director's office, introduced himself, and pulled out what he calls his "calling card." His strategy is to let his art do the talking, so he dug into his shopping bag and unrolled a painting on the director's desk. As always, Morrisseau was confident that his audience could not help but be transfixed by the intensity of his vision. And he was right.

Before fleeing Red Lake, Morrisseau began experimenting with his brothers-in-law—Henry, Goyce, and Joshim Kakegamic—to produce prints on cloth and paper from his paintings. While he was in jail in Kenora, and then recuperating from his burns, they were dealing with miles of bureaucratic red tape to secure an economic development grant from Indian Affairs. They have since used the funding to purchase equipment, rent space, and hire a master printer to teach them the printmaking process, and the Triple K Cooperative is finally up and running. They now have a small silkscreen print shop on Howey Street and are actively producing prints from their own work. Morrisseau had some of his own paintings run off, and although the Kakegamic brothers are still learning the process, he was impressed by the results—the luscious wet imprints sliding smoothly off the roller. He found the whole process fascinating, and he was astounded that out of one painting he could get fifty or even a hundred prints. The potential for his work to be distributed far and wide was unlimited. He hadn't even thought about the money.

Again Morrisseau relies on his calling card. He walks into Great Grasslands Graphics, a small independent print shop on Francis Street that has done work for other Native artists in the city, and unfurls another painting. And he is not the least bit surprised to hear that Bob Checkwitch, the owner, would love to print his work. The phenomenal interest in the new Woodland Art is at its height and as prints roll off the press like counterfeit money, Morrisseau is again flush with cash. Booze for all his new friends in any bar he enters. Posh hotel parties into the wee morning hours. Twenty-seven floors up to the penthouse of the Northstar Inn, Winnipeg's destination hotel, and there's Morrisseau and company, a gaggle of bodies plunked down on leather sofas and easy chairs, between them cases of beer and wine. During this time he has a remnant of family with him, the last sip in a glass that was once full, and among the partiers is his kid brother Wolf. At one point Morrisseau sends him to the corner store with a thousand-dollar bill for a package of cigarettes. But instead of the cigarettes he returns with the police, who think the young man has stolen the money. As though tearing a page from the great English poet William Blake, who expounded that the road to enlightenment is through the door of excess, Morrisseau dives into the well of it, spitting up liquid gold. He doesn't stop until he finally drinks himself sick enough to end up in a Catholic detoxification centre in Ste. Rose du Lac.

By the mid-1970s Morrisseau is well familiar with Odjig's Gallery of Native Art, and not only has his work on display there but has participated in group shows coordinated by Odjig. He had heard that there was a store on Donald Street that sold Indian art and was run by none other than an Indian—and he thought to himself, it's about time. And when he learned that it was owned by Daphne Odjig, he remembered meeting her years before at the Lakehead Art Centre in Port Arthur, where he had attended her first solo show. It had been organized by his friend Susan Ross, who'd told him specifically that he should attend. He'd also heard that Odjig's shop was a kind of drop-in centre for Indian artists, so he decided to drop in with a couple of his paintings. When he arrived at the store Odjig greeted him warmly, taking both his hands in her own. An elegant woman in her mid-fifties, dark hair flecked with grey, she was wearing a black turtleneck sweater and a striking silver and turquoise necklace. Morrisseau could not take his eyes off it.

Odjig told him that she was originally from Manitoulin Island in Ontario, and that she had followed his work since his first exhibition with Pollock in 1962. She showed him around the gallery and they stopped in front of one of her recent paintings, called *Massacre*. He didn't realize that she had actually painted it herself until he noticed her signature. Modestly, she said the painting was inspired by the history of her Potawatomi people: "If we don't tell our stories, who will?" Morrisseau, who for the most part stayed away from painting history, simply nodded and looked over to another painting that caught his eye. She told him it was called *Nanabojou and His Daughter*. "Sexy!" he said, moving up closer and outlining the breasts that dominated the picture with a finger, making them both laugh. As they continued around the gallery and he looked at her work, Morrisseau thought of the books that he had read at the Weinsteins', on French modernism, cubism, Picasso, Braque, and he was in his element talking to her about them. Alone with Odjig in the quiet of the gallery, surrounded by her paintings, he realized then and there what was different about her. Like him, she was a born artist.

Odjig was more than happy to carry Morrisseau's work, and in fact had a proposal for him to consider. She asked him if he would like to be part of a group of artists who were in thinking of incorporating themselves as an association. Morrisseau already knew something about the offer because Odjig had called Jack Pollock, who had passed on the message to him, but not without a smirk of cynicism. As far as Pollock was concerned Morrisseau could have all the success he wanted on his own, if he would only show some self-restraint. And he certainly didn't think an artist of Morrisseau's stature should have to share his royalties with less established artists. But as Pollock knew well enough, neither he nor anyone else could lead Morrisseau around by the nose, and Morrisseau would do damn well what he pleased.

Odjig told him that they didn't have a name yet, but were thinking of something like "Professional Indian Artists." Morrisseau agreed that the word "professional" should be a part of the title. Whatever he was, he was a professional artist. She said that the focus of the group would be to expand their horizons through the sharing of ideas and to promote their work collectively, as well as to provide encouragement and support for the next generation. Odjig explained that she was tired of being treated as a second-class artist simply because she was Native and having her work relegated to museums rather than art galleries. She said it was laughable that they were considered "ethnic artists" when the French and Italians weren't. She had spoken to Carl Ray about the idea a few years ago when they were teaching art on Schreiber Island in northern Ontario. And she mentioned other painters like Jackson Beardy, Joseph Sanchez, Eddy Cobiness, and Alex Janvier, who had all agreed to join. Morrisseau remembered Janvier from the Indian Pavilion at Expo 67. The Ottawa bureaucrats didn't think his work was traditional enough— all they saw was modernist abstraction—and relegated it to a side wall. He shook his head thinking about their stupidity and the arguments that ensued. There was Janvier pointing to the influence of beadwork and teepee designs, and the powers-that-be closing their eyes and their minds.

Odjig was well aware of Morrisseau's unpredictability and was surprised when he said sure, it was a good idea. He then asked her where she got the beautiful necklace—he wanted one for himself.

Over the next few years, Morrisseau managed to make it to a couple of the group's meetings in the conference room of the Northstar Inn, where he often stayed anyway. The name Professional Native Indian Artists Inc. was now official, but they were beginning to be known simply as "the Indian Group of Seven," a name Carl Ray had joked about. Morrisseau doesn't know if this is a good or a bad thing and simply smiles. It doesn't matter how you're called for supper, he thinks, as long as you're called. He enjoys hanging out with the group, going for drinks and talking about art, and they enjoy his company as well, and his take-no-prisoner attitude about art and life. Until he gets out of hand. Morrisseau is merciless when it comes to teasing. Like the time they were all up in the Northstar's Paradise Lounge on the twelfth floor, red leatherette seats, plush carpeting, fancy, and Morrisseau was getting drunker and drunker and started calling Janvier a mere a graphic designer, and then with a grin as big as a window, he turned to Odjig and called her Picasso's grandmother. As for him and Carl Ray, they ended up arguing when Morrisseau poked and prodded him by calling him his protegé.

But for Morrisseau it's all in the spirit of Nanaboozho, and he believes that together they have a better chance of breaking through the prejudice that has corralled their work. One of the group—he thinks it was Jackson Beardy—held up his two fists in front of him as though holding an arrow, and said that one arrow alone snaps easily, but a quiver of arrows is a different story.

Whenever Morrisseau is in the city he drops into the gallery with work, or to purchase supplies that Odjig sells at cost to the artists. And in the summer of 1974, he paints in the small studio space upstairs and prepares for group shows at the Eaton's department store in Winnipeg and the Anthropos Gallery in London, England. The interest in Native art continues to grow nationwide, and in the coming months Odjig expands and renames her shop, establishing the New Warehouse Gallery. Then, Max Stern of the Dominion Gallery in Montreal, considered by many the voice of Canadian arts, hosts a show for the group. With the door of opportunity thrown open, they charge forward with two more exhibitions.

Following the lead of Morrisseau, who is no stranger to the press, the "Indian Group of Seven" is by now commanding national attention. But even with recognition, the money tree does not sprinkle its golden leaves down upon other members of the group as it does upon the father of Woodland Art, who sells four hundred dollars' worth of art at the Dominion Gallery. Attempts to secure government funding for its members from Indian Affairs and other agencies meet with little success, and their work remains shut out of major public institutions, such as the National Gallery of Canada and the Art Gallery of Ontario.

For the next couple of years Odjig's New Warehouse Gallery is the creative and social hub for artists either living in or passing through Winnipeg. But after two more exhibitions, in Ottawa and Vancouver, the Professional Native Indian Artists Inc. unofficially dissolves and its members go their own ways. Without financial support it becomes too difficult to hold meetings and coordinate exhibitions. Odjig herself becomes frustrated and sells her gallery, moving to British Columbia to devote herself to painting. She will always remember Morrisseau dropping into her gallery when the spirit moved him, and how he once made a beeline for the bathroom to down a bottle of rye, and then approached a fashionable lady in a mink stole and whispered something devilishly naughty into her ear. Only to see her fluster and scurry off.

Meanwhile, Morrisseau continues to ride the crest of interest in the new Native art, and if any work is purchased by private collectors or galleries, his name remains at the top of the list, signalling even greater things to come.

Bad Medicine

ALWAYS THE THUNDERBIRD MAN, Morrisseau is always on the move, always changing into someone else in the process. After the trial in Kenora he is in Toronto, Vancouver, Winnipeg, and in the blink of an eye, the flap of a wing, he lands in Thunder Bay, and by autumn of 1974, he is visiting Curve Lake Reserve, halfway across the province. Alice Olsen, originally from the Red Lake region, married and living in Curve Lake at the time, tells of meeting him while visiting her sister in Thunder Bay. Morrisseau recognizes her from Red Lake where ten years earlier she was director of recreation for the Indian Friendship Centre. By this time he is separated from Harriet and their relationship is beyond mending, and when Alice introduces him to her younger sister Doris, a long-haired beauty in the process of embracing her identity, Norval remembers her from Red Lake as well and cannot take his eyes off of her.

Having lived in the same community, knowing the Ojibway language, knowing the same people, Morrisseau and Alice Olsen quickly become friends "We got along so well I invited him back east for a visit," she says, "I didn't think he would come." But as the conductor is closing the door to the train taking Alice home, Morrisseau and his sixteen-year-old daughter Victoria come running down the platform and jump on board. Morrisseau knows that Doris will soon be heading east too, and stopping in Curve Lake. She is planning to join the Native People's Caravan, a cross-country trek protesting broken treaties and land rights grievances, which is due to arrive in Ottawa and march on Parliament Hill. When they arrive in Curve Lake, Norval and Victoria bunk in with Alice Olsen and her young family.

His daughter hung around with him, Olsen says, and joked with him all the time, and like a typical teenager got things she wanted out of him. There was only one time Olsen ever saw him get really angry with her: "We were sitting in at the kitchen table, and he had just come out of the bathroom with his hair sopping wet. I didn't think anything of it, assuming he had just washed it. That's when Victoria piped up and began teasing him that he was dyeing his hair so he could look younger and fool the ladies. He must have been doing it for my younger sister, who was expected to arrive any day, because, boy, did he get mad at her. He quickly forgave her though. You could tell he really loved her."

Constantly making art, Morrisseau sets up a table in the basement and paints every day. Some of the paintings he sells to Whetung Ojibwa Art and Crafts Gallery on the reserve, establishing a relationship with them that will become useful to him later on. Other pieces he sells to whoever will buy them—on the reserve, in Peterborough—and some he gives away. Indicative of his enormous talent he carves Olsen a large wooden spoon, and, as though hearkening back to his Red Lake years, he also gives her an etching done on a sheet of birchbark. Doris telephones to say she is on her way, and Morrisseau cannot contain himself, his anticipation and anxiety getting the better of him. He takes a taxi into Peterborough and purchases the brightest red shirt he can find, a tie, and a pair of checkered pants, along with a bottle of wine. His hair dyed, a set of new clothes—he wants to be stylish and as primed as ever for her. His love for Doris builds unabated, and he falls for her like a stone. Perhaps he lets it happen consciously, doesn't bother to catch himself because he feels it is the only medicine that will cure him from his break-up with Harriet. Perhaps he's thinking about her when he paints *Self-Portrait, Devoured by His Own Passion*, depicting the artist's constant struggle with his emotions. Morrisseau, the hopeless, obsessive romantic. In a gesture of seduction he writes Doris a love letter on the back cover of his Grumbacher art pad, a surprising song of fresh love:

> Refreshing Light upon a Man's lost Soul your beauty your Lips and Eyes—the Very Look you gave me burns deep Inside of me. A flame a Touch that no Liquid could ever Put out. One look Upon those Angel like Eyes gives me. Life to Exist another 20 years of Youth. My Beloved. You would make anyone very happy even to have you as a friend only.
>
> Norval.

> PS, What a Joy To this searching Heart to See in Reality and the soul Who bears That Beauty. Doris my secret Love.

That night Morrisseau gets into the wine, his tie askew, his pants-fly open, but he appears happy enough. He and the Olsen family pose for a photo among a stand of white birch. The day is blue and beautiful. Alice is sitting near his feet with her two children, Doris is standing beside Morrisseau, laughing. But otherwise the visit does not go well for him. Doris has little romantic interest in Morrisseau and soon leaves with a young man from the reserve. Morrisseau wakes to discover they have gone off together to meet the caravan to Ottawa. He becomes extremely upset, and Alice Olsen sees another side of him. He broods all day and goes out and then stays away until evening. When he returns he has a paper bag with him, a heavy one, the kind from a liquor store. He opens the paper bag for her to look inside. She cannot make out what it is. Feathers, something dark, she is uncertain. He tells her to look closer and she realizes with the shock of surprise that he has a mallard's green head in the bag. It stares up at her with its dull, dead eyes.

"What're you doing with that?" she asks, stepping quickly away.

"I'm going to fix her," he says. "I'm going to make something bad happen to her, take away her looks."

Alice can see that he's not joking. This is serious. She becomes frightened, and beseeches him not to do anything. "In the name of our friendship," she says. "Think of my parents up north in Trout Lake, please don't do anything." She explains that Doris is young and didn't mean to hurt his feelings.

For a while Morrisseau just sits at the table not saying anything, brooding like he's been doing all day, until he finally mumbles, "Okay," and goes outside and buries the bag in the backyard. He and Victoria leave the next day.

Alice Olsen cannot recall how many paintings Morrisseau completed during his two-week visit with them, but he always seemed to have money, and by the time he leaves there are five half-finished paintings on the table in the basement. His creativity a river constantly flowing through his hands, he has no need to take them because he knows there will always be more.

At the McMichael

BY 1975 EVERYONE involved in the arts in Canada has heard of the Indian painter Norval Morrisseau. He has had fifteen solo shows and thirty-one group shows since his first big sell-out in 1962. He has attended at least five of the shows personally and is always a big draw. Since encountering Morrisseau's work in 1969, Robert McMichael, the founder and director of the McMichael Gallery in Kleinburg, Ontario, becomes an enthusiastic supporter of the artist and purchases his *Misshipeshoo–Earth Monster,* making the McMichael one of the first major institutions in Canada to acquire his art. McMichael, upon leaving the latest exhibition at the Pollock Gallery, gives Morrisseau his card and says that he should come and visit his gallery sometime. It so happens that Morrisseau is tired of the noise and crowds of Toronto, and looking for a place to paint out of the city. Finding out exactly where the McMichael Gallery is located is easy enough; Morrisseau learns that Kleinburg is around twenty-five miles north of Toronto. A mere cab ride for the artist, who is famous for travelling across the country by taxi.

One might even go so far to say that for Morrisseau, taking taxis is part of his very nature, something he does naturally without a second thought. To buy groceries, to buy a bottle, to sell his art, to visit his friends, to go partying, to go sightseeing, no matter how close or how far, when he has the money, he does it all by taxi. It is also part of Morrisseau's contradictory nature to be generous beyond compare, and this is no better exemplified than in his attachment to taking taxis. After spending hundreds or even a thousand dollars on a ride, he has been known to give the taxi driver a tip equal to the fare itself—and wake the next day without a dime in his pocket. (He will then ask the hotel or wherever he's staying for a pencil and paper, do a quick sketch, sell it to buy paint and art paper, and start all over again.) It is easy to understand how Morrisseau's eccentricity might attract all kinds of people—how by the strength of his magnetism he can be likened to a fiery star, a sun, with all the people he meets revolving around him like planets.

There is a story that Brian Marion tells about Morrisseau and his love affair with taxis. From the time Marion meets Morrisseau in Winnipeg at his show at Gallery 115, in 1976, until their parting in the early 1980s, Marion is Morrisseau's adopted son, apprentice, companion—whatever that implies—and travels constantly with the artist. One time he and Morrisseau were on the Fort William Reserve, adjacent to the city of Thunder Bay, where Morrisseau liked to visit the elders and share stories. He had been visiting the reserve for more than ten years, dropping by whenever he was in the area. This time he was there partying and, as the evening and conversation progressed, a young woman started to boast about how many friends she had. Perhaps it was because she was in the company of Morrisseau, who rarely travelled alone, that she wanted to show off. One of the band councillors—or maybe it was the chief himself—jumped in and started talking about how many friends he had and what he'd done for them: he had given them money, bought them vehicles, fixed up their houses. Yes, indeed, he was also very popular. Morrisseau admitted that he had never done anything like that, and he wasn't sure how many friends he had or how popular he was, but he was willing to find out. He picked up the telephone and to everybody's surprise called a taxi driver in Peterborough. This particular driver was always driving Morrisseau around to God-only-knows-where, and he had received some pretty hefty tips along the way in the form of money and paintings. In any case he had given Morrisseau his personal number and told him to call him anytime. Morrisseau asked him to come and pick him up in Thunder Bay. Some 900 miles away. The taxi arrived the next day.

When Morrisseau steps out of the taxi at the McMichael he is wearing a beautifully embroidered moose-hide jacket, his unruly mass of black hair surrounding his craggily striking face. Always conscious of his appearance when he is sober, he is as flamboyant as ever. He's only recently left the Ste. Rose du Lac detox centre in Manitoba, so for the time being he is not drinking. An elaborately carved wooden staff in his hand, he strikes the floor with each step. And as is usual these days he has a young companion with him carrying his case of paints and board. Once inside he marches up to the front desk and asks to speak directly to Robert McMichael. He grins broadly as McMichael approaches and from a plastic grocery bag he again withdraws a giant-size calling card, this time a brilliantly painted, highly stylized self-portrait. McMichael will always remember this moment as "a startling and unforgettable introduction."

Morrisseau has a proposition. He wants to paint for the gallery. He says he will do three paintings, and they can choose whatever they want. He doesn't know what he'll do yet; that will come to him when he's painting. Although he seems to show little interest in what happens to his work after he sells it, he is nevertheless absolutely sure of himself and the value of his work. McMichael and his assistants are more than happy—they are enthralled. When Morrisseau speaks about his people and their legends, "it is in the present tense as though the event were unfolding before him, flowing naturally as if he were reciting a favourite poem or recalling a memorable experience," Jeanne Pattison, the gallery's director of education, later says about the encounter.

There is a slight problem, however. Morrisseau does not necessarily work on acid-free materials, so the gallery has to prepare new boards for him. He prefers to paint large, he tells them: "the work is bigger, freer. You can proportion it better." The following day Morrisseau and his companion return to the gallery and pick up three boards of primed Masonite measuring 40 by 32 inches, along with some additional acrylic paint, since he is nearly out. (Raw sienna, yellow ochre, cadmium yellow deep, cadmium green light, chrome oxide green, cerulean blue, permanent violet light, alizarin crimson, cadmium deep red, cadmium orange and mars black.) They hole up for three days at the Twin Elms Motel, just south of Kleinburg, and during that time Morrisseau executes two paintings: *The Artist's Wife and Daughter* and *Self-Portrait*—which is still damp when he delivers it, having finished it that morning. He returns the third board still blank as snow, shrugs, and says that he ran out of steam.

Morrisseau makes it clear that he wants the gallery to purchase both of the paintings outright. Or he will take them somewhere else and sell them immediately, saying he needs the money to get back to Thunder Bay. In typical Morrisseau fashion, though, he does not get involved in the negotiations and lets his companion take care of it. Instead he has coffee in the dining room with Jeanne Pattison, an avid art collector herself—who will subsequently purchase work from him—and goes off into another realm altogether, talking about his visions while answering her questions about the aesthetics of his work. He tells her that the colours in the two paintings are pure, not mixed. It is clear to Pattison that unlike some of the younger Woodland artists, who are experimenting with figure-ground representation and multiple planes, Morrisseau is much more interested in colour. "I love colour," he tells her, "all those fancy names, cerulean blue, Venetian red, magnesium brown." And he remembers one of his recent visions: "it was about a beautiful holy chalice made of gold with brilliantly jewelled reflections of diamonds, rubies, and amethysts appearing on it," he says. "Colours like in a cathedral." Pattison picks up on the theme of religious iconography and its influence on his work. Mentions that the dark outline and the dignity of the figures, the segmented colour, the two-dimensional flat plane combined with the luminosity achieved from over-painting, all tend to carry the impression of stained-glass windows. "Many religious visions inspire my work," he answers matter-of-factly, and then adds, after a short pause: "And not just Christian. I'm also an Indian. My culture is my world."

This point makes him go on to discuss the two paintings specifically. In *Self-Portrait* he is wearing an elaborate headdress. He says that he did not paint any specific headdress. "It's the way I would like to be when I am dressed like an Indian, or at the Happy Hunting Ground. It is a vision of myself in perhaps a spirit world, somewhere, maybe the dead world." He explains that in his hand, he holds a sign of authority, which could be a rattle, but it also represents a sign of power. The other painting, *Artist's Wife and Daughter*, he says is a visionary portrait of his wife and unborn child. "The facial spirals represent the ancient Indian symbol of continuity, as in the power of thought. Sacred, no beginning and no end. It was instinctive to use it."

As for the birds in the paintings, he says they are ravens. "I remember seeing many ravens in Red Lake, maybe fifteen or twenty on the street at the same time." As though far away for a moment, remembering, he suddenly looks over and remarks that the woman in the painting could perhaps be a visionary spirit wife, and not necessarily his actual wife. And it is a vision that haunts him. "I've seen it on many occasions and the wife is always presenting me with another unborn child. The baby is angrily telling her mother she wants to be born. She is saying: 'When are you going to take Dad back?' But the mother is not paying attention." Pattison knows that Morrisseau has recently separated from his wife. She wants to say something to console him, but he stands and simply adds that he is happy that his paintings are going to hang in the collection, where so many people will see them: "Maybe for a thousand years." He has talked enough, and it is time to leave.

Eckankar

The Indian people were very close to being a community of ECKists. That is to say they had more freedom and there was nothing to tie or bind them to dogma or religious superstition or anything like that.

—Norval Morrisseau

AFTER SIX MONTHS on the wagon, Morrisseau hits the ground with a wallop and he is back in Thunder Bay holed up in a hotel, drunk out of his mind with a prostitute and a life-size blow-up doll for companionship. When the call comes from the hotel manager, Pollock is away and Eva Quan, his administrative assistant, takes it upon herself to fly to Thunder Bay to sort things out. Quan is furious. Although a petite woman, upon arriving at the hotel she throws the other woman out of the room and gets the hulking

Morrisseau into the shower, and then organizes his flight back to Toronto. While he's sobering up with cup after cup of black coffee, she packs up his things—including the blow-up doll, which she plunks on Pollock's desk, asking, "Now, what do we do with this?"

It turns out that Quan is a member of Eckankar, referred to as a New Age religion of light and sound, and on the chance that it may help with his drinking, she invites Morrisseau to attend a meeting with her. Nobody knows better than he does that he has to do something about his drinking. "Less alcohol, less confusion," he admits, and he is grateful to her for the invitation. The meeting they attend is at the Four Seasons Hotel, and the hotel's ballroom has been rented for the occasion. Rows of chairs have been set up on the carpeted floor, which serves to dampen the sounds of attendees' footsteps. Fabian Burback, the head of the Toronto chapter of Eckankar, stands at a lectern in front of the assembled group. Dressed in a nondescript blue suit, heavy and balding, he is nonetheless a commanding presence. A hush pervades the large room. He welcomes everybody and then goes on to explain the central tenets of Eckankar. It's not a New Age religion, he notes, not a religion at all, but a belief system older than organized religion itself. Welcome to Past Lives, Dreams, and Soul Travel.

Morrisseau hears things that evening that resonate with his own core beliefs—a light goes on that illuminates the world and confirms everything taught to him by his grandfather Potan all those years ago. He connects Eckankar's emphasis on soul travel through the astral planes to his traditional Ojibway teachings, which also emphasize the ability to move outside the corporeal body (as witnessed in the Shaking Tent ceremony). He finds in Eckankar a level of acceptance that he has never had before, and begins to reflect on his personal transformation. His freedom. In Eckankar terminology, he is now free to be true to his reincarnated self, to move beyond karma debt, and attain the seventh level of the astral plane.

In addition to a new metaphysical language, Eckankar gives Morrisseau leave of Christianity. It helps him overcome the pangs of sin and guilt that he wears like a crown of thorns, and as he portrayed himself in *Indian Jesus Christ* two years earlier. Laying to rest his Catholic guilt, he reverses earlier statements he made—that no Indian was ever a homosexual—and embraces his sexuality. He talks freely about it. "To the Indian, a homosexual is one of the most gifted persons there is," he announces. "I think all shamans are homosexual, or, anyway, bisexual." In Eckankar Morrisseau receives confirmation and blessing—he is secure enough to say that "as far as sex goes, I did everything under the sun"—and in 1976 he is initiated into the faith.

As he paints he reflects deeply on the process of his illumination: "Here is a man in the gutter. Drunk and all this. So confused and lost. And one day what happens, he sees the light, that's the way he's developing. The man who was suffering on the physical side cannot be compared to the man who's inside. The one who is inside which we call Soul is a very highly developed Soul. Sometimes though I have to fall down because some part of me is still there. But as I say, today, I realize that Norval from the gutter to what he is as an ECKist had to change. And that is a great process." For Morrisseau existence is fundamentally about spirit, and in Eckankar he finds a spiritual outlet to assuage his terrible craving. But more than help sober him up, Eckankar has a profound and irrevocable influence on his art.

Morrisseau begins incorporating the precepts of Eckankar into his work with *Spiritual Self Looks Beyond* and *Spiritual Self Emerges,* two paintings executed in 1976, which feature a "pale astral blue background" and in the foreground, a figure whose enlightenment is emphasized by the primary colours red and yellow, gushing from his mouth or eyes. The artist's exploration of Eckankar's belief in soul travel and otherworldly dimensions will continue to be expressed in his art, as indicated in the titles of two paintings done the following year, *Levels of Consciousness* and *Door to Astral Heaven.* The divided circle of early work, representing the dualities of life, and the complete circle, representing the circularity of life, are eventually combined in startling ways to express his new consciousness. And in 1978, the artist will pay homage to his grandfather Moses Potan Nanakonagos in the masterful diptych *The Storyteller. The Artist and His Grandfather,* where he literally incorporates the word "HU" into the circle, a chant that ECKists believe is the key exercise in unlocking the ability to move through the levels of the "Astral Planes." Perhaps more than any painting from this period, it unequivocally reveals his attempt to establish a new visual vocabulary to express Eckankar's key concepts while acknowledging his dept to his own Ojibway heritage.

Throughout his career, Morrisseau continues to push at the borders that circumscribe the "woodland" style he has invented. And his best work will prove that he is far from the primitive painter that some label him to be—Pollock going so far as to call him "a highly sophisticated painter marked by an incredible capacity for constant growth and development"—and with his introduction to Eckankar his art moves in an astonishing new direction. A direction the painter embraces. "I may never paint the things I used to paint because this is a great turning point in my life," he says. "My responsibility today is to be a great artist. What I'm gonna paint is the Indian spiritual version, the Indian way of what the physical universe looks like, and the astral heaven on top, and all the things we believed in up there. There'll be men and animals and there'll be thunderbirds, they'll be everything. This way towards the Indian!" And with this Morrisseau plunges fully into what he now calls his "psychic state" and the circles that stood off in the corners of his early paintings become central. Soon they will open up and become portals where humans, fish, and animals move through levels of existence. It is a theme that he will continue to develop as he explores what he calls the "healing power of colour."

Thunderbird and Inner Spirit

His Inner Master guides him
to higher consciousness.
A spiritual helper,
a dreamtime
he learns to call upon
as a loon calls in evening.

Beyond the physical universe of objects
weighted and measured.
Outside the realm of electrons
and neurons,
chemically charged synapses.

Like a Buddha he sits at the genesis of consciousness
Embodied as a brilliant Thunderbird.

He is quick to speak
with his new vocabulary,
pressed into him like a leaf.
Of Astral Visions, House of Invention,
Seventh Plane, Deep Dreaming.

And the unbelievable becomes believable.
Faith is everything.
Proof in a brush of colour
that can heal anyone
but himself.

Man Changing into Thunderbird
(Transmigration)

FROM THE VERY FIRST TIME he heard the story about the man who changed into a thunderbird, Morrisseau has wanted to paint it. But as yet he has had no idea how to squeeze the essence of it onto canvas. How does one go about doing something so daunting? As early as 1964, he pondered this question, noting that such "large works would require much thought to concentrate the story pictorially." It is something that haunts him, dangles in front of him, but gets caught in the dream catcher web of a spider, or escapes through a hole in the night sky and slides down a path of owl feathers, into the world of myth and creation.

The story says there were seven brothers. One day
the youngest, Wahbi Ahmik,
went hunting and met a beautiful woman
named Nimkey Banasik.
They fell in love at first sight
and the young warrior took her home to his wigwam
where they lived as man and wife
and were happy.
All the brothers cherished her except one,
Ahsin, the oldest,
who felt only hatred for her.

The idea grows inside Morrisseau the way a butterfly grows inside a chrysalis. Except it is not about a butterfly, it is about a thunderbird, and more about a whole way of seeing, about perception and belief. When it finally cracks open, or rather when he cracks it open, the idea is so large he knows instinctively it will be one of his most important pieces. Not junk commercialism done for a quick buck. Not twenty paintings on a clothesline, him jumping between them like a jackrabbit. Not another set of nesting loons or another

multicoloured trout. Not something he can paint with his eyes half
closed. Half in stupor. Once in the moment his eyes are wide open
and burning with possibility, as though giant talons are digging into
his memory and stirring his imagination. As though clamped onto
his shoulder muscles, with the steady beat of locomotive wings, they
are lifting him high above the ground.

> One day Wahbi Ahmik returned from hunting
> and discovered the campfire near his wigwam
> stained in blood.
> Panic-stricken he rushed to his wife
> but discovered her gone.
> Knowing what his brother Ahsin felt for her
> he stormed into his tent
> and demanded to know what happened.
> I see a trail of blood leading into the forest.
> What have you done?

The year is 1977, and Morrisseau is again showing with the Pollock
Gallery but he is hardly under Pollock's tutelage, their relationship
strained by their giant personalities. With his home in Red Lake far
behind him, Morrisseau is lapping up the good life like a saucer of
sweet milk. And his art has become little more than a means to an
end, more commerce than calling. He sells it to buy the basics like
cigarettes, groceries (though he eats little for a man his size), shoes or
a shirt when he needs it. More often than not he simply trades paintings for whatever he needs or wants, a week's rent in a flop house,
a bottle, a meal, an English Derby plate, a Spode teapot, a blowjob,
a fuck, everything and anything. The moment the only thing that
matters.

> Ahsin was not afraid of his younger brother's anger.
> You brought this woman Nimkey Banasik to our village.
> We were all happy together before she came.

201

Now she is gone for good.
When you left this morning I sent our other brothers away
to be alone with her.
Then I saw her cooking for you
and I got out my sharpest arrow,
which found its mark in her hip.
I would have chased her down and killed her
if not for the roar of thunder
that filled the sky
and frightened me.

As for Pollock he is still smarting from the Kenora court case a few years earlier—though he knows Morrisseau didn't instigate it. By this time Pollock's gallery and personal life are in shambles, his blatant honesty and vanity making him *persona non grata* in what he calls Toronto's bitchy art scene. His own life of flirting with excess has scarred both his body and mind, inside and outside. So honest and vain he later admits in his own book, printed in England where nobody knows him personally, that if he were to drop dead tomorrow the single most important thing he would be remembered for is the art of Norval Morrisseau.

Oh Ahsin! my foolish brother, cried Wahbi Ahmik.
Even though I am mad enough to kill you,
I pity you.
Did it not ever cross your mind who Nimkey Banasik was?
You must know her name means Thunderbird Woman.
I would have told you
if not for your blind hatred.
I would have also told you
she had six sisters.
Can you not imagine the power our children would have had?
What it would have meant for all of us?
For this woman was a thunderbird

in human form.
And now it is too late.

To say that Morrisseau is Pollock's cash cow and he is only in it for
the money would be unfair, unless you put it in perspective and add
that Morrisseau is everyone's cash cow. No, safe to say there is something more between them. For Morrisseau their initial meeting was
no accident. There is no room for accidents, or luck for that matter,
in his life.

I am leaving to never return until I find this woman,
Wahbi Ahmik said, as he turned his back on his brother
and followed the blood trail
that led far into the great forest.
For many moons he travelled until he came to a huge mountain
that reached over the clouds and beyond.
And he began to climb higher and higher,
until the earth disappeared and he reached the summit.
And there before him on a blanket of cloud
stood a towering teepee
shooting forth
lightning
and thunder
across the sky.

To be sure, whatever Morrisseau's and Pollock's frailties, together they
are magnificent. As if they walk on clouds. Pollock routinely reads
Morrisseau's mind like a cup of tea leaves and reminds him of his
purpose and stature, prodding and coaxing to get the best out of him.

From the majestic edifice came the laughter of women,
which suddenly stopped.
For they felt his presence.
Then the teepee flap opened and there stood Nimkey Banasik

looking more beautiful than ever.
With concern she asked why he had followed her.
Because you are my life, he answered.
She smiled upon hearing his words
and beckoned him forward.
Come inside, she said,
and we will give you the power
to walk on clouds.

Pollock knows Morrisseau can handle scale, which he has proven in *The Artist and His Four Wives* and *Some of My Friends*, each of them marvellous at 43 by 131 inches. What he doesn't know is that Morrisseau has also done sets of paintings, diptychs, like *Merman and Merwoman*, and has played with perspective in *The Land (Land Rights)*, where he divided the canvas into two panes. The problem is, Morrisseau is back living in Winnipeg, which makes it impossible for Pollock to keep track of him. Pollock knows the challenge is not to keep him painting, which he does constantly, but to make sure that he sends the gallery what he does, as Morrisseau would just as likely sell to anyone who comes knocking on his door.

Inside the wigwam were seated two old thunderbirds
in human form.
Light radiated from their eyes
suggesting a presence full of power and wisdom.
They saw Wahbi Ahmik's hunger
and offered him food.
In an instant a roar of deafening thunder erupted
as they stretched out their arms and changed into thunderbirds
and flew away,
to return with a big horned snake with two heads and three tails.
They offered it to Wahbi Ahmik to eat
but he quickly turned away from the writhing mass of flesh.
The next morning they again asked him if he needed food.

and the thunderbirds returned with a black snake sturgeon
and later with a cat-like demigod.
And Wahbi Ahmik grew weaker
and weaker.

Pollock flies back and forth between Toronto and Winnipeg, making sure that Morrisseau is not going astray and taking whatever paintings the artist has finished. Bob Checkwitch of Great Grasslands Graphics is also working with the painter during this time, doing a series of prints, and helps to keep him in check. Through meetings, telephone calls, and letters, Morrisseau and Pollock talk over the concept for *Man Changing into Thunderbird (Transmigration)*, and after much discussion Morrisseau decides to translate the story into panels. He knows this will be his greatest work to date.

Finally the old woman, who feared that Wahbi Ahmik was starving,
told her daughter to take him
to her great medicine uncle
Southern Thunderbird,
whom she knew would have strong medicine for the human.
They laid Wahbi Ahmik on a blanket of cloud
softer than rabbit fur and wrapped him gently
so that he would not see.
And with the thunder suddenly erupting
Wahbi Ahmik felt his nest of cloud move.
After what seemed like a mere moment
they stopped
and his wife Nimkey Banasik
removed the cloud from around him.
And there in front of Wahbi Ahmik,
perched on a cloud,
stood a great medicine lodge.

Three weeks before the opening of the exhibition, which is scheduled for August 10 at two o'clock, Morrisseau sends four panels to Toronto. Pollock's constant nudging has been well worth it: the complex multicoloured thunderbird-man against the brilliant orange background in a shrine of the natural world almost vibrates off the canvas. It is a feast for the eyes. But after staring at the images Pollock realizes that Morrisseau has yet to complete the story. Morrisseau tells him not to worry, the man will be transformed into thunderbird. Another two weeks pass and Pollock starts to become anxious. He telephones Winnipeg and Morrisseau assures him that he will bring the last two panels to Toronto with him. Pollock warns him that he needs time to prepare the paintings. That they have to be stretched and framed. Again Morrisseau tells him not to worry.

Wahbi Ahmik looked around him and saw many lodges,
the homes of many different kinds of thunderbirds,
all in human form.
Entering the great medicine lodge
Nimkey Banasik brought her uncle greetings from her mother
and beseeched him for help.
My mother said that you would have medicine for my husband
so that he may eat as we do
and perhaps even become one of us.
The old thunderbird stood in silence, pondering the love between them
and the consequences
of such an action.
Let it be known that if this human takes my medicine
he will never return to earth
but will become a thunderbird forever.
Then the medicine thunderbird took two small blue medicine eggs,
mixed them together
and advised Wahbi Ahmik to drink it.

On Friday, August 9, Morrisseau saunters into the gallery about lunchtime. Under his arm is the roll that Pollock is expecting. Everyone takes a break from installing the show and gathers around to see the last two panels. Morrisseau grins as he unrolls two blank canvases. Pollock is stunned. It's the last straw. He barks and growls at Morrisseau, who calmly tells him that the pictures will be finished in time for the show. Pollock exclaims that the other panels are still at the framer's and he won't be able to use them for reference. "No problem," Morrisseau says, unmoved by the calamity that Pollock foresees.

> The moment the potion entered Wahbi Ahmik
> he felt a strange power surge throughout his body.
> Looking at his hands and feet he saw
> they were no longer human
> but the claws and wings of a thunderbird.
> With the next drink the change was complete.
> He was now a thunderbird.
> His human form, the wigwams, the great medicine lodge,
> all disappeared.
> Everyone was now a thunderbird
> inhabiting the realm of thunderbirds.
> And so Wahbi Ahmik and Nimkey Banasik
> thanked Southern Thunderbird
> and flew home together
> where Wahbi Ahmik feasted
> on thunderbird food
> and lived out his life with this beloved wife Nimkey Banasik.

Morrisseau purchases three brushes and about twenty tubes of paint from Daniel's Art Supplies up the street from his hotel. For the life of him Pollock cannot fathom how Morrisseau is going to execute the paintings, and asks himself, "How can he possibly carry in his head the complete chromatic palette of the first four panels?" As Pollock is leaving the hotel room, Morrisseau tells him to come back at one o'clock in the morning and he'll have the paintings ready for him. Not knowing what to expect, Pollock returns at the exact hour. Morrisseau swings open the door to his room, and there they are, spread out on the floor. He has finished the series with two more panels. The moment Pollock sees them it becomes clear to him that Morrisseau has not only successfully recreated the colours of the first four panels, but he has somehow managed to match their composition and scale. They are exactly like the others.

And the people who remained below
in the world of humans
generation upon generation
remember Wahbi Ahmik
as the Man Who Changed
into
a Thunderbird.

With the canvases still wet, Pollock carries them back to the gallery in his outstretched arms and brings them to the framer's the moment they are dry. The show opens on time with Morrisseau touching up the new panels with dabs of paint on the tip of his right index finger. Within one hour the complete set of six panels is sold. And as Pollock predicted, everyone who is witness to *Man Changing into Thunderbird (Transmigration)* cannot look away. As one reviewer describes it, "the brilliant stained-glass colours and the visionary fluidity of its tangled shapes give the work a joyous force that overwhelms." Only later will Morrisseau confess to the press, "I didn't think I'd finish it," and then add, displaying his customary confidence, "I had a right to see all those visions. I am a Shaman. I am part Thunderbird. It is me."

The Garden Party

AT THE HEIGHT OF HIS CREATIVITY Morrisseau is one of the most popular and sought-after painters in the history of Canadian art. And in the midst of it all, he is back living in Beardmore and on the telephone to Pollock, discussing their latest success and planning for the next one. Which turns out to be Morrisseau's famous garden party—how to describe it other than to say it's the stuff of drama, theatrical realism pushed to the limit, a glimpse of the surreal, a one-of-a-kind performance. In any case it's something you marvel at as you sit down on one of the two dozen mismatched chairs he's collected from neighbours and set in a semicircle in the yard beside his house. If you can call it that—the two-room structure covered in red asphalt siding is little more than a shack. A half-tumbled-down outhouse set off to the side. Where you gather the grass has been recently cut, a hand-scythed island in a wild sea of dandelions and weeds two feet tall. A threatening sheet of overcast cloud has unexpectedly broken to reveal a brilliant northern Ontario sky. The spring day is unseasonably warm enough for you to remove your jacket, as others have done. Loosen your tie. Pollock jokes that it's the shaman's doing.

Beside you are the twenty guests who have also made the trip and, because of the flight, whom you feel you've known forever. Everyone is spectacularly awkward, and absurd in contrast to the surroundings, the women in long dresses, flowered sun hats, and white gloves, the men in three-piece suits, fedoras, and scarves. Attire befitting a Mad Hatter's tea party. You shake your head, smiling to yourself, and think, "How did I get talked into coming to such a godforsaken hole?" The one answer: Morrisseau—and Pollock of course, his bon vivant agent, who orchestrated it all.

As a long-time patron, certainly one of the earliest supporters of Morrisseau's work, Pollock made sure to include you on his list of invitees. You had heard rumours that something was afoot, something was being organized, and you thought it might be a celebration for the upcoming thirtieth anniversary of the Pollock

Gallery. Then again, word had it that Morrisseau was going to be receiving the Order of Canada later in the year too, which made you think that might also have something to do with the party. Whatever the reason, it was all fairly hush-hush—perfectly natural, pending confirmation—and then a couple of weeks ago an official invitation arrived with *Pollock Gallery* embossed on the envelope in gold lettering. At first you didn't believe what you were reading and thought it had to be some kind of practical joke. Fly 750 miles for a tea party? To some isolated airstrip that's not even on the map, and then take a bus for another half hour to Beardmore, north of Thunder Bay, where Morrisseau was supposedly recharging his creative batteries? It sounded positively ludicrous, and you immediately called Pollock to inquire what it was all about. But what you had read in the letter was the gospel truth. It turns out that Morrisseau was in the midst of purchasing an antique silver tea service to go along with his twenty-one-piece serving set of Royal Dalton china when someone said he should throw a garden party, just like the queen.

He took it to heart, and who else but Pollock would set out to implement such an outlandish plan. He had it all figured out: he would charter a DC-3 for $3,300 and divide the cost by inviting twenty-one friends, patrons, and admirers of the artist. At the airstrip in Jellicoe (wherever that was) the guests would be met by one of those yellow school buses and transported to Beardmore. Everyone would spend the afternoon there, participate in a once-in-a-lifetime Morrisseau-style "happening," and then fly back to Toronto that evening.

In addition to supporting Morrisseau's art, you have known Jack Pollock since he opened his first gallery on Elizabeth Street in 1960. You know something of his rather unconventional lifestyle, and that whatever he does is always first class, if not extraordinarily outrageous. "Sure, why not," you said. "I wouldn't miss it for the world." And so you too became one of Morrisseau's band of merry tricksters.

As you boarded the plane, everybody was handed a big, Sunkist orange, which must have recently come out of the refrigerator because it was cool to the touch. Something to quench your thirst perhaps, since there would be no stewardess on board serving drinks—liquor is strictly forbidden on smaller planes. You smiled affably, thanking the young man who gave it to you, and took a seat and belted up. Some of the people on board you recognized from either Les Copains, the restaurant Pollock frequents, or the gallery—people such as Eva Quan, the gallery administrator; Brian Schieder, the young artist who also works there; Robert Houle, the curator of contemporary Native art at the National Museum of Man in Ottawa; Kay Kritzwiser, art critic for *The Globe and Mail*; architect Spencer R. Higgins; lawyer Richard Baker; Mr. and Mrs. Higgins, who are big Morrisseau collectors from Hamilton; artists Madeleine McDowell and Helen Duffy; and the always elegantly dressed Stephen Cory, whom you met at the restaurant. Most of the others you do not know.

A middle-aged woman sat down beside you and introduced herself. She was wearing a long red skirt, a paisley blouse, and a couple of rows of bright beads around her neck that gave her a gypsy look. A friendly sort, she introduced herself immediately as Barbara Stimpson, and she said she was living in Ottawa and worked as a recording secretary in the House of Commons. She too was a collector.

When you were in the air, Pollock came down the aisle and with a wink told everyone to enjoy the oranges. You and Barbara looked at each other—not fully grasping the implication—then someone behind you exclaimed, "It's vodka and orange!" The smell of the alcohol mixed with orange rose up to greet you like a kiss. Always full of surprises, Pollock admitted that he had injected the oranges the evening before the flight. And announced to the general merriment of everyone that there were plenty more. By the time the flight landed everyone was grinning cheek to cheek and you really didn't much care where you were.

Pollock planned every last detail with precision, and after

reaching the airstrip, which turned out to be a strip of tarmac and a small white shed in the middle of nowhere, you filed aboard the school bus and bounced along a gravel road until you hit the highway to Beardmore. Driving into town was a surprise: one tiny street; one hotel with a bar, called the Crestwind Hotel; one motel, the Roxy Place; one restaurant; one café; one liquor store; one movie theatre—abandoned; one gas station; one store here and maybe one store there. This is not to say that it wasn't a picturesque little town in a rustic northern Ontario kind of way, but only that it had seen better days. Its skeletal streetscape showed the tell-tale signs of a typical northern Ontario boom-or-bust economy. At one time it may actually have been prosperous and offered quality living, but now it was barely hanging on to life.

The bus turned up Walker Street, a gravel road, and the bus driver, who had brought his two young daughters along for the adventure, called out that Morrisseau's place was up ahead. You'd arrived! And were more than a little surprised to see where he was living. By this time you were feeling dehydrated from the alcohol, your mouth as dry as the weeds outside, and rather nauseous, having been shaken and stirred for the whole ride. The day did not look promising. But as the bus approached you could hear the steady beat of a big Indian drum. And there was Morrisseau with his little entourage, waiting to greet everyone. With the swoosh of its air brakes the bus came to a jarring stop. All the guests stood to exit like children arriving at their first day of school, and were barely able to conceal their anticipation.

Dressed in a beaded leather vest and a shirt with long ribbons flowing from it, along with an elaborate headdress of finely sewn quills on birchbark and replete with feathers, Morrisseau looked splendid and beamed with pride—which he did not try to conceal in the slightest. Twenty-one people had travelled to the ends of the earth to make his garden party a reality, and he was happy and excited to see everyone. As you descended from the bus he welcomed and hugged each guest, making each person feel special.

Then he proceeded to give everyone a rare American buffalo nickel from a finely hand-hewn bowl. "This is to honour you for coming, a small token of my gratitude," he said, as he placed the silver piece in your palm and wrapped your fingers around it. Then Pollock hopped off the bus and they hugged like brothers, and Morrisseau gave him one of the nickels as well. "Where did you get these?" Pollock asked, excitedly. Morrisseau only smiled and handed the bowl to his apprentice Brian Marion, an attractive young Native man wearing a red shirt and white jeans, his raven hair braided.

As the drum continued you were guided to the field behind the house, where Morrisseau, the master of ceremonies, the maestro, told everyone to take a seat. He asked if everyone had met Fabian Burback, the head of the Toronto chapter of Eckankar, and taking him by the arm, sat him down in a flowered sofa chair, a place of honour beside his own seat. Once everyone was settled he said he was going to do a traditional Anishinaabe welcoming ceremony. He and his apprentice then laid down two blankets, one red and one blue, in the centre of the yard. Kneeling on them, they removed various items from a small red suitcase to complete their preparations, including a leather bundle that contained a long-stemmed pipe, a pair of eagle feathers, and various kinds of herbs. He then took up a fan made from what looked like partridge feathers, and a rattle made from a turtle shell, representing power and protocol in his culture.

Laying out the last of the things he needs Morrisseau lets everyone know what's going on, and announces that sweetgrass, sage, cedar and tobacco are traditional medicines. As he is doing so, he asks Robert Houle something in Anishinaabemowin. Robert is Saulteaux and must understand because he gets up from his chair, looking rather formal and incongruous in his blue suit and tie, and joins the two men on the blankets. A flash of a wooden match, and herbs are set ablaze in a tin pan. The smoke rises in a small cloud. Morrisseau bends down towards the pan to greet it and sweeps the smoke over his head and chest. Brian Marion does likewise, and finally Robert. You cannot make out what Morrisseau is saying but it has the rhythm of prayer. He then stands and informs everyone that they are going to smudge everyone in the traditional Anishinaabe way, and approaches each guest with the pan of sweet-smelling smoke. You see some people removing their glasses and jewellery so you do the same. Morrisseau tells you to think of something beautiful. So you think of your grandson, who is two years old. When the smudging is complete he puts aside the medicines and says, "Let's party!" And after a moment, "I'm hungry." And laughs to relieve any apprehension anyone might have when it comes to Morrisseau and his reputation for partying.

Before too long, amid the chatter and laughter, Morrisseau and a helper begin to make the rounds with the antique silver tea service and the Royal Crown Derby cups and saucers, serving a homemade raspberry tea, along with platters of fresh golden bannock and nutty brown wild rice. "A repast fit for the queen herself," you announce as Morrisseau comes around and provides a special blessing with the feather fan. Meanwhile, Morrisseau's brother Wolf, Brian Marion, and a couple of other Native helpers circle around the drum, and on a "one, two, three, four" they begin drumming in unison. You listen to the song they play rise and swell to crescendo heights, punctuated by four beats, boom, boom, boom, boom. As you enjoy your tea, Brian and Wolf entertain everyone with what they call "happy songs," both of them singing to the beat of the drum.

Then Morrisseau, sitting down by this time with a feathered staff in his hand, says he will perform some ancient medicine songs he learned from the old people long ago. You finish your tea listening to him chant in his own language, the collective breathing slowing as nobody wants to make a move. As soon as the songs come to an end, Morrisseau jumps up reinvigorated and rushes around getting everyone up and dancing in a huge circle around the drum. He calls this an "intertribal" and all the guests, especially Pollock, seem to be having the time of their lives. The drumming continues, and as you get closer to the drum itself you realize it is made from a modern bass drum that has been refashioned, painted and adorned with symbols and feathers, to make it look Indian. One does what one has to do.

It must be coming up on late afternoon when the blackflies descend, looking for their own lunch. It feels like you're getting at least a pint of blood siphoned out of you, and there's a lot of swatting going on. By this time your bladder is to the point of bursting anyway. You stare at the outhouse off to the side of the shack and make your way towards it by going around the periphery of the circle. The little building looks like it's about to topple over so it's one experience you're not cherishing. A couple of yards away you can already smell the stench. You open the door, hold your breath, close the door, but you are overpowered and dash out, gasping. You decide to check the house. Judging from the condition of the outhouse, you figure there has to be a washroom inside.

The house is small, with two rooms on the ground floor and a simple staircase leading to an upper floor. In sharp contrast to the dismal look of the exterior, the clapboard interior is filled with an assortment of what you can only describe as Victorian treasures, rich dark furniture, and oil paintings in gilded frames. Amazed by the incongruity, you enter the second room, which is dominated by a large wooden table with Morrisseau's artwork scattered across it. Brushes standing in a Player's tobacco tin, empty tubes of paint lying on the floor. You don't see any sign of a washroom so you ascend the staircase, lowering your head as you cross the threshold to the upper floor. It takes your eyes a second to adjust to the darkness, but as a single room takes shape you make out an unmade double bed, sheets and blankets askew, a row of dressers, and then what looks like a statue in the middle of the room. You take a few steps and soon realize that what you are looking at is really a giant carved penis mounted on the floor, its base covered in black fur, a little sign on the shaft of it saying "extra seating." A joke, you think, maybe a gift. You start laughing, and that's when it hits you: the walls are covered with gay porn, pictures and advertisements for all sorts of sex toys cut from magazines, and it dawns on you that you really shouldn't be up here. You are heading back down the stairs when you meet one of the women in her finery, also looking for a place to relieve herself, and you tell her there's no washroom up there.

Together you decide to pay a visit to the gas station down the road, which you saw while driving in. When you arrive you are not alone: half a dozen of the other guests are lined up along a grimy cinderblock wall in their long dresses and suits, waiting to use the single stall. The gas attendant looks like one of the boogie-woogie Andrews Sisters, tight white blouse, beige slacks, and string sandals, a beehive of hair stacked on her head, a glass of scotch in her hand. She says she knows Morrisseau well. "Quite the character," she says, looking you over. "A real trickster, that one."

By the time you return to the garden party, jackets and shawls are strewn over the backs of chairs, ties loosened, shoes kicked off, and everyone is dancing in a long conga line, trying to keep hold of the shoulders in front of them, snaking their way around the yard. Morrisseau is in the lead, laughing and calling, and everybody is panting and red-faced but at the same time filled with laughter as they stumble and try to keep time to the beating drum. You watch the hilarity for a moment, and then jump in at the end of the line with the rest of the stragglers and do your best to keep up. Finally, the drumming stops with its mandatory four beats, and you disengage and collapse panting in a nearby chair. And then, after more raspberry tea to quench everyone's thirst, the garden party comes to an end.

The plan is for the group to go to the Crestwind Hotel on the main street for a quick dinner and then hop on the bus for the trip back to the airplane. But before the guests leave, Morrisseau says he has another gift that he would like to bestow on everyone. "A gift from the Thunderbird," he says. Each person is to go over to where he is sitting, and he will do a tailor-made sketch for them. You stand back and watch him with his Grumbacher sketch pad on his lap and a black felt marker in his hand. He touches the hand of each person who approaches him and in a couple of minutes produces what he calls a portrait. Of the inner self. The deftness and speed of his execution is nothing short of remarkable, if not magical. Once set down, his pen never leaves the paper. Jack Pollock and Robert Houle stand beside him like sentinels, talking to him in confidence, and you get the impression they may be trying to get him to tone down his inspiration. From what you saw upstairs in his house, you can only imagine what he is capable of drawing.

You are finally next in line, and, like the others before you, your drawing is completed in mere minutes. "For you, power and potency," he says dramatically, tearing the sheet away from the pad and handing it to you. At first glance it appears to be his signatory montage of animals, a bear, a serpent, and a half-human bird person receiving spiritual power from a shaman. You thank him and he shakes your hand warmly. (Only later do you notice that protruding from the shaman is a massive penis entwined among the figures, its knob-like eyes giving it the appearance of a comic-book insect, which leaves you wondering if he sees something in you that you don't see.) Like everyone there, you are touched. The whole day has been a gesture of pure generosity, and you and the others gather around to hug Morrisseau goodbye. By way of explanation he says that it's the Anishinaabe way to treat your guests with respect and hospitality, and that's all he is doing. And on that note Morrisseau concludes his primordial performance. Naturally you would like to see some devious underbelly to the lovely afternoon to slake your cynical nature. But Morrisseau's sincerity has far exceeded your expectations. By the time the guests all leave for dinner, there's not a dry eye on the bus.

The Crestwind Hotel's restaurant is a typical northern bar, dark wood panelling, leatherette-backed chairs, small rectangular tables. The food arrives on platter-size plates and looks pasty, but as promised by the bus driver, who it turns out is also the hotel's owner, it is hearty fare: roast beef, mashed potatoes, canned gravy, canned peas, and a small dish holding iceberg lettuce and a slice of almost-red tomato, doused in French dressing. Your eyes by now have adjusted to the darkness of the room, and what almost flattens you is the wall behind the bar—it's jam-packed with Morrisseau's paintings. More than a dozen of various sizes, all of them unframed and mounted with thumbtacks.

And maybe it's the beer but later you wonder aloud if anybody actually paid for them. If anyone really gives a shit about the artist. To this there is a sudden silence at the table. Maybe everyone feels a little guilty, or maybe a little embarrassed. You are reminded of the full-colour coffee-table book that Pollock and Lister Sinclair are about to release. Pollock undoubtedly has high hopes for it. And what better way to attract attention? What better publicity than a happening garden party in Beardmore?

Fame

ON A SPRING DAY in 1979, Morrisseau is invested into the Order of Canada. Invited by Governor General Edward Schreyer to come to Rideau Hall in Ottawa for the ceremony, he travels with Brian Marion, whom he introduces as his companion. Befitting his contradictory nature, and despite everything that has happened to his people, Morrisseau makes it known that he is a proud Canadian. And he is dressed for the occasion in a snow-white suit, with a feather and a band of mink fur in his hair, a bear claw dangling from a bone choker. Morrisseau loves the attention and the palatial residence, and is as gracious as ever to the governor general and his wife.

Later, however, when reporters asks him about the honour, he responds angrily. And philosophically. He tells them that he feels so much confusion: "First the white man drives my people down to the pits of hell with an army of missionaries, and then they honour him, lift him up on their shoulders, with this medal. What has been lost is lost," he says, "and no matter who he was before, that person is gone." He also makes it known that it is the white man who must take responsibility for what has happened. And then, in a gesture of reconciliation, he adds that if he had never hit rock bottom he would not be the great artist he is today. For Morrisseau there is a reason for everything.

And maybe this is how he feels about his disintegrating relationship with Pollock. By this time Pollock has made sure that their garden party has hit the newspapers and circulated throughout the Canadian art scene, making critics and artists alike sit up and take notice of the painter's outlandish artistic temperament, where everything and anything goes. Something a New York artist might have pulled off, but here in Canada? Brighter than ever before, Morrisseau shines like silver lure cast into dark water, attracting all kinds of interest.

And when Pollock and Sinclair also release their stylishly framed coffee-table book *The Art of Norval Morrisseau*, reviewers use words like "magnificent" and "extraordinary" to describe the striking publication. Pollock is smart, and in recognizing this project as the bones of his legacy, he spares no expense. With an insightful essay by Sinclair, a memoir of Pollock's first meeting Morrisseau, and an interview with Morrisseau himself, the book is composed of the painter's best work to date, laid out in pages of vivid colour and bold black and white.

For Morrisseau and Pollock, though, rather than this period being the beginning of a new chapter in their relationship, it turns out to be the culmination of their careers together, and the beginning of the end. With the surge of popularity comes a barrage of interviews, and when Morrisseau is asked about his career, he points to Pollock: "Jack became my blood brother, my agent, and my friend." But with so much new interest in Morrisseau and his art, rolls of paintings passed from seller to buyer to buyer, and Pollock losing grip of his own life, they soon find themselves spinning in different directions. Two brilliant comets flaring and burning off into the night.

Tom Thomson's Shack

FOUR YEARS AFTER HIS FIRST VISIT, Morrisseau shows up again at the McMichael Gallery, but this time to serve as artist in residence. The short yet tumultuous period has seen him paint some of his greatest work to date, like the visionary *Artist and His Four Wives* (1975), done in high-contrast red and blue, featuring the artist's four dream-wives beseeching him to stay in their lives, while thunderbird and bear sentinels stand at each end and support the panel; the provocative *The Land (Land Rights)* (1976), a single canvas separated into two distinct spaces, emphasizing political discord between the Native and the Settler, one of Morrisseau's few overtly political paintings; the iconic six-panel *Man Changing into Thunderbird* (1977), based on the concept of transformation, which in terms of composition and narrative power is one of Morrisseau's greatest works; and the evocative diptych *The Storyteller: The Artist and His Grandfather* (1978), an homage, displaying Morrisseau's earliest influence while pointing to new directions. These and other spectacular paintings have consolidated Morrisseau's reputation as one of Canada's greatest painters, despite his reputation for living so hard and heavy the concrete sidewalks sometimes crack under his feet.

When Morrisseau arrives this time he is practicing the spiritual teachings of Eckankar and walking the red road of sobriety. "I haven't been drinking much lately," he tells a reporter at the gallery, who is quick to seize on the subject. He answers the reporter's questions without dismissing him for what he usually calls the media's junky thoughts. "Of course, some people fall off the wagon every six months. It's surprising—the more times I fell off the wagon, the less it got to me. I may have fallen off three times after I joined AA. The first time I might have drunk for two months. The second time, only for a month. You do learn something. Physically you go down; spiritually you go up. You are much stronger when you overcome these things. I have done it!"

As far as Morrisseau's concerned, he is beyond it all. Encircled by a coterie of assistants who placate his every need, his wife and family surrendered to loss, at age forty-seven he feels like a reincarnation of his former self, freed from Christian fear and guilt, with original sin pushed aside in favour of another kind of belief system. "You see I feel I have outgrown Christianity," he says to the reporter. "Christ never enters my mind much anymore. I loved him. I worshipped him, but I had been brainwashed into it. For me something else was better. Furthermore, Indians don't have a devil. There is only Manitou, God." And when asked to describe his present state of mind? "Serenity," he answers in a word.

Standing in one of the McMichael's honey pine galleries, feeling the warmth of the smooth wood as he glides his hand over it, he breaks into a smile when Robert McMichael congratulates him on his recent appointment to the Order of Canada. Morrisseau was happy to accept the invitation to be the official painter in residence for the gallery, which comes with the opportunity to work in Tom Thomson's famous shack for three weeks. And frankly, he is happy to be out of the city. When asked if he is excited to be working on the same easel that Thomson used, he says casually that he feels good about it. It is only later, when he is alone standing in front of Thomson's *Windy Day* and works by the Group of Seven, like Johnston's *Sunset in the Bush*, that he comes to understand why the painters are revered by so many. Listening to his own breath, the paintings carry him back to his home in northern Ontario, spruce and granite, rivers and snow, thunderous Nipigon waves. Knowing these paintings only though art books and then seeing them come alive in front of him, Morrisseau is so impressed that for his first few days at the gallery he revisits these particular paintings regularly. He sits quietly and contemplates the greens of spring, the blues of summer, the reds of autumn, and the whites of winter, all places the paintings bring him to remember.

At the same time, though, he wonders where all the life is. Clearly, what they saw and what he sees are entirely different things. For Morrisseau the land is full and teeming with life. Reality but a blink—a slight shift sideways and it is transforming into something else, something grounded in belief and story. Worlds within worlds. Fish people swimming through the human world in the midst of transforming into bird people, into a leaf, everything sliding through the other's reality and becoming each other. Not empty and void of life, as though the land had never been inhabited by his people for thousands of years, or by the other-than-humans.

For the next week Morrisseau is preoccupied by such thoughts as he paints in Thomson's shack. Then one night, after working for ten hours straight, he has an unexpected medicine dream and finds himself entering one of Thomson's paintings. Finds himself inside the geography of a landscape that he knows intimately. His soul travels to what he now calls "the House of Invention," the source of his creativity, or what reporters who write about him call "the bewitched territory of his imagination," and he awakes knowing that he's had another vision. It has always been his belief that nature is our best teacher and that we can tap into its power to come to some understanding of our life and purpose. To know that nature is not *out there* somewhere, but inside you, and to realize what it means to be in perfect harmony with nature, as his ancestors knew it. For Morrisseau this is the lesson of his vision. That same day he holds true to his vision: he lays a new blank board on Thomson's easel and paints his multicoloured *Soul in Form of Fish Swimming the Cosmic Sea*, which the McMichael purchases.

The days pass and Morrisseau continues to paint in Thomson's shack—though not always uninterrupted. With the Order of Canada, headlines about his famous tea party, and a CBC special all happening in the space of a year, his star has once again ascended. To coincide with his well-publicized tenure at the McMichael Gallery, the *Toronto Star Weekend Magazine* does a full spread on him called "The Pride of Norval Morrisseau," excerpted from Pollock and Sinclair's *The Art of Norval Morrisseau*, and the art-buying public flock to Kleinburg to meet him. And although he likes the attention, at times he feels he's on display. Still, he never lets his audience interrupt his work. "I can live anywhere. I can paint anywhere," he says when asked about the crowds. "I don't need to isolate myself."

One afternoon Morrisseau is deep at work and turns to find a young boy, not much more than ten, staring at him, and he is reminded of his own children, who he rarely sees. "What a pretty picture," the boy says, stretching his neck to examine the bird-like chimera spangled with bright yellow eyes, a body of brilliant greens and oranges. "Here, have a piece of my cookie," he says, turning to the painter, as though responding to what he has just seen. Morrisseau will tell this story to a reporter who comes to interview him the next day. Reflecting that he favours childlike simplicity in people, he will say: "Children are perfectly natural... As we grow up we are taught not to react naturally... Modern civilization separates us from nature and our spiritual source of power. We forget the beauty of a fleeting look on a child's face. We begin to think other things are more important." Dwelling on his encounter with the boy, he will once again lay a fresh board down and give himself over to what he calls "the source." From this blank canvas will emerge *Manifesting from Within Childlike Simplicity*, another painting that the McMichael Gallery will purchase.

During his residency, Morrisseau paints from morning until late afternoon and then returns to his motel by taxi. There is always at least one apprentice at his side to come at his command, and some-times there's a whole entourage. Never being alone physically, he believes, helps to assuage his spiritual loneliness. These companions of his are always good-looking young men who are keen on learning the secret of his creativity. His personal relationship with them depends entirely on the individual. Some are lovers, some are sons, some are long-time friends, some are merely acquaintances passing through. There is no expectation and no judgment. Morrisseau believes that we are all spiritual beings just as he believes we are corporeal human beings with physical needs. First and foremost has always been the question "Who am I?," a question that has taken him down the less than navigable road to "I am." "You constantly have to sort out your thoughts and ideas," he says, and it is these ideas that Morrisseau puts into his paintings, and no matter the excess, he believes that he has always been spiritually strong. Believes that no matter what happens to him, the goal of his painting is to pass on his sense of spirituality to his people.

It is with this in mind that he again takes up another blank canvas and slips it onto Tom Thomson's easel. The last painting he does at the shack he calls *Shaman and Disciples*. In it, he is the shaman-master on the astral plane, near the city of light, with some of his chelas—student-disciples. He paints himself as the bearded figure in the middle ground, while on his left is his apprentice-son Brian Marion and on the right is his musician friend Shingoose. It is the largest painting he does at the gallery, measuring 71 by 83 inches, and one of the most impressive.

Taking one day off each week to rest, he completes sixteen paintings in three weeks. When asked about his phenomenal output, he remarks that when he is tired and wants to stop, he lets his inner master, or spirit, take over for him. It is something that he is now able to express through the language of Eckankar. In the end, the McMichael purchases five paintings, and Morrisseau is grateful for the residency.

Doctor Morrisseau

IN 1980, Morrisseau is living in Toronto when he receives a letter through the Pollock Gallery from McMaster University in Hamilton. When he opens it he sees that it comes directly from the university's president, Dr. A.N. Bourns, who writes, "Dear Mr. Morrisseau: I take pleasure in informing you that the Senate of McMaster University has by unanimous consent authorized me to invite you to accept the honorary degree Doctor of Laws... In authorizing this award, the Senate wished to pay tribute to your rare artistry in expressing the legends and traditions of your people.

Senators deeply admired your superb ability to focus the eye and mind on the spiritual power of the traditional beliefs and wisdom of your ancestors. They wished also to honour your inspiration and leadership... We would, therefore, be honoured if you would accept our invitation."

And for an instant Morrisseau sees himself sitting in a small wooden desk at St. Joseph's residential boarding school in Fort William. Even after all these years, the words "dumb Indian" still clang in his head like a school bell, as though he were too ignorant to know the value of an education. So he embraces the idea of receiving the doctorate. Above all, it means he will be recognized not only for who he is as an artist, and what he has done for his people, but as an intelligent human being. Two years earlier, when he was appointed to the Order of Canada, and attended the investiture ceremony at Rideau Hall, it was one of the proudest moments in his life. Unlike other recipients, who more often than not keep their medal tucked away in a little box, Morrisseau wears his almost daily, so often the ribbon is beginning to look tattered. But for Morrisseau, the point *is* to wear it. As he says matter-of-factly, "I'm very proud of it." And he is just as proud to receive an honorary doctorate.

The convocation is held in the spring, and it is a formal affair with the requisite pomp and ceremony, signalling a bright moment in the lives of the graduating students. This year two honorary doctorates will be among them. University officials are beginning to worry, however, because there is less than a half-hour to go and there's still no sign of Norval Morrisseau. Before proceeding to the polished gymnasium, the graduating students and honourees are fitted with traditional academic gowns and hoods. The officials in the fitting room stare nervously at the door, waiting for Morrisseau to appear. Dean of Social Sciences Peter George decides to go out to the parking lot in case Morrisseau is lost, and it is there that he sees the artist getting out of a car and strolling across the lot. George rushes over to him and to his surprise Morrisseau greets him with a pat on the back, acting like he has known him for years. For

Morrisseau all is well with the world, and his attitude and bearing give the impression that it would stop spinning and wait for him at his command.

Dressed smartly for the officious occasion, he is wearing a pair of dark dress pants, a white shirt, and a floral-patterned leather vest. His thick, unruly hair is combed back and his mustache trimmed. He is hurriedly fitted with a McMaster burgundy and white gown and hood, and he immediately takes an interest in the hood—a piece of clothing included in one of his very first birchbark paintings of the Shaking Tent ceremony—and pulling it over his head for a moment he admires himself in a nearby mirror. He then takes his place in the procession of officials and graduating students, and follows the sound of bagpipes into the gymnasium, past a throng of beaming visitors and proud parents.

Addressing the assembly, Dean of Humanities Alwyn Berland reads the citation: "The fragmentation of modern society and its dependence on transitional values based on utility in place of time-tested values rooted in tradition and historical experience have been the cause of much of the anxiety and anguish of our times. No group has been more vulnerable than the native peoples of Canada... Yet some have found ways to cope... have turned back firmly to the faith of their ancestors, inspired by fresh perceptions... among the latter is the gifted artist who stands before us now."

Morrisseau does not speak during the investiture, but by now he is deep into the teachings of Eckankar, and if he were to speak he would tell the students that whatever they want is at their finger-tips, all they need to do is dream deeply and travel to the House of Invention. He would say that you don't have to worry about the astral plane, just go there and see for yourself—just be—that's the whole process. Prove it to yourself. Instead, upon hearing "I present you a Canadian artist... a gifted son of a great nation, Norval Morrisseau, that you may confer on him the degree of Doctor of Laws, *honoris causa*," he strides up to the chancellor and accepts the award graciously with a smile and a handshake.

Afterwards Morrisseau lingers and shakes more hands with various officials and students who want to meet him. When Dean Berland says that he will be Morrisseau's guardian for the evening reception, Morrisseau remarks, "No, you're not, my guardians are over there." Everyone present is perplexed to see the artist pointing into thin air, at nobody in particular. "I'll go with my friend here," he then says, as he reaches out and gives Peter George, the man who found him in the parking lot, a quick hug. Morrisseau has no interest in attending the banquet for the honorary graduates and special guests; instead, he decides to go home with Peter George, who in the meantime has called his wife, Gwen, to let her know that they will be having company. When they arrive, she is taking muffins out of the oven and their children, Michael and Jane, soon arrive home from school. Morrisseau eats muffins and drinks tea with the family while telling them stories about his life, plunging into stories about travelling by canoe to encountering his spirit-bear helper to travelling through the astral planes. When one of the children asks him what he means by "astral plane," he points to the patterned glass of the French doors in the room and says that the astral plane is like looking through those doors. Morrisseau is in good shape and gregarious, and he mesmerizes both the adults and the children with his tales.

At the same time, sitting in the dean's beautiful home, a part of him cannot help reflect on what he has taken part in today, and where he has come from, and the incongruity of it all. All the bright-eyed students he has just seen at the convocation flash before him, all of them walking proudly across the podium, their futures laid out like promises. And what of his own children? Morrisseau thinks back to the early days in when he took an interest in their education. He remembers attending parent-teacher interviews and inquiring how they were doing. At least for the first few. Victoria, David, Pierre, Eugene, Christian, Michael, Lisa—seven kids now, and the thought of them suddenly causes him to cough and choke, which sends Gwen running for a glass of water. Unlike all the graduates he's just seen, and even the dean's kids, not one of his own children will ever go to university and receive a higher degree. The door of opportunity will never be thrown open for them. He looks back to Michael and Jane, who sit listening to his sugar-coated stories of growing up in the north. And that's when he abruptly announces that he has to go and asks his hosts to call him a cab. A container of muffins under his arm, he stands on the sidewalk smoking a cigarette until the taxi arrives, which takes him wherever he is going.

The Bear

In Toronto, and preparing for one of his last shows with Pollock, Morrisseau is out hunting. Daniel's Art Supplies, at 430 Spadina Avenue in the heart of the city, is just down the street from the Waverley Hotel and the Silver Dollar Room, and just ten minutes away from his studio on Baldwin Street. The door opens with the delicate chime of a Chinese bell. Daniel is at the counter serving a young woman who is wearing a royal purple beret and matching scarf. Normally colour like this would make Morrisseau stop and take notice, but he is in a hurry this morning. He has a show opening tomorrow at First Canadian Place, presented by the Pollock Gallery, and as usual he is down to the wire. Without so much as a glance at the woman, he pads to the counter and mumbles to Daniel that he wants 24 yards of primed canvas, 12 yards of unprimed, Gesso, then quickly grabs a gallon of white paint and a gallon of black from a nearby shelf, swinging them onto the counter like they are bags of beans, and turning again grabs a few number 4 and 8 brushes and four medium-size stretched panels. Morrisseau likes that the store is unpretentious, a place for working artists—organized disarray, art supplies stacked every which way.

Daniel is a first-generation Chinese Canadian who never dreamed of getting into the art business, but having stumbled into it, he likes the people he deals with. The look of them, their temperaments, never cease to amaze him. Daniel values Morrisseau's business, his prodigious output leaving him always in need of art supplies, and over the past ten years they have developed a cordial relationship. Morrisseau regularly joking about the red and yellow peoples being related. (For Morrisseau every stripe of humanity is related.) Daniel making sure he is well taken care of. Having seen Morrisseau in all kinds of conditions and moods, he knows that this bear of a man has indeed the temperament of a bear.

Today Morrisseau's movements are swift and silent as he plunks the rest of the supplies on the counter then digs into his pocket and pulls out a crumpled wad of cash. Filthy stuff, he sometimes calls it, and Daniel thinks that only an artist like Morrisseau would say such a thing. When Morrisseau doesn't have cash he will often have a note and phone number from Pollock, or whoever he is dealing with at the time. When he doesn't have a note, Daniel just gives him credit, because he knows Morrisseau will always be back for more supplies.

Daniel acknowledges Morrisseau with a quick smile before turning his back to him in order to finish up with the young woman. He doesn't sense the mood Morrisseau is in today. In his own mind Morrisseau is already out the door and down the street with his supplies, walking into his studio, laying down the canvas and taking up the brushes and paint. His back turned, Daniel doesn't see this. Doesn't see the hurried look in Morrisseau's eyes. Doesn't see him stuff the money back into his pocket. Doesn't see him abruptly leave. Daniel turns when he hears the chime of the bell above the door. It is a lesson he remembers well, and the next time Morrisseau comes in—as he does when all is forgiven and forgotten—he politely excuses himself from the other patrons and greets the bear.

An Open Embrace

MORRISSEAU'S LAST EXHIBITION at the Pollock Gallery closes on July 16, 1981. The profits from Morrisseau's almost yearly solo shows have been blown on excess, with both him and Pollock going through money as though the Windigo creature itself were devouring it. Pollock living a life of extremes, cocaine orgies, lavish costume parties, the best restaurants, a room at the Waldorf Astoria. Morrisseau spending upwards of five thousand dollars a week. No longer the camera-shy youth from the bush with the blue blazer and tie, Morrisseau's hair is now permed, his dress an elaborate fusion of his own design, pseudo-modern-primitive, beaded vests and bright shirts, silver and turquoise bracelets, broaches, necklaces, and amulets. His persona as father of the Thunderbird School of Shamanistic Arts cast in precious metal.

From that point on Morrisseau does what he has learned to do in the name of survival and belief in his own physical and psychic bliss. He goes wherever the leaves of the money tree rustle loudest— not for the money itself but for the creature comforts it affords. And so he turns away from the Pollock Gallery and moves to the Palette Gallery, while still selling to private collectors. And then, in the midst of living high, he hooks himself to a black limousine and begins selling his work to the Nexus Gallery, run by Albert Volpe—whose family has been associated with the American mafia since the turn of the last century—and any lingering connection with Jack Pollock is effectively severed. By this time everyone wants a piece of the action. Morrisseau is a bankable star who has never receded from public interest. He is as much a personality as he is a painter, his identity as artist and shaman inseparable, and promoted to an eager group of collectors and followers. And the rewards are fabulous: money in his pockets bunched like Kleenex, a shaman-artist surrounded by a coterie of good-looking young people who become his apprentices and disciples—and are portrayed in such paintings as *Shaman's Apprentice* (1980) and *Grand Shaman and His Apprentice the Blond Person Tala, Sunshine for the Group* (1980).

Selling to the Volpe family, Morrisseau paints out of numerous locations: the studio on Baldwin Street, the basement of the Nexus Gallery, and a posh Spanish-style villa in Vandorf, north of Toronto. All of it either paid for directly by Albert and Violette Volpe or indirectly from money paid to Morrisseau for his paintings. But when it comes to Morrisseau's relationship with the Volpes, it has to be considered through the thick fog of opinion. For some it is a terrible time for him. For others it is the time of his life. Robert Houle, the Saulteaux artist and curator, visits Morrisseau during this period at the Town Inn in Toronto, which he assumes is paid for by the Volpes. "There was a very pretty Italian boy there with him who would serve us tea," he recalls. "Whether he was a lover, I'm not sure, but he seemed to be there to please Morrisseau. One time I had to use the bathroom, and he said he had a little treat in there. He had some hash in a penis pipe he'd carved."

Houle says that he got to know Morrisseau quite well because he speaks Ojibway and Morrisseau enjoyed dropping by to talk. "One time I was listening to Bach when he happened to come by and he knew all about him. His music, his life. He said he had astral travelled to visit him."

The two Anishinaabe artists become close for a couple of years, but then there is a break in their friendship. Houle wants to commission Morrisseau to do a performance piece as part of a Toronto arts festival, and Morrisseau agrees but wants to get paid in drugs. "He was going to paint a teepee and then sit in it. I was all for it," Houle says, "until he told me that he wanted to be paid $3,000 in cocaine. He didn't get the coke. I refused to do it. It made for some bad blood between us." He further adds that as director of the contemporary Native art collection at the Museum of Man in Ottawa, he went to the Pollock Gallery to purchase five pieces of art and only ended up purchasing one because "Eva Quan, who was working for Pollock at the time, and was a specialist in Morrisseau's art, did not want to authenticate it."

Morrisseau's earliest and only Ojibway apprentice, Brian Marion, known as Little Hummingbird to Morrisseau and his followers, and as Disco Dick to Pollock because of his tight white pants, says that he and the other apprentices all lived out in a mansion in Vandorf and painted with Morrisseau. "Of the nearly ten years I spent with the artist," he says, "I learned a lot of stuff from him, but he was so eccentric, he was hard to live with. When he was drinking it was not always positive. I didn't want to take part in those things, didn't want to spend time with him when he was on his escapades, and I'd leave." He stresses that "lots of times he was completely sober. I don't want to give you the impression he was drunk all the time. It wasn't like that. He was often more sober than drunk, and we had lots of good times."

And while many speak of Morrisseau being mired in addiction, especially during the Volpe years, Ritchie Sinclair (Stardreamer), another apprentice and painter who lived out in Vandorf, goes even further to refute Morrisseau's use of heavy drugs. On the contrary Sinclair speaks of Vandorf with reverence, as a time shrouded in mysticism, and says that "to know Norval you had to know he was on a mission for God."

Brian Marion also speaks of the artist with awe and respect, as his memories of those years linger: "One time in Vandorf he was meditating by a window in the middle of the night and the next morning the owner of the house we were renting drove up and thanked him for sending her a message informing her that her mother was dying. She got to see her mother before she died. How he contacted her, I don't know; we didn't have a telephone."

And for a while the villa is indeed a godsend, a haven, where Morrisseau is surrounded by his family of apprentice-disciples and free to paint collaboratively and develop his Thunderbird School. He is secure in Vandorf, not a worry or care in the world, and the Volpes supply him with everything he needs or desires. Their big black limo rolls up the driveway with canvases, paint, money… and leaves with the completed paintings. Morrisseau can paint whatever he wants, experiment with theme, scale, and colour—the market for his work is a blue flame. As long as he does his part everything is taken care of, and every wish is granted.

However the retreat is eventually overrun by visitors seeking out the famous shaman-artist, and the group finds itself caught in a cacophony of activity. Sinclair remembers that "ECKists gathered by the hundreds to meditate and make their 'HU' sound beneath the thunderbird paintings, Native groupies were sleeping in cars and becoming self-proclaimed bodyguards, while 'wannabe Native' New Age seekers camped out on the grounds. Noise and nightly bonfires became the norm." Humorously, as though the spirits are watching, it is not the crowds but the clogged toilets (from both paint and people) that make Morrisseau abandon the villa in Vandorf.

By 1983, Morrisseau is back in Toronto, installed in a massive Victorian-style house in Riverdale, near Broadview Avenue, where he continues to party and paint, apparently oblivious to everything he does disappearing into the coffers of the Volpes. That year he paints his incredibly luminescent, otherworldly *Androgyny*—mammoth at 144 by 240 inches—his largest painting to date, which with a master's stroke exemplifies Morrisseau's exceptional ability to control space and balance colour. In brilliant reds, blues, and yellows, *Androgyny* combines Anishinaabe cosmology with Eckankar philosophy, where the astral planes of consciousness are represented by portals opening to other worlds. Brian Marion recalls living on Richmond Street in downtown Toronto with Morrisseau, and how this painting came to be. One night there was a knock at the door and he went downstairs to answer it but nobody was there. About ten minutes later came another knock, and still nobody. The third time he goes down, there is a huge roll of canvas at the door. He figures it's from the Volpes. Morrisseau uses the canvas for a painting that he wants to give to the people of Canada. He completes it, but he is drinking again, and the painting disappears. "Somebody took it," says Marion, "because I remember he had to do another one, which turned out to be *Androgyny*, the one hanging at Indian Affairs. Things like that happened to him."

And that same year, in a twist of fate, Paul Volpe—the brother of Morrisseau's benefactor and head of the family—is murdered and stuffed in the trunk of a car at Pearson International Airport. And in the pandemonium that ensues among the remaining family,

Morrisseau is momentarily forgotten. According to some he simply walks out the door and catches a cab. For others his departure is more dramatic, fleeing under the cover of darkness and waving down a passing car.

It is when Morrisseau leaves Toronto that the fog of opinion clouds the ensuing events. Having visited the Curve Lake Reserve previously, he makes arrangements to sell his art at the Whetung Ojibwa Art and Crafts Gallery on the reserve and ends up renting a small isolated farmhouse from the Whetung family, a couple of miles from the tiny community of Buckhorn, and six miles from the reserve itself. According to Michael Whetung, Morrisseau shows his work in the gallery to cover living expenses, but continues to produce for the Volpe family. Snowed in all winter, a mile from the nearest neighbour, the road to tiny Buckhorn long and desolate, Morrisseau settles into an extremely quiet life compared to the life he has just left behind in Toronto. And whatever the arrangement is between Morrisseau and Albert Volpe, it is clear that Volpe knows where he is living and continues to back him financially. Upon occasion Morrisseau calls the Whetungs and asks them to bring him some money for living expenses, but it is always repaid promptly. According to Michael Whetung, "he stayed at the farmhouse for the better part of two years, off and on, and then he picked up and left without letting anyone know."

Locals from Curve Lake Reserve, like Alice Olsen, say members of the Volpe family eventually showed up, their black Mercedes banged to hell from coming up the long potholed dirt road. What is clear is that whoever came calling had no trouble finding the place. Some say that when the family discovered that Morrisseau had skipped out on them, they came looking for him and trashed the place. There are others, however, who don't recall them ever trashing it. Michael Whetung, although busy with his own life at the time, remembers Morrisseau himself doing major damage to the house by taking a chainsaw and cutting out a wall between the kitchen and the living room to make more space to paint. "If there was damage, it's Morrisseau who did it," he says. "He didn't ask. He didn't care."

To this end, Whetung says Morrisseau was so busy painting all the time, he didn't even bother to get rid of his garbage; he just piled it in a big heap on the side of the veranda. "I took some money up to him once in the middle of winter and he was out in the front yard. He looked to be doing a ceremony. He had a big bonfire, and he was standing in the snow just wearing his jeans. No boots. No jacket." Whetung scratches his beard as he thinks back to those times, and although it was his deceased parents who dealt with Albert Volpe, he says he thinks "Morrisseau was on good terms with him."

Ritchie Sinclair, Morrisseau's former apprentice, goes even further and claims that "Albert Volpe and his wife Violette were kind, soft-spoken people. Norval respected them immensely." How the Volpes would have found the farmhouse seems indisputable: they knew where he was all along and they kept track of his paintings. So what did happen between Morrisseau and the Volpes in the chaos following Paul Volpe's murder? Maybe they had a business arrangement that Morrisseau walked out on? Maybe someone eventually noticed that he was not holding up his end of the bargain and took it upon themselves to collect a debt? Or is it all just part of the myth of Morrisseau?

The idea that Morrisseau was some sort of captive is suspect. Sinclair is quick to refute the myth of him playing the helpless Indian, while Marion stresses "he chose what he wanted to do." Both apprentices emphasize Morrisseau's independence. So whether or not Morrisseau was seduced in any number of ways by the Volpes, it appears that painting under their sponsorship, at least for a while, gives him the space and means to incorporate the concepts of Eckankar into his visual vocabulary on a scale never before realized—as witnessed in his incredible *Androgyny*. And perhaps in any number of so-called missing paintings from the early 1980s that passed through the hands of the Volpes.

If Morrisseau has any feelings of helplessness, they arise because of his family. His grandparents, gone. His wife and children, gone. Brian Marion becomes Morrisseau's companion and adopted son—his new family—as will many others who flow through his life. His idea of family an open embrace. And yet, as Marion says, "he never stopped thinking about his own children and he always painted them." As he does in *Ojibway Family* (1977), *Victoria and Family* (1978), *The Storyteller* (1981), *The Children* (1982), *Daughter-in-law Holding Raven Granddaughter* (1985). And he never stops believing that he did not abandon them, but they abandoned him. The echo of this rupture something Morrisseau turns into art.

A Bridge

It's been a long time coming but the Art Gallery of Ontario has finally recognized the existence of Canadian Indian Art. After years of deafening silence, their work dismissed as anthropology, Anishinaabe artists finally hear they are going into the groundbreaking exhibition Norval Morrisseau and the Emergence of the Image Makers.

—*TORONTO STAR*, FEBRUARY 1984

AFTER MUCH CONTROVERSY, in February of 1984 the first group exhibition of Native artists opens at the prestigious Art Gallery of Ontario in Toronto. In the local art circle it becomes common knowledge that the gallery does not want the exhibition. Those in charge, both directly and indirectly associated with the gallery, consider painting by Native peoples inferior to Canadian art of the European tradition and a mere fad that will not last. But after pressure from influential collector Helen E. Band, and Roy McMurtry, the Attorney General for Ontario, the exhibition goes ahead anyway. Morrisseau's popularity has put Native art on the Canadian public's radar, and although the Professional Native Indian Artists group has disbanded, the individual artists' reputations have done much to promote the art nationally.

The exhibition is curated by Tom Hill, the Seneca artist involved in making the 1973 documentary on Morrisseau, who is now Director of the Woodland Indian Cultural Education Centre in Brantford, and Elizabeth McLuhan, the curator of the Thunder Bay National Exhibition Centre and Centre for Indian Art (later renamed the Thunder Bay Art Gallery). They are promoted as experts in the emerging field of contemporary Native art. Hill and McLuhan take it upon themselves to organize the show without any curatorial input from Jack Pollock, who considers himself the foremost expert of Morrisseau's art. Taking the oversight as an affront, and by now realizing that Morrisseau was his finest moment, and it's over, Pollock attends opening night intent on making a spectacle of himself, wearing a bearskin coat and carrying a wooden staff that he uses to wave at friends. He feels disregarded and neglected after having helped create the field by discovering Morrisseau, and he makes his displeasure known. He is appalled by the selection of works presented—particularly Morrisseau's—and later says that he "came away convinced that they had deliberately put on a mediocre exhibition."

Not all agree. While the work of other artists, with the exception of Daphne Odjig, is greeted with mixed reviews, Morrisseau again takes the spotlight. Whatever his personal demons, his artistic genius continues to be applauded. Kay Kritzwiser, an early supporter, writes in *The Globe and Mail* that in the "space devoted to Morrisseau's paintings, a stunning retrospective look is provided. His work becomes a bridge between two Morrisseaus. There is the tentative, almost primitive work... but now here is the assured painter, with a brilliance of colours, known not sensed, and a confident, clean technique." Morrisseau is there to be congratulated and he takes it all in stride. Oblivious to any controversy, he is simply pleased to be exhibited with old friends like Daphne Odjig and his former brother-in-law Joshim Kakegamic, along with younger artists like Roy Thomas and Blake Debassige. He does make it clear, however, that there is only one Norval Morrisseau.

Thunder Bay Motel

To COINCIDE WITH this first full examination of contemporary Woodland Indian Art in Canada, Heather Pullen, a freelance journalist working for CBC Radio, searches out the father of the movement. She finds him holed up on the edge of Thunder Bay at the Sea-Vue Motel, in unit 21, sandwiched between highway and railway. A constant barrage of trains, trucks, and cars just a step outside his door. She phoned Morrisseau to set up the meeting so he is expecting her, but she's hesitant. Like nearly everyone, Pullen has heard stories about him. Knows he can be temperamental when he wants to be, cranky, rude, uncooperative. When he opens the door, she is surprised by his hulking size, and his huge hands—which he extends in welcome.

Ever the nomad in the midst of transformation into one of his many selves, Morrisseau is happy to be back in the north. The north is home. Here he will say hello to old and new friends, and in the process sell a few paintings to the Thunder Bay National Exhibition Centre, among other places. The Four Seasons Hotel in Toronto or the Sea-Vue Motel in Thunder Bay, it makes no difference to him— after living the high life, he welcomes the modest little room like the fresh air blowing off Lake Superior. Pullen is astonished, and will ask her countrywide audience, "How can this be the famous Morrisseau?" At first glance she thinks the room is shabby, but as Morrisseau walks her around it, pointing out his treasures, she begins to see what he sees. And so she reports: "The tiny room is crammed with run-down furniture, an old shag rug, dingy velvet wallpaper. But with an artist's instinct for beauty, Norval Morrisseau has filled this room with an amazing clutter of Indian artifacts and white man's antiques. Beside him on the night table is a big ceramic washbowl filled to the brim with nuts and dried corn. The dressers and tables are covered with fragile pieces of china, glass and silver."

Morrisseau the collector, who walks in beauty and surrounds himself with beautiful objects, items heavy with history, kettles and teapots, plates and platters that other hands have touched and cared for. Or with simple things, like a piece of smooth stone or coloured glass, and all the wonderful foods of the earth, like apples and oranges that a child sees brightly for the first time. "My objective is to beautify the world with colour. This is what I'm here for," he stresses. But he also admits that even though he has left Christianity behind, he has to constantly fight the old feeling that he is a sinner: "no better than a maggot in the beard of God." Religion and spirituality are always at the forefront of Morrisseau's thoughts.

Not far from where he sits is the St. Joseph's Residential School. And although he rarely speaks of his experiences there, he believes it is his destiny to remember, and thinks it might have something to do with ridding himself of what he calls "psychic detritus." The stuff left stuck to his spiritual self that hangs on to him like seaweed, curls around his ankles, up to his thighs, and wants to drag him to the bottom of another bottle.

And so he focuses on spirit travel in the psychic world beyond human limitation: "I cannot worry about Greenpeace… the Atomic bomb… because now is most important of all. Now!" This is his concern. This is his calling. These dream journeys that he must paint for the world. "Every time you buy my paintings you're buying a psychic television," he says with a grin to the young reporter, pointing to a table covered in paintings. "Look at those round symbols, every time you turn on you tune yourself into that," he says with the utmost conviction. Like Picasso, the one artist Morrisseau admires, he cannot stop himself from painting. And he paints everything: coats, vests, cups, plates, bowls… constantly creating. He shows Pullen his latest: a hand-painted elk-hide cloak with bear paws, turtle shells, and human figures symbolizing his status as a shaman. "A magic shaman's cape," he calls it. For the moment it is his prize possession. He holds it up as though he could disappear if he put it on. It's a cape you'd wear to "travel to Egypt to sit with Cleopatra… speak with the kings of ancient Babylon," he says. And then, as quickly as it began, his animated conversation grinds to a halt.

With the sound of a train rolling through the walls, Morrisseau lights a cigarette, takes a long slow drag from it, and speaks as though remembering episodes from not so long ago. Maybe a posh hotel in Toronto. A villa in the country. "I don't paint to make money, I think it is really a very, very filthy thing. I walked away from $285,000!" he says, as though pulling the figure from a hat. "An eccentric they called me! But enough comes to me when I really need it." And then he adds, after another pause, "But it's a drag to have to wait for it." He laughs, and the reporter giggles. She is young and blank to his past, and he mentions only what he prefers to remember. Speaking now as though he has just taken off his magical cloak and materialized into the room from one of his seven astral planes, he hearkens back to the time he joined Eckankar. He tells her that he hasn't drank for seven years, never mentioning the lapses, and that he has won his long battle with alcohol. He says he is finally at peace with himself. He is philosophical about his alcoholism and has no regrets. Without it, he says, "Is it possible for me to be what I am now? The great change I see now, the artist, the self confidence, to be free, respectful, to never have the desire to drink."

As for the whole Woodland Art movement Morrisseau is credited with creating, with a swipe of his cigarette he disavows himself from it and dismisses the younger painters following in his footsteps as "psychic leeches." His reasoning is as mysterious as his life, as is the gesture he makes with his hands, reaching up to the ceiling as though pulling it down around himself. In the tiny rundown room on the side of the Trans-Canada, he makes it known that his only concern is for *his art*—which he sees from the perspective of someone looking down into the room from the open ceiling. He speaks of himself in the third person: "There is no other Indian artist except Norval Morrisseau as far as that goes, because he gets these images from somewhere else." The painters he's met and mentored throughout his career—Carl Ray and the Kakegamic brothers, his many acolytes, including Brian Marion and Ritchie Sinclair—brushed away like the fallen ash from his cigarette. His statement an announcement to the world that he is ready to begin with someone new at his side. "It would be so nice when my apprentice finally arrives at the door. I would say, okay, walk in guy and let's get to work." And so the reporter announces that "More than anything Norval Morrisseau wants an apprentice," that "he has had a vision and he is ready to pass on his magic." The artist's magic embodied in his antique objects, his elk-hide cape, his paints and brushes. Everything he cherishes fitting into his one trunk. The rest of it left behind.

As a parting gesture, Morrisseau says, "While we are on the air, I wish there was someone out there, somewhere who would come to me and say, 'Look Norval, here's some money, paint.' And I'd say, 'Sir, thank you very much.'" In doing so, Morrisseau again conjures his own reality. He has already done the appropriate ceremony, laid down tobacco, burned sweetgrass. He has spoken to Bear, his spirit guide, and the ancestors who look out for him. He has wrapped his shaman's cloak over his shoulders and cranked up his psychic television. And he knows it is just a matter of time before someone arrives to fulfill their destiny.

Fall from Grace

MORRISSEAU IS BACK in Winnipeg visiting Bob Checkwitch at Great Grasslands Graphics when he learns that Galal Helmy, a self-made Egyptian businessman, is keenly interested in his work. Standing beside the silkscreen table, he looks up from a wet print and stares at Checkwitch as though a light has just gone on. Checkwitch tells him that since purchasing his first Morrisseau print, *Spiritual Feast*, from Great Grasslands Graphics in 1977, Helmy has always wanted to meet the artist. Morrisseau is always looking for signs, and he has recently dreamed of Egypt's pyramids. What he saw was not ruins, but structures shimmering in gold and silver like newly minted coins. And he thinks that Helmy must be the one: the manifestation of his call for a patron.

Far from Egypt as one could possibly be, Helmy is now living in the mountains near Jasper, Alberta, operating a restaurant and gift shop (which he will later expand into an art gallery), and when Morrisseau calls he insists that they meet. "Send me a ticket, and I'll come," Morrisseau says. The only idea that he has about where he is going is through his soul travel, but he has absolute faith in it, and he doesn't hesitate to get on the bus and turn westward into the sunset of his life. On the way to Jasper, though, Morrisseau decides to get off the bus in Edmonton. His ear always to the ground, he hears about Agnes Bugera's recently established Bearclaw Gallery, specializing in Native art. In typical Morrisseau fashion, he grabs a cab to an art supply store, and with some paint and board under his arm, he rents a cheap room near skid row, not far from the gallery. There he does six paintings and brings them to Bugera the next day. Also typical is that along the way he picks up a handsome new friend. "He showed up with a young, long-haired blond man. I don't know who he was." Bugera says. "He wanted quite a bit for the paintings because they were originals, but settled for $2,000. He really didn't care about money."

A week later, when his money is gone, and the young man forgotten, Morrisseau arrives in Jasper and meets Galal Helmy, who comes face to face with Morrisseau's reputation for random acts of eccentricity. "The moment he steps off the bus, he says he wants to paint, and I take him to purchase art supplies, and there at the store he suddenly says he wants eighty-one canvases." Helmy looked at Morrisseau dumbfounded, thinking "Why not fifty, or eighty, or even eighty-five?," but Morrisseau was adamant that it had to be eighty-one. Not more. Not less. From there, Helmy drives him to his small gift shop and restaurant in the heart of Jasper National Park. And in a dramatic shift from the streets Toronto and Edmonton, Morrisseau finds himself floating in the magnificent verdant forest of Maligne Canyon, surrounded by the splendour of the Rocky Mountains. For Morrisseau, Galal Helmy is the perfect patron at the perfect time and place, their relationship as perfect as his Red Lake years with Joseph and Esther Weinstein. People who know culture. The kind of people Morrisseau summons in his dreams.

Settled in Maligne Canyon, in a room at the rear of the gift shop, Morrisseau begins working on a dozen paintings at the same time, sets up an assembly line of production. He amazes Helmy with his ability to create and remember the contents of each image simultaneously, and apply each colour precisely and concurrently, while moving back and forth between the panels. Helmy watches the artist juxtapose and layer pure colour, squeeze it straight from the tube and apply it with a finger in thick swabs to a point where it is vibrating off the canvas. Morrisseau finishes all eighty-one canvases in a month, all of them done in the dull light of the restaurant, away from the windows, because he says the intensity of the colours can be blinding, even to him.

It is during this time that Pope John Paul II comes to Canada, and Morrisseau tells Helmy that he has issues with the Catholic Church and he is going to stop him from landing in the Northwest Territories. "He wants to go there and see my people! He'll never land." And Helmy dismisses it as crazy talk until one evening he is watching television and learns that a blanket of heavy fog has unexpectedly rolled into Fort Simpson, making it impossible for the Pope to land. Helmy again finds himself enthralled and mystified by the artist. As for Morrisseau, when he learns that Helmy's family is related to Egypt's ousted King Farouk, and that Galal has studied the prophetic writings of Nostradamus, he is convinced he is meant to be living in Maligne Canyon. As Helmy puts it, the bond between him and Morrisseau "was cemented by the mysteries of ancient civilizations and esoteric rumination," with their long talks ranging from Helmy's interests in prophesy, Egyptian history, and Old Testament genealogy to Morrisseau's interests in world cultures, spirituality, and the ancient Ojibway pantheon of manitous. And because family is always on Morrisseau's mind, he adopts Helmy's family as his own and even offers to name Helmy's newborn son.

A year after leaving Toronto, and settled into artistic solitude in

Jasper, Morrisseau announces to the local press that the mountains have given him back his sanity. "Here, I'm being fed spiritually," he says, pointing around him. Far from being magical, Morrisseau's routine at Maligne Canyon is simple: he eats his meals in the restaurant, steak and potatoes almost every day; he sits on the little balcony of his room that looks out on the mountains, smoking his "Indian herb," as Helmy calls it, and eating raspberry ice cream, sometimes feeding the lone elk that comes to his window; he goes for long contemplative walks in the bush with Butch, the stray German shepherd he has adopted; he reads voraciously (and never watches TV); and above all he paints long into the night.

What Helmy finds odd, though, is that Morrisseau never once mentions that he misses anyone. In fact it is quite the opposite. One evening Helmy asks him about his grown children in northern Ontario, wondering if he has contact with them, if he sends them money, and if he sees his grandchildren. Morrisseau dismisses them outright for not being interested in the world. And Helmy, born in Egypt and raised in Austria, cannot help but see the irony of it all. The way he sees it, their lack of worldliness is a result of their lack of education, their poverty and isolation, and Morrisseau himself is responsible for it. The painter's voice cracks with emotion only for his daughter Victoria—and she is still the child of years ago.

But Morrisseau is not unaffected, and whatever it is he keeps to himself, it comes leaking out of him before long. On the night of their conversation, the ghosts of memory come howling. Anxious and pacing, Morrisseau calls up Helmy to come and pick him up and bring him into town because there are too many coyotes crying and it's a bad omen. And later when his dog Butch gets run over, he sits on the roadside cradling him in his arms, as though confirming he really can care, then carries him into the forest to do a ceremony for him, and stays up all night crying with the coyotes outside his door.

For three years Morrisseau lives in Maligne Canyon, where Helmy not only gives him a place to live and paint, but buys most of whatever Morrisseau produces, paying him by the square inch of canvas. Or he trades for it. He becomes cautious, however, about trading when Morrisseau pawns a David Wong sculpture for a few hundred dollars. Aware that such an arrangement could come back to haunt him, and being an astute businessman, Helmy makes sure to document every transaction and has Morrisseau sign receipts for the money he receives. "To ensure nobody can say I took advantage of him," he says.

As far as Morrisseau is concerned, he knows exactly what he is doing, and without having to take care of ordinary necessities of life he paints in the white heat of creation. Each year that he is there, from roughly September to May, he glows like the rocks in a sweat lodge before stopping, exhausted, "out of steam" as he puts it. He then quietly packs his bag and leaves to visit friends and galleries across the country. Always returning in a few months' time to his sanctuary in the mountains. Helmy tells the press that during these years he averages about $200,000 a year in purchases and expenses, which include the artist's food, lodging, and art supplies.

Morrisseau spends the money he makes from Helmy on anything he wants—a white leather suit, a Rolex President watch, bracelets and necklaces, antiques, artifacts, art—whatever catches his fancy. Six months after meeting Agnes Bugera, he again shows up at Bearclaw Gallery in Edmonton, but this time with the intention of buying. Morrisseau has not forgotten something he saw on his first visit, and trades Bugera a couple of paintings for a heavy turquoise and silver necklace with a matching bracelet. "He always appreciated beautiful things," she says. And although Morrisseau continues to drop in from time to time, telling her stories about his out-of-body experiences, events as ordinary to him as sleeping, she remains wary of him and comes to think of him as someone with multiple person-alities. "As far as I'm concerned he's a bastard with a twinkle in his eye. Nice to you one minute but wouldn't give you another thought a moment later." And so she learns not to ask about the ideas behind his paintings, which makes him turn red with anger, or even when he might return.

Morrisseau's pattern is to leave Maligne Canyon with thousands of dollars rolled up in his pockets and fastened with an elastic band and go off to Thunder Bay or Vancouver or Toronto. And a few months later return flat broke, worn out, and exhausted. Morrisseau is philosophical about this lifestyle, saying that money is a river you dip into when you need it, and there will always be more, but you have to be careful not to drown in it.

When asked specifically about all that cash, Helmy shrugs and says he thinks that he gives most of it away. He says that after a show at the Manulife Centre, "I gave him thousands in cash and in a couple of hours he was back asking for another $400. You tell me where it went." It is a question that is answered for Helmy quite by accident. One day Morrisseau is talking about his art and unexpectedly says that he could no longer endure the "assembly-line syndrome in Toronto," and he feels safe in the mountains where nobody will come looking for him. And as though by premonition—echoing the cautionary sentiments of Jack Pollock, who warned the artist to leave Toronto—the RCMP arrive at the restaurant looking for him. They explain to Helmy that Morrisseau worked for the Volpe family and they may be looking for him, and Helmy realizes why the painter is content to live in isolation, as inaccessible as possible. The police also explain how the family took care of his every need and desire, and Morrisseau's spending starts to make sense. It is later confirmed when the artist himself mentions that he bought a bag of cocaine that turned out to be baking powder.

Whatever Morrisseau's lapses during his mysterious sojourns into the world of shady friends and shady deals—in 2013, Gary Bruce Lamont, one of his Thunder Bay acquaintances, and Benjamin Morrisseau, a nephew, would be implicated as chief suspects in a Morrisseau art fraud ring; Lamont would be later charged with eight other criminal offences, including sexual assault—above all, Morrisseau manages to stay away from alcohol. And contrary to popular belief, the 1980s are one of the most prolific periods of his career. He sells paintings to dealers like Bugera at her Bearclaw

Gallery, and at exhibitions in Edmonton at the Manulife Centre and in Calgary at the Gulf Canada Gallery, and to associates of every stripe, and still leaves hundreds of paintings behind in Maligne Canyon. And as many others have done before him, Helmy will resell some of these paintings, and go so far as to make silkscreen prints out of them to cover his initial outlay of cash and recoup his investment. In addition to the art gallery in Maligne Canyon, his own EA Studios Timberwolf Gallery in downtown Jasper will carry an unimaginable selection of them. Being a proud Egyptian Canadian and sensitive to a nation's patrimony, he will also say to the press, "my plan is to donate many of them to Canadian museums because they are part of Canada's heritage." He goes further to say that like the Picasso Museum in Paris, there should be a Morrisseau museum in Canada, and he believes firmly that one day such a museum will become a reality. Morrisseau smiles when Helmy tells him this, and looks around at all his paintings on the walls, and says he should just name the restaurant after him.

In early 1987, Helmy escorts the painter down to California for a high-profile exhibition of Native art at the Southwest Museum of the American Indian, a Spanish-style building perched on a hilltop overlooking Los Angeles. Organized by John Vernon, a successful Canadian actor, and a cohort of museum and embassy officials, the exhibition features Canada's most renowned Native painters: Norval Morrisseau, Daphne Odjig, Alex Janvier, Eddy Cobiness, and Jane Ash Poitras, among others. A preview of the exhibition is hosted by Joan Winser, the Canadian consul-general in Los Angeles, at her Beverly Hills residence. For the four exclusive openings that follow, featuring traditional Native singers and dancers to kick them off, numerous dignitaries, Hollywood actors, art collectors, and expatriate Canadians jam into the hilltop museum. Morrisseau is one of the big stars of the exhibition, with a room of his own and a follow-up solo show starting the next month in Santa Barbara. When the press catches up to him he is relaxing on a bench in the upper level of the museum, watching the flow of visitors below as the light from the desert streams in. Although the champagne is flowing freely, he is in a serene alcohol-free mood, reflecting on the significance of the occasion. "What's nice is so many of us are being shown together. It's about time," he says, revealing the generous side of his nature, his ability to rise above the clamour of the crowd.

To develop a market for his art, he and Helmy plan to remain in Los Angeles for three months and stay at the Marina del Rey Oakwood after his show in Santa Barbara. During this time Morrisseau doesn't touch a drop of alcohol, and together they tour the coastal area. The length of the stay, the strange environment, and the constant people, however, take a toll. Later, when he is settled back in Canada, and after his infamous period on the streets of Vancouver, he will say with his wry sense of humour that he found the whole trip "boring, boring, boring." And that "anybody should start drinking in California."

The exhibition at La Casa de la Raza in Santa Barbara is scheduled from March 5 to March 11, 1987, partly overlapping with the group exhibition in Los Angeles, and Morrisseau is there for the opening. The *Santa Barbara Visitor Press* challenges the public to come "if you care to see duality dance with unity singing the spectrum of the sun." Again, Morrisseau is the feted star, but this time it is different: he is without the other painters to help absorb the shock of American adoration; he is alone and cannot avoid the spotlight. He initially enjoys the attention, then starts feeling like a dancing bear chained to a post. He decides to go into a Native American sweat lodge to cleanse himself, but it is a ceremony like no other he has ever known. He is offered a drink of mescal. He takes it. Drinks it in one gulp. He takes another. And another. And before he knows it he cannot stop. Helmy has never seen anything like it in his life. He has heard the stories but this is unimaginable. Morrisseau transforms before his eyes, becomes other-than-human, and Helmy can do nothing about it. Morrisseau starts to drink everything in sight. He grabs a bottle and won't let go, guzzles the wine in less than twenty minutes. Helmy manages to get him into a cab and back to his room at the King Inn in Santa Barbara, but that night he disappears. With no idea where he has gone Helmy is at least relieved to know that Morrisseau has little cash on him.

In the morning he receives a phone call from the police in Santa Barbara: the artist is in jail for drunk and disorderly conduct. The chief of police makes it clear to Helmy that he doesn't give one iota about who Morrisseau is. As far as he's concerned he's going to rot in jail. Helmy calls Joan Winser at the Canadian Consulate in Los Angeles but it turns out she cannot do anything. Morrisseau has broken the law, and the chief of police turns out to be a hard-ass who doesn't like Indians.

But Morrisseau has Bear on his side, has faith that his ancestors have not abandoned him, and it turns out that one of the senior policemen on the force is married to a Canadian who just happens to be an admirer of Morrisseau's work. She talks to her husband, who talks to the chief of police, who gives the okay for Helmy to come and pick him up. "Get him the hell out of the country," he says. Helmy arrives packed and ready to go and lures Morrisseau into the car with a bottle of Coke mixed with rum and he drives twenty-seven hours straight to the Canadian border. When he looks over at Morrisseau he realizes that his Rolex President watch, worth thousands of dollars, is gone. Sold or traded for drinks in a bar.

Helmy stops to rest at a motel in Surrey, BC, and gets a room for each of them—but Morrisseau is not in a resting mood. He is on a rampage for more drink. He tosses the bed across his room as if it were as light as air, throws chairs against the walls. He wakes up everyone except Helmy, who is exhausted from the drive. But wake up he does when the desk clerk calls him in the middle of the night to say that the Surrey police are on their way, and that he has to pay for damages.

The next day Helmy is at the police station trying to convince them to release Morrisseau into his custody, explaining that he's just had an exhibition that brought in 27,000 people. That he's sick and needs treatment. That he's a member of the Order of Canada. No sooner are they on their way when Morrisseau demands to get let off, demands money, saying that Helmy owes him, saying that he needs to be free to stretch his wings. Helmy offers to get him help, pleads with him to come back to Jasper—but Morrisseau has other plans. By the time they reach Vancouver, he is burning in his seat for more alcohol and Helmy finally breaks down and gives him one hundred dollars. To Helmy's surprise Morrisseau guides him to the east end of the city, to skid row. It is as though he knows where he wants to be. He tells Helmy to have a safe trip back to Jasper and gets out of the car and briefly waves goodbye—as if the years they have spent together in the mountains never happened. Morrisseau will never again return to Maligne Canyon.

Oranges

LIVING ON WHATEVER DRINK he can get his hands on as if it were steak and potatoes, Morrisseau wanders downtown Vancouver selling what the press call his "booze sketches." Filthy, gaunt, long hair matted, clothes smelling of urine, he flops down on the street with an outstretched hand. Those who think he's just another down-and-out Indian make a point of stepping around him. The passersby who recognize him are quick to capitalize on his condition and stop and pay him five or ten dollars for the erratic felt pen and paper drawings he whips off on the spot. As soon as he has enough money stuffed in his pockets for a bottle he staggers off to the nearest liquor store.

On tottering legs he makes his rounds, often sitting outside the Vancouver Art Gallery in Robson Square. Sometimes, when the weather is especially wet or cold, he heads over to the Marion Scott Gallery on Howe Street and draws on a little table in the back room, selling his work to Judy Kardosh, the manager, who tries to talk him off the alcohol. But before the conversation is over he is out the door and in an alley guzzling a bottle of tequila in twenty minutes. And by evening he is again passed out in a park under some bushes or curled up on a hot-air grid on a sidewalk.

Nights like this he dreams that his thunderbird self is flying high above the clouds, soaring over Lake Nipigon, his great expansive wings brushing the spirit world, when Misshipesheu, carried on a mighty tidal wave, springs up and clamps its fierce jaws around his legs. He tries to fend it off with a bolt of lightning, shooting out of his razor-sharp eyes, but he is powerless against the beast and down, down he goes, tumbling through cloud and sky, unable to shake off the great weight wrapped around him. He hits the lake full force and goes down like a white stone sucked into a black void. And there he is in print, fallen from grace—May 13, 1987—a Canadian Press photograph showing him in stark black and white, sitting in a filthy alley with a sketch pad on his lap, a pencil in one hand and a mickey of whiskey in the other. The acclaimed shaman-artist, "the grand old master," as the press calls him, member of the Order of Canada, presented as the epitome of a lost soul. The stereotypical drunken Indian.

It has been six weeks since Galal Helmy dropped him off on skid row but with all the press he is getting it could have been six years. The photo and article make it onto the newswire and reporters looking for an easy story pounce on him. The CBC's *The National* does a special, and the "Famed Native Artist on Skid Row," clutching his dirty grey blanket, is broadcast across the country. When asked if he would like to sober up and go back to Jasper, Morrisseau says, "Oh God, no, I don't want to go back there. I want to be drunk every day. I love it." He is sick of the assumptions about him. He is sick of a world fuelled by money. He would rather drink it away or give it away—which he does, daily. His interviews draw national attention and everyone is aghast at the sight of him. Distressed to see what he has become.

One of Morrisseau's oldest Anishinaabe friends, Frank Meawasige, flies in from Toronto to rescue him. He tracks him down on the street and brings him to his hotel to sober up, and makes arrangements to fly him back east for treatment. Morrisseau uses the occasion to raid the bar fridge in the room and gulps down the tiny bottles of liquor as if they were dessert before disappearing into the night. "There's nothing better than being drunk in Vancouver!" he says and gets quoted across the country. And shortly thereafter he hobbles into the Marion Scott Gallery, unsteady and gasping, and collapses without response. This time he is on the verge of dying. They rush him to Lions Gate Hospital, and lying in bed with his guts on fire, retching bile and blood, seeing the walls melt before his eyes, thinking it's better to die than suffer like this, Morrisseau wonders how all this came to be—and he swears off booze.

When he is feeling better one of the doctors offers to put him up in his house on Salt Spring Island. He says he's an admirer and would be happy to give the artist a place to recuperate. Besides, he says, it's empty. Morrisseau finds himself ensconced in a huge glass and cedar structure overlooking the ocean. Next to him on a glass table are fresh tubes of acrylic paint and sheets of blank canvas. He is encouraged to paint. And he does. It's the only thing he knows how to do. He remains in the house for a couple of weeks painting, staying dry, and getting healthy. Then one day he feels it is time to leave and asks for payment for the paintings he assumes the doctor wants to buy, and he is told that they will barely cover his room and board. More disillusioned than angry at being used by the doctor, he guzzles whatever alcohol he can find in the house and with a paint-brush in hand he signs his name in big black Xs across all of them. And ends up back on the street where he began.

At Hill's Native Art Gallery, near the Gospel Mission on the edge of skid row, where Galal Helmy dropped him off months earlier, Morrisseau finds a place to warm himself and paints in the back room beside west coast masks and a rack of Inuit prints. They buy whatever he produces with no questions asked. It is far from his best work but clients buy it all the same. It is still "a Morrisseau" and worth more than the work of most artists. At this point in his life, Morrisseau couldn't care less. And to those who want to take advantage of him, he says take it and go away, because in truth he pities them for their small, money-grubbing lives, and with equal disdain he dismisses the reporters who don't understand him and write that "he is remarkably free of regret, resentment or rancour."

The reporters who do seek him out make sure to stand far enough back to avoid the stench of him. When they ask Morrisseau about why he's living on the street, he is quick to tell them, and the whole country, that he likes the street because he's free to do whatever he wants. They make sure to record every detail. His six-foot-two frame is shrinking, they write, he is skin and bone, wearing a ragged hide of urine-stained jeans and a mouldy blanket. No matter what anybody says or does to try to help him, he shrugs them off because the way he sees it, he is his own person. And his physical welfare should be of no concern to anybody else. And if it is true that he is shrinking, then it is into the molecules of everything: shoe, gum, bottle, car, cement, earth, shit, bone, blanket, tree, star…

And then one cold and wet night, warmed by nothing more than the shrubbery around the courthouse complex where he has passed out as sodden as the ground, he dreams so vividly he can smell Christmas. He is five years old again, waking to his first orange. He has never seen anything like it before. He presses his nose to the beautiful globe and the aroma fills him with its sweet-and-sour tanginess. He holds it up in his fingertips, its radiant colour against the sheer whiteness of a northern Ontario winter. The dream is so vivid that he wakes up weeping, speaking in Anishinaabemowin to his grandparents, thanking them for their love, and the gift of beauty.

Left: Norval Morrisseau recovering his health and painting at Coghlan Art Studio in Aldergrove, BC, in 1992. *Bryant Ross photo, Coghlan Art*

Right: Norval Morrisseau as a happy grandfather, holding Robin, son of Gabe and Michele Vadas, at their home in White Rock, BC, 1993. *Courtesy Gabe Vadas*

IV 〇 NIIWIN

Born Again

MORRISSEAU IS WEARING a brown blanket draped over his head and shoulders and half-drunk from downing a mickey of whiskey a few hours earlier. He is lost on a crowded street going no place in particular when he sees him: a curly-haired teenager with a beard sleeping in a cement stairwell at a McDonald's restaurant. The afternoon light spread around him, the blanket draped over his head, Morrisseau gazes down at the young man huddled in the corner, who in turn looks up into the silhouette above him and thinks the drunken painter must be a monk of some kind. Maybe Morrisseau is feeling sorry for the world again, for his family, for all the plants and animals, or maybe he's just feeling sorry for himself, but he can sense that the young man is carrying a burden as heavy as a sack of stone. To the artist everyone has both their physical and spiritual selves, the two sides of a coin, and he recognizes the young man's need for someone. He sees it in Gabe Vadas as clearly as if he were examining an X-ray, or the interior of one of his paintings, because despite what he may say he has the same need. Their eyes meet and Morrisseau calls out to him.

Vadas quickly realizes that the guy before him is not a monk at all, but just another drunken Indian with a bloated face, long matted hair, and a straggly beard. He almost turns away, dismissing the drunk, but instead he asks if he needs help—as clear as the night is long, anyone can see he needs help. But to his surprise Morrisseau waves the question away, and in a gesture reminiscent of concern or insight he says that "all is well." To Vadas, it is as though he were saying, don't worry, what you're looking for has arrived. Nobody has ever said this to Vadas before, and especially not with such an air of confidence. How could someone dressed in rags, looking so hard-pressed, think everything is okay? What happens next surprises Vadas even more. The Indian standing before him, wrapped in his filthy blanket, points to him and says that he has seen him in his dreams. That he has appeared in his visions just as he is now, with curly hair and a red plaid shirt. Like so many before him Vadas is mystified. Like so many before him Vadas feels the magnetic pull of Morrisseau's personality. Slowly, cautiously, he takes the few steps up the stairs.

Morrisseau knows how he must look so he explains that he's a famous artist. He's got the Order of Canada. He just had a show in California. He walked away from $285,000 in Toronto. The young man doesn't believe him so Morrisseau decides to convince him. He gives the young man one of his sketches and then takes him over to Robson Street where he begins hawking other ones for the requisite five or ten dollars. To his surprise Vadas sees people stop in their tracks, talk to the artist, wish him well, and dig into their wallets and purses. Turning the tables, Morrisseau now asks the young man if *he* can help *him*, and holds out the money he's collected in his huge bear-paw hands. They start to hang out together. They go for coffee and talk. There is something about the drunk besides having his pockets lined with gold that compels Vadas to speak from the heart.

It is during one of their conversations that something cracks inside Vadas, and he tells Morrisseau that what he really wants is a father. "That's all I've ever wanted," he says. Morrisseau responds in a way that is not out of character for him. Vadas will remember that with the swipe of his hand the painter somehow manages to take his pain away, as though sweeping it under his tattered blanket and holding it there. With his gaze now locked upon Vadas, all concerns of his own family, and his countless friends and apprentices, are given to the wind. All thoughts of yesteryears forgotten. The shaman-artist and master of transformation pronounces from the depth of belief that "karma is precise," and that he is meant to be Vadas's father, and Vadas is meant to be his apprentice-son. And so begins the relationship between Gabor Vadas, the young gypsy-like Hungarian, and Norval Morrisseau, the old worn-out Ojibway, a relationship that marks another turning point in the artist's career, and his seventh and final cycle of life.

The artist sees that the beautiful curly-haired youth is eager to learn and not yet bloated with questions. Morrisseau hates it when people constantly ask him stupid questions, such as why he's on the street—although it is something he is almost ready to shed like the blanket he is wearing. Maybe he feels it is time for another trans-formation. Or maybe he feels love or infatuation. Maybe he feels it is simply time to clean up. These days, when he sees his grizzled reflection in windows, he has to turn away. "Soon, but not now," he says to Vadas, "I will return in a few months' time," indicating that everything in the artist's life has been a convergence of events at a precise time and place. And right now he is still drinking heavily, not yet ready to go down his next path.

When he does finally return that summer and find Vadas, he is temporarily living on the University of British Columbia campus as artist in residence, and he is no longer the tramp that Vadas knew, with a river of dollars flowing through his hands. Now transformed back into a renowned artist and living humbly but comfortably, Morrisseau invites Vadas to move in with him, and together they find an apartment in the east end of the city. Although Morrisseau still loses himself to the bottle at times, Vadas helps keep some semblance of order to his life and takes it upon himself to manage his affairs and help guide him to sobriety. It is no small feat for Vadas, a high-school dropout, but he takes it on with a passion and a vengeance when he hears Morrisseau's stories about all the money his paintings have made over the years—for other people.

With street life now behind them, Morrisseau and Vadas begin living off the revenue Morrisseau generates from his art. They make the rounds selling and trading to galleries including Vancouver's Marion Scott Gallery, Lattimer Gallery, and Hill's Native Art Gallery, and Edmonton's Bearclaw Gallery, as well as to individual collectors such as Bonnie Edwards Kagna, who in one year amasses a collection of twenty-two paintings, which she publishes in a catalogue called *My Year with Norval Morrisseau* and advertises for sale in limited-edition giclée reproductions.

In late September, two months after leaving the street, they show up in Jasper and meet Galal Helmy at his Timberwolf Gallery. Helmy initially thinks—as does Agnes Bugera at Bearclaw Gallery—that Vadas is Morrisseau's latest lover, and their affection for one another makes it appear that way, but the artist introduces the young man as his son. He tells Helmy about having an affair with Vadas's mother years ago, but Helmy considers it far-fetched. Whatever the story, he is happy to finally see Morrisseau off the street and invites him back to Maligne Canyon. But the artist is not interested. He and Vadas have other plans, and they strike a deal with Helmy for a suite in the Jasper Inn where Morrisseau will paint, with the cost of the room to be deducted from the price of the paintings they will sell to Helmy. As is usually the case when it comes to business, Morrisseau takes little interest in it, and Vadas is very much part of the negotiations.

Back on his feet and re-transformed from street person into shaman-artist, Morrisseau surrounds himself with the accoutrements of shamanism: rattles, drums, eagle feathers, braids of sweetgrass, tobacco ties, and other traditional items. Around the hotel room are dozens of canvases in various stages of completion, and on a small table are other boards and brushes in containers. The painter will work long into the night when the spirit of creativity moves him. And it is during his time at the Jasper Inn that Morrisseau tells the press that he is back to painting and in good form. "When I travel the ancestors tell me to go down into the world and paint. So this is what I do, whether I'm drunk or sober, as long as I hold the brush this is what I do." With a majestic view of the Rockies, room service, plush carpeting, and satellite television, Morrisseau and Vadas are now as far away from street life as they can get. They remain in Jasper for twenty-one days, with Morrisseau back to painting daily. Upon leaving they sell a dozen paintings to Helmy and trade him another eight for his Dodge van, which takes them back down the highway to Vancouver.

When asked about his life on the street, Morrisseau will say that he was simply looking for a "heart of gold," while humming Neil Young's song of the same name, and go on to describe the amazing technicolour visions he had during those times. Ruby red mountains.

Sapphire blue bears. Legions of sun gods in multicoloured head-
dresses. The sun itself shining like a jewel in the reflection of their
armour. "I don't see why what I did should affect anyone but myself.
It involves me and my head up here," he says, gesturing to his forehead and then to his heart, "I found what I was looking for." He is
referring to his life with Gabe Vadas. And with this, the miles recede
behind him, and he moves into the centre of a creative life.

After four months off the street and getting healthy again,
Morrisseau has a successful exhibition at the Gulf Canada Gallery
in Calgary, and he and Vadas move from the rundown east end of
Vancouver to the cultural hub of Gastown. With Vadas's companionship, Morrisseau now finds himself with money in the bank that
he can draw upon when he feels like it. Unlike Galal Helmy and
innumerable other art dealers and collectors who never concerned
themselves with the artist's personal finances, unlike all of the lovers
and apprentices in the artist's life, Gabe Vadas takes on the role of
Morrisseau's personal manager and oversees everything: he will
manage their living expenses, pay bills, rent apartments, purchase
groceries and art supplies, and even squirrel money away for a
rainy day—a concept as foreign to Morrisseau as a cat with hooves.
Something Morrisseau will grin about when he slaps his backside
and says, "I've got a bank card in my back pocket. I'm still waiting
for the person to come along with two money bags but I've found I
don't need that anymore."

Morrisseau has always believed that his drinking was a temporary setback and he would get his career back on track, and he made
sure to say as much: "All those guys are afraid I'm not going to get
out of it... I'm going to show them." And never once did he feel
that his work would suffer. On the contrary, for Morrisseau drink
provides inspiration: "Can you imagine the paintings I'm going to
do, the visions I've had?" he announced to the astonished public.

Although he is on the road to recovery, Morrisseau knows that
what he really needs to do is get out of the city, live as he did in
Maligne Canyon, and he is thinking about this when Bryant Ross

re-enters his life. A heavy-set man with a white goatee and an easygoing manner, Ross, like so many others before him, comes at the just the right time and offers Morrisseau a way to stay healthy and pick up his career. Ross had initially met Morrisseau through a mutual friend who lived in Vancouver and later went out to the University of British Columbia to see him while he was artist in residence. Entering the artist's room he was nearly knocked off his feet. "Every square inch of the room was filled with paintings," Ross remembers. For Ross there was a disconnect between the destitute Indian and Norval Morrisseau, the famed artist. And like everyone who comes under the spell of the artist's best work, he immediately wanted to buy some of the paintings.

But their relationship soon goes deeper than a mere business transaction: Ross and Morrisseau strike up a friendship based on art—not the buying and selling of it, but the making of it—and Ross offers the artist a place to paint and live outside of the city. It turns out that Ross is an artist himself and in the midst of purchasing the abandoned Langley Power Station, built at the turn of the last century. Having lost his own studio in Vancouver to urban development, he sees potential in the old power station as a studio for working artists and a gallery. But there is one problem: he lacks capital. He tells the painter that the massive concrete structure with its huge panels of windows and floor space is an ideal location for creation and contemplation—an ideal location for his Thunderbird School of Shamanistic Arts, which Morrisseau has been talking about reviving with Vadas. So he elicits Morrisseau's support and invites him to move to the power station property.

Morrisseau jumps at the chance to get out of Vancouver. By mid-October, Morrisseau and Vadas have moved to Coghlan Art Studio, an hour east of Vancouver in the vanished community of Coghlan, near Aldergrove in the Fraser Valley—a quiet rural neighbourhood of farms and acreages that is now part of Langley. There Bryant Ross becomes Morrisseau's business manager—and fifteen months later he will coordinate a show for Morrisseau at the Marion

Scott Gallery that will net upwards of ten thousand dollars. Enjoying the community of artists who come and go—like Stan Hunt, the master Kwakiutl carver, who does a totem pole there that Morrisseau helps to paint—and inspired by the natural beauty of the region, Morrisseau dives back into his art and paints on the station's expansive floor, allowing him to once again work on a massive scale.

At times he falls off the wagon and goes on a drinking binge for a day or two, ends up trading paintings for cab fare and drinks at Bob's Bar n' Grill down the road or any number of bars in Aldergrove. But these bouts are infrequent and rarely severe. On one binge nastier than most, however, he won't stop drinking, carries on, pisses himself, and Bryant Ross has had enough. He decides that he's going to force him to dry out by packing him into a car and driving up the Sunshine Coast. He figures that the spectacular scenery of the Pacific Ocean and the Coast Mountains will be enough to get the artist back on the path of sobriety. Along the twisting highway, watching waves lapping the shoreline, they pass Gibsons, then Sechelt, and Morrisseau tells Ross to stop so that he can buy a bottle. Ross ignores him and in the ocean-blue light of day, darkness spreads over Morrisseau's face. They keep going, and when they do finally stop for gas, Morrisseau hightails it into the convenience store. He returns with a paper bag and, as they are driving away, he pulls out a bottle of Listerine and chugs it down while staring Ross in the eye. Ross can see he is making himself sick. "Okay, okay," he yells, and in Powell River, the next town along the way, they stop at the first liquor store they see. Ross is expecting Morrisseau to buy a case of something cheap, or at least a forty-ounce bottle, but instead he comes out of the store with a small bottle of Dewar's Special Reserve, which he drinks in tiny sips for the rest of the trip. Never stopping, but never going overboard either. His message to Ross: *I am the master of my own fate and it has nothing to do with you or anyone else.*

Up at the north end of the Sunshine Coast they stop at the ocean to stretch their legs and go down to the beach, Morrisseau with his tobacco. Five teenagers hanging out spot them and begin to approach. As they get closer Ross sees that their heads are shaved, their faces pierced, and their black T-shirts are ripped off at the sleeves, showing off homemade tattoos scratched into their arms. Native punks, he thinks, and he braces himself for what seems inevitable. But to his surprise they are much more interested in knowing who Morrisseau is and what he is doing. Ross tells them he's a grand shaman of the Ojibway Nation and that he's doing a ceremony.

Morrisseau is now in the water and speaking in his own Anishinaabemowin language. The teenagers gather around and stand silently, their fists moving back into the shape of hands that seem to want to reach out and touch the tobacco that Morrisseau is holding. Without losing a beat, Morrisseau moves from his own language to English and begins explaining the significance of the ceremony. That it is for the fish, and the people here who are traditionally fishermen. He takes up a pinch of tobacco for each of them and tells them to hold it in their left hand. At first they step back, unsure of themselves, look at one another, but then they cautiously take the tobacco and hold it as instructed, their hands again clenched into fists but now with a different purpose. By the time the ceremony is over, the biggest and toughest of the youths, the leader of the gang, unexpectedly takes Morrisseau's hand and kisses it in a gesture of gratitude and goodbye. On their walk back to the car, Ross wants to say something to the artist about what just happened, but he doesn't know what to say. It is Morrisseau who opens the conversation. He says that the kids are starving and there is nobody providing the kind of food they need.

Ross and the other artists at the Coghlan Art Studio learn to leave Morrisseau alone when he is drinking, knowing full well he will do what he wants to do and there is not a damn thing they can do about it. They also know that inspiration will soon come calling, and it is just a matter of time before he sobers up and returns to work. Coming off a drunk he says he is at his most creative, and overnight shifts from alcoholic to full-blown workaholic. And as is customary, he amazes everyone with his ability to work on up to thirty paintings at the same time. Everyone marvels at his youthful agility as he crawls across the huge station floor from one painting to the next, carrying a whole bank of imagery and colour in his head. When Morrisseau is not painting they often find him sitting outside under a tree having a cigarette and reading books on mythology, philosophy, or history by authors such as Joseph Campbell and Vine Deloria Jr.—and more than willing to discuss them with anyone who is interested. In the planter boxes around the A-frame house that he and Vadas rent from Ross on the property, he grows a garden that reminds him of his grandmother, and even puts away jars of crabapples and cherries from the trees in the yard. The window ledges of the house are filled with his collection of blue carnival glass. A potted ornamental orange tree sits in the kitchen.

When Vadas's girlfriend and future wife, Michele Richard, meets Morrisseau—remembering him from the couple of times she served him in Opus art supply store in Vancouver—she cannot believe how much he's changed. How is it possible? No longer ragged and gaunt, he looks like a completely different man. What she notices above and beyond his washed hair and clean clothes, his new sports jacket and snakeskin boots, is that he's baking bannock. He's planted a garden. That he's rebuilding his life.

An International Artist

MORRISSEAU IS TAKING A MORNING WALK in the quiet of the Langley countryside when the sight of a pool of lush cranberries brings him to a full stop. The crimson blood-red beads floating on the surface of a flooded bog make him shudder with surprise. An instant burst of childhood revisited and he is again a barefoot boy helping his grand-mother pack the traditional Anishinaabe medicine into canvas sacks, to be later dried and boiled. He is in a good mood when he returns to the old station house, where he has been living for the last year, and finds an official-looking letter waiting for him. He sees it's from the Department of Indian and Northern Affairs in Ottawa and for a moment considers tossing it away. But today is a good day, and he rips the corner open with the end of a paintbrush and reads that the Cultural Affairs Section has been trying to locate him for the past year. To mark the bicentennial of the French Revolution, the government of France is organizing Magiciens de la Terre, an exhibition at the Centre Georges Pompidou in Paris. It will feature artists from around the world, and in all of Canada only three artists have been invited, Morrisseau the only painter. They would like him to attend.

Morrisseau's first reaction is to say no; he doesn't want to go; it is too far, too foreign, too big of a thought to wrap his mind around (the same response he gave Galal Helmy in Jasper when asked to go to Vienna). Bryant Ross, however, will not take no for an answer and convinces him that it is an honour like no other. He promises the welcome of Europe and offers to escort him and introduce him to Paris, the City of Light, and Amsterdam, the City of Red Light. But it is the promise of London, Buckingham Palace, and the Crown Jewels that finally convinces him, and despite his trepidation of flying across the ocean he decides to go.

Morrisseau's exact birthday remains a mystery, though, and he does not have a birth certificate, so it becomes a nightmare of nego-tiation to get him a passport. After a barrage of bureaucratic phone calls and letters, Secretary of State for External Affairs Joe Clark finally intervenes at the last moment, and Morrisseau finds himself at the Vancouver Airport boarding a plane for Europe. And there he is being escorted into the monstrous, space-age, postmodern, high-tech Centre Pompidou in Paris. And he fits seamlessly into the crowd. Flame-red sunglasses, white shirt, beige corduroy sports jacket, white pants, turquoise necklace, greying hair tied back in a ponytail, he arrives looking every part the artist he is, confidently supervising the installation of his artwork and fielding a host of interviews. This moment of belonging to the international art scene is a highlight of his career.

Besides meeting other Indigenous artists from the United States, South America, Africa, Tibet, Japan, Australia, Europe, from all over the world, Morrisseau uses the opportunity to visit some of Europe's most famous galleries: the Louvre and the Picasso Museum in Paris, the Van Gogh Museum in Amsterdam, the Tate Gallery in London. During this time he never touches a drop of alcohol, afraid as he says to get lost in a foreign country, and to Ross's pleasant surprise he is enthusiastic about all he sees. Everything is like a new page or a new painting for him. To the point where he comes out of a cannabis café near Amsterdam's Red Light District and detours into a street of jewellery shops, mesmerized by the prehistoric amber, finally settling on a bulky necklace that looks like it weighs a ton—which he takes apart back at his hotel and resets in his own design. It is the Picasso Museum in Paris that leaves the greatest impression on him, because standing in front of Picasso's paintings he is again the young man kicking off his rubber boots in Joseph and Esther Weinstein's home in Cochenour, the afternoon sun streaming round him, and he sees himself opening one of their art books for the very first time and losing himself in Picasso's *Femme en Chemise*, in an unnamed *Figure*. In a world of art that he never knew existed. In a world he never knew existed.

As he stands in the seventeenth-century Hôtel Salé, in the palatial gallery of the Picasso Museum, surrounded by the sway of foreigners, the languages of the world, he can barely believe where he is. His life in the bush of northern Ontario is light years away. The distance between that curious youth with the dream vision of making art and the galleries of Europe marked by his craggy features, his grey hair, his slight stoop from painting a thousand canvases. He sits down on a polished wooden bench and contemplates the master's work, and he sees it not from the inexperienced perspective of youth, new to the very idea of making art, but rather from that of a mature painter at the height of his power. And to his surprise Picasso's paintings are not as he anticipated. What stands out for him are muted tones of black and grey, brown and white, blue and green, a play of tones and shades, and he asks himself, "Where is the colour?" It is a question he will continue to ask himself when he arrives home invigorated, knuckle-white in his eagerness to paint.

On his return he tells the press that he thought the Picasso Museum was like a dark room. He says similar things about the Van Gogh Museum. And in a moment of reflection, he lays out a personal manifesto: "Everything looked so grey so I said to myself, I'm going to do something about colour. I'm going to beautify the world with my paintings. We can learn how to heal people with colour." Profoundly affected by his European trip, Morrisseau embarks on his next cycle and throughout the 1990s, and into the next millennium, his paintings become saturated with what he calls "real colour." His palette changes to floodlight brightness, ghost white, stovepipe black, yellow gold, tomato orange, deep pink, firebrick red, magenta, orchid purple, fuchsia, steel blue, bottle green, as he experiments with layers of paint and repainting to heighten the value and intensity of the colour. His innate sensibility allowing him to plunge into the power of his creative vision. His best work vibrating off the canvas, making the viewer blink and marvel at the spectacle. This period sees him move even further away from the earth tones of his early years, from nature's primary palette, to a synthetic spectrum that illuminates his many canvases with technicolour brilliance.

The couple of years Morrisseau spends at the Coghlan Art Studio prove to be a peaceful and productive time for the artist, and the income he generates from his work, including that from a solo show at Vancouver's Art Emporium, and numerous private sales, allows Ross to purchase the power station outright. But as Morrisseau has done with everything in his life, he leaves this too behind, and by 1990 he and Gabe Vadas are gone. Despite the passing years, though, Morrisseau will continue to stay in touch with Bryant Ross and return from time to time to paint. In 1994, for example, he will paint one of his masterpieces on the station floor, the massive 93- by 202-inch *Observations of the Astral World*, which will come to hang in the National Gallery of Canada.

Observations of the Astral World

By the time he finally grinds to a halt
he is down on all fours swinging side to side.
He could wring out his body like an old rag
and have enough whiskey to fill a bottle.

A month of serpents licking his face,
sucking his brain, and his only hope
to summon his bear power
and paw his paintbrush back to life.

He closes his eyes and prays, and in a burst
of everlasting light he is in the midst of soul travel.
He sees a family, the same happy family
he always sees in this delicate dream.

They are entwined by the sacred tree of life
    — in full bloom,
apples bright as red-lip kisses,
branches the shape of robins and bluebirds.

Grandparent, father, mother, child, observing
their spirit selves among the other-than-humans:
a bear, a bird, a fish, a man,
a bear-bird-fish-man.

The astral world projected like a map
of the mind, seven planes up
to a separate reality, where cement grey
does not exist and colour heals.

Where the moon is a portal
you can slip through. Watch!

As a school of fish appears and disappears
like children playing a game of hide and seek.

Eyes in the shape of an O. Mouths
saying Hello.
          Here I am.
Let me show you the way.

The Shaman's Return

My works are icons that help focus on spiritual powers
generated by traditional belief and wisdom.

—NORVAL MORRISSEAU

BY 1989 GABE VADAS has learned enough about the art business
in Canada to negotiate with Donald Robinson of the Kinsman
Robinson Gallery in Toronto's upscale Yorkville district, who signs
an exclusive representation agreement with Morrisseau. The artist
becomes their master colourist. Robinson is well aware of what
Pollock went through in representing Morrisseau in the sixties and
seventies. He remembers "Pollock sitting at his desk, holding his head
in his hands, lamenting that the artist had not arrived and neither
had his paintings." He also knows "Norval's reputation for being
extremely difficult, unpredictable and self-destructive." But whatever
doubts he harbours about working with the artist are tempered by
also knowing that Morrisseau is one of the few living artists who
has managed to capture the imagination of the nation. Although his
boozy knock-offs have undermined the market, his best work is still
very much in demand, and he's still capable of producing masterpieces. Morrisseau is money in the bank. The plan is therefore to
restrict future off-market sales and try to bring order to the chaotic
Morrisseau marketplace across the country.

Much of this relies on the relationship between Morrisseau
and Vadas, which Robinson characterizes as "mutually beneficial."
For while Vadas benefits financially from their arrangement, living
a lifestyle he could never have imagined—not to mention that
Morrisseau has made him his sole heir, with power of attorney—he
nonetheless provides stability to Morrisseau's life. Kinsman Robinson
begins to promote itself as Morrisseau's official dealer with national
advertisements, and within a year they organize their first sell-out
show for the artist.

As with everyone who meets Morrisseau, Donald Robinson is

pulled in by his mammoth personality. Finding the artist to be more than a business associate, he is unprepared for what he calls "the immediate empathy that we felt for each other." To bond their relationship, the artist smudges Robinson with sweetgrass, and later gives him an eagle feather, and he too comes to believe that Morrisseau is as much shaman as artist, "a living treasure and a living bridge to the oral traditions of the past." Robinson will go on to tell a story about taking the artist to Midland to visit the archaeological site of ancient Huronia there. Morrisseau is wearing a white summer suit at the time and upon arriving at the site, he suddenly heads off into the woods and plunks himself down on the ground. He begins digging into the earth with his bare hands and retrieves a piece of pottery. Robinson is at a loss to explain how the artist knew it was there. He does remind everyone, though, that Morrisseau's grandfather Potan was a sixth-generation shaman.

Morrisseau's own evolution into a shaman and eventually to "Grand Shaman" is as steady as an iceberg moving across the ocean. Although it is something he denied in his earliest interviews—his earliest advocates like Selwyn Dewdney pointing out that he had no formal training—and something that was not promoted in the early days of his career, by 1979 he was stating matter-of-factly: "I am a shaman-artist." By the time Kinsman Robinson comes to represent him, his two identities, artist and shaman, have become merged and are inseparable, and it is a reality that does not elude Robinson, who calls their first exhibition *The Shaman's Return*. And return he does. His sell-out show proves once and for all that he is one of the most sought-after painters in Canada. Kinsman Robinson's bold move in signing an exclusive deal with Morrisseau does not, however, go unchallenged. Maslak McLeod, a Toronto gallery dealing in the Morrisseau resale market, which also begins exhibiting work in 1990, balks at the claim and hosts its own retrospective exhibitions in 2003 and 2006. Donald Robinson is undeterred, and the Kinsman Robinson Gallery follows the first Morrisseau exhibition with solo shows regularly thereafter. Morrisseau will also become the subject of continuing retrospectives with accompanying full-colour catalogues. Now in his late fifties and enjoying a stable home life with Gabe and Michele Vadas, and the guidance of Donald Robinson's business acumen, Morrisseau once again returns to the spotlight. And the public flocks to purchase his artwork.

Grand Shaman Grandfather

AFTER LEAVING the Fraser Valley community of Coghlan, Morrisseau and Vadas move to the town of White Rock, about an hour south of Vancouver on the southwest coast, and with all the changes they have gone through in the last few years, they might have drifted ashore from another world. The relocation coincides with sales from Kinsman Robinson, along with other select exhibitions, and they move into a Spanish-style house with a stone courtyard and a blossoming orange tree. Gabe Vadas and his fiancée Michele have just given birth to a son, Robin, and Morrisseau is delighted and names the boy "Ogeegi Debenesie Peedasigay" (He Who Comes Shining). The cries of new life fill their home, and he takes on the role of grandfather with enthusiasm. It is a role he's never imagined for himself, despite having seven adult children who have their own children. This new domestic life takes him back to his first few years with Harriet, and he embraces it wholeheartedly, showing up one day with a wooden cradle carved in west coast designs for baby Robin, and, as in Coghlan, he goes about cultivating a garden behind the house, growing roses and canning tiny crabapples with cloves. And he again covers the ledge of the kitchen window with his collection of blue carnival glass, allowing the morning light to fill the room with colour.

But this period is not without grief and turmoil either, which come with bouts of thinking about his own children. Remembering when he used to sit at the kitchen table and let them watch him paint. When he used to carve them toys, a flute or a spinning top, out of a piece of wood. Or tell them stories that his grandfather told him, making them laugh or run for cover. Although that never lasted—waking up in jail in Nipigon, or Geraldton, or Longlac—camping beside the tracks with other drinkers—whipping up something on birchbark to buy cigarettes and a case of wine—Harriet and his kids left to fend for themselves. That's what he also remembers.

Morrisseau has made no effort to keep in touch with his family. For all he knows they could have dropped off the face of the earth. And so it is more than a surprise when Pierre, Eugene, and Christian use what little money they have to fly from Ontario and Manitoba to visit. For Morrisseau, it's as though they have suddenly fallen out of the sky and landed beside him—and it makes him curious. Why now? The last time he saw them they were paper-thin kids, and here they are big thick men. Who sit together on the sofa, barely speak, spend their days watching afternoon talk shows on television. Who stand soundlessly when he gestures to the open case of beer on the floor. Who do not utter a word of what he thinks may be on their minds. Thoughts of long ago come at him like a snowstorm or a television channel gone off the air—something his guests, his sons, could never tune into or understand. What he would like to do is reach out and explain to them who he is, what he stands for, and why he left their lives so long ago. But he wouldn't know where to begin, and besides, he can see that it's too late. All the same he tries to strike up a conversation, but it is like a creek running dry and soon meanders into silence. The damn TV, he thinks, and he reaches for the remote and abruptly turns it off.

And naturally turns to painting.

Oddly, not one of his three sons has ever held a paintbrush. This surprises him. And it hurts him to think that of all the apprentices he's had over the years, not one of them was of his blood. He offers to teach them. And they pile into Vadas's van and drive to an art supply shop where Morrisseau purchases additional supplies. Back home he takes up a pencil, lays out a dozen sheets of paper, and in typical Morrisseau fashion spontaneously sketches various images on the paper. A bird. A fish. A bear. He then goes about labelling the background colours, which his sons are instructed to fill in: B for blue, P for purple, G for green, Y for yellow. When they complain that they need thicker brushes because it's taking too long, he shrugs and gives them thicker brushes. When one finally asks for a mini roller, he shakes his head; he does not use a roller. All the same the painting goes well and serves to occupy their time, and binds them together. They leave a few weeks later, but by then Morrisseau is drinking again.

When Gabe and Michele see what's happening they intervene and try to talk him down before the bender begins, which they know will hit like a tsunami of nightmare proportion. Michele has known Morrisseau now for three years, and she cannot deal with his binge drinking—unlike her husband, who has pledged himself to the role of unwavering caretaker with monk-like devotion. She has already seen him wreck the house once before, wreck himself, and the sight of him and what she witnessed was beyond her comprehension. Nothing in her life had prepared her for it.

Once he got into the whiskey it was as though he had suddenly turned himself inside out, and whatever was inside him, whatever pain and anger that had built up, was unleashed like a rabid dog, growling and snapping at strangers and loved ones alike, black bile spewing for all the world to see. And all they could do was stand by and watch helplessly while he waved them away and pissed himself, pissed on the floor, fell over furniture, knocked his precious canning shelf over, shattered glass everywhere, to the point of breaking his arm. And then the glare of the hospital emergency, and Morrisseau too drunk to feel anything, bloated up like a sick bullfrog. Michele had had enough. That was when she told her husband flatly that she refused to raise her son in such an environment.

After unsuccessful attempts to talk the artist down again, Gabe, Michele and the baby are in their van in the yard, about to leave, when Morrisseau grabs the garden shovel. "Nobody is going to tell me what to do," he slurs. And standing there in the middle of his beloved rose bed, he turns in uncontrollable red-faced anger and whacks the shovel against the windshield with all his might. His arms raised above his head, he hits it again and it shatters. Grains of glass fly through the air over Gabe, Michele, and the baby. Huddled over her son to protect him, Michele screams and calls out baby Robin's name. And Morrisseau is hit with a bolt of recognition. His arms go limp and he lets the shovel fall to the ground. Waking from his drunken trance, he realizes what he's just done and looks inside the van through the broken glass and sees that the baby is in the front seat. Thankful to see that he's unharmed. Without a word he flees inside the house. Weeps in shame for what might have happened.

It is after this incident that Morrisseau finally quits drinking for good. With the help of friends like Bryant Ross, who drives over from Langley and takes him on a road trip to Harrison Hot Springs, Morrisseau finally weans himself off alcohol and moves into another productive phase. By now he is financially solvent, and in 1992 he and Vadas purchase a house on the Semiahmoo Reserve, beside White Rock. Throughout this period, he takes care of his health and goes on what Michele Vadas describes as "crazy diets of wild rice and sardines and lemonade." Builds a sweat lodge and a firepit in the backyard. And as in previous times, family, friends, apprentices, followers, helpers, and hangers-on continually move into and out of Morrisseau's life.

Pulled into the fold by Morrisseau's reputation and generosity, people like Wolf Morrisseau, Shawn Ellis, Paul Schellenberg, and Karl Burrows arrive at different times to fulfill a role in the Morrisseau household, and they are welcome. (Though not all are: Brian Marion claims he was not allowed to visit the painter.) From helping to cook and clean the house to weeding the garden, to painting, everybody takes on a specific task, and Morrisseau is content. He has always enjoyed the company of others, and in his role as shaman-artist he is always the blazing sun around which everyone orbits. Like a modern-day da Vinci, Michelangelo, or Raphael, with an atelier of assistants and apprentices, Morrisseau sees no issue working with other painters. And it is this shifting stream of helpful visitors that will eventually be put under a microscope when it comes to the authenticity of Morrisseau's vast body of work.

In Healing Colour

MORRISSEAU BELIEVES that everybody can be an Indian. Everybody has the potential to see the world through Indian eyes. Just as everyone is born a shaman but soon forgets.

Settled on Semiahmoo Reserve in a sun-drenched house with a panoramic view of the ocean, the surf crashing below, the southern Gulf Islands off in the distance, in a studio of glass and cedar, he paints in the healing colours of the world as he goes about mending his life, stitching it together like a birchbark scroll. Sliding into the old grandfather he is. His new family beside him, their new baby, he hasn't seen or felt this much light in years, having lived through what he calls the dark period, when every day was grey as the streets of rain-drenched Vancouver, the grates he slept on, the cardboard he took shelter under. Now when he sleeps, he likes to say he dreams in technicolour.

The world we live in is dark, and it's getting even darker. It needs to be brighter, he thinks, as he lays a canvas down and readies his brushes. Morrisseau recalls his trip to Paris, the galleries he visited, coming away thinking everything was so gloomy, a sodden streetscape, a dull café, a butcher's shop, a life of suffering, and he is determined more than ever to brighten the world.

He thinks back to *Victoria and Family*, the painting he did in 1978, his daughter's first baby, his first grandchild. He remembers a baby boy in the embrace of his mother, suckling the milk from her breast, a protective robe wrapped around them, birds connecting them to the sky world, a radiant halo indicating the divine love of parenthood. He keeps his mind focused on this sacred birthing moment. Dipping his brush into a jar of pigment, he begins, painting his beloved theme of mother and child, embroidering the figures in the leaves of the learning tree, berries of knowledge, butterflies hovering overhead, his ever-vigilant bird-spirits watching with their bright eyes. Together all the humble creatures of the earth—insect, bird, human—joined in kinship.

We can learn how to heal with colour, he affirms, laying naphthol red over the cadmium yellow as he dresses the figures in the painting with the power of the spectrum. Cobalt blue streams from the woman's hair into a circle of life-giving connection.

Morrisseau is not surprised at where he is today. It is all part of the great plan, the order of the spirit world, and the love he feels for his new family is the love he feels for all creation, something so vast it has almost killed him. Though he knows it is not easy to die, with the trail between past and present scarred and twisted from living. Today he is full of belly laughter seeing his new grandson's first steps, holding up the child and looking into his white bubbly face. There is so much to teach, so much to learn. Long-ago memories from his own childhood flood him, his grandfather Potan's comforting voice, a fur blanket spread on the plank floor, the glow of a woodstove, the old stories burrowing into the room. It is this he wants to remember, as he applies the paint intensely, not the other stuff, not his own kids, one, two, three, four, five, six, seven, he never saw grow up. Not them. Not here. What he must do is let Spirit take over. Like it always does. Let the painting become everything.

His new-found family life makes its way into his paintings, and he settles down into painting scenes of harmony, as in his candy red and sun yellow *A Tribute to My Beloved Daughter-In-Law*, featuring a mother and child circumscribed by a portal of consciousness, his signature Tree of Life, birds and butterflies of happiness. But having entered the House of Invention, travelling into dreamtime through the seven levels of the astral world, he's hardly laid down the last stroke of paint when he turns his attention to something else.

Morrisseau has always made a point of living in the present. "It is the now that counts," he is fond of saying. And he's the happiest he's been in years surrounded by his new family, by his extensive collection of whatever catches his fancy—Haida masks, paintings, a bentwood box, a bear cloak, a shaman's drum, a hand-carved staff, strings of turquoise, silver bracelets, brass amulets, amber necklaces—all this at his fingertips when his daughter Victoria sends him a black-and-white snapshot of Harriet. It is 1995 and she has just died. In the photograph she is sixty-six and wearing an old T-shirt and slacks over her sagging plumpness, a toothless smile, the tell-tale signs of poverty and hardship across her face. He picks it up, stares at it. He turns it over and sees her name written in blue ink on the white back and traces his finger slowly over it. After a moment he flips it over and looks at it again, and the weight of forgetting comes crashing down on him with such force he drops it on the table.

He knows he could never be the straight and narrow Pentecostal she wanted him to become. Knows there has never been an inkling of doubt about his mission in life. That he could never have fulfilled his destiny without moving on. And yet he cannot help but think back to the letters he wrote to people such as Selwyn Dewdney, Paul Okanski, to his artist friend Roy Thomas, about trying to win Harriet back after she had given up on him. "I am now starting down a fresh road again, and I am awaiting Harriet's reply," he wrote to anyone who would listen, but more to himself than anyone else. Half believing at the time that with Christ's help he could change.

His hand reaches for the photograph again, and he sees her not as she is today, but as the young woman he met in the Fort William tuberculosis sanatorium, who once filled the room with sunlight. And it is as though time has stopped. He is still living up in Red Lake in the company house, on the dirt road, days working in the gold mine, nights sleeping in her arms. *It was a good life… it was a good life for a while*, he thinks, as he takes the picture and slips it between the pages of an art book he's been reading, then shelves it.

Medicine Man with Bear (The Poisoned Bear)

In the old days when a shaman gave an Indian medicine, he often told a story. I was given such a story called The Poisoned Bear.

—NORVAL MORRISSEAU

HE IS LIVING with Gabe and Michele Vadas in the British Properties in West Vancouver when he gets sick. They see that something is wrong with him and call a doctor, who after examining him at his clinic tells him that he has Parkinson's disease. Morrisseau wants to know how this could have happened to him, but the doctor cannot give him an explanation.

That evening, or the next, he lies down and has a dream. He is back in northern Ontario and finds himself in a small clearing among the trees. A shaman is sitting beside a fire. Though they are surrounded by darkness, the shaman's blue cloak looks like the sky on a bright, clear day. He tells Morrisseau to look into the fire.

Morrisseau turns to it and looks closely, and there in the red embers he sees a trapline that is about a hundred miles long, and every twenty-five miles there is scaffolding with dried fish on top. It must belong to the Indians of the area, he thinks. Somehow he knows that his Bear spirit found it, climbed on top of it, and ate some of the fish. He can't tell exactly when this occurred, but he knows it probably happened quite some time ago.

The Indians, tired of having their fish stolen, had decided to poison the bear and kill it. But the bear was strong, it had power, and it didn't die. It was still alive.

Morrisseau looks away from the fire, and the shaman explains to him that his Bear spirit, the bear part of him, is poisoned. In the white man's words, his central nervous system is now damaged.

Later he has another dream, and he stares into the same fire. This time he is walking through a forest of cedar and poplar trees and sees somebody walking towards him. It is an old woman with a pleasant, kind face. In her hands she has a tray, and on it is a dish with good things to eat, like blueberries, fish, and bannock. She offers the food to him, and he eats.

When he has had his fill, she asks him, "Do you know what you just ate?"

Morrisseau looks at the tray and it is crawling with little white insects. They grow wings and start to buzz around the food before flying off. The old woman suddenly turns into a woodpecker and flies into one of the nearby trees. With her beak tapping the trunk she begins to dig under the bark for the bugs. He turns away from the fire.

And again the shaman is there to interpret the dream for him. He tells him that the woodpecker is a good medicine woman. She gave him the plate of bugs to keep him alive. He is sick because of the poisoned fish and she was trying to help him. She tried to dig the sickness out of him, but there is too much.

This was Norval Morrisseau's medicine dream.

One Last Time

AT THIS STAGE IN HIS CAREER, having survived his highly publicized and infamous six weeks on the streets of Vancouver, his popularity renewed, and surging with sales through the Kinsman Robinson Gallery—a large work selling for up to $50,000; smaller pieces for up to $8,000—Morrisseau's return is routinely referred to in the newspapers with the phrase Donald Robinson used for their first exhibition: "The Shaman's Return." Morrisseau enjoys the attention, but believes that he never went away, and he makes certain that others are aware of it.

But that's the way it's always been for him. Consider August 1995, when Morrisseau is in Ottawa to receive the honour of an eagle feather at the Assembly of First Nations' National Chiefs Conference. He telephones Barry Ace, the chief curator of the Indian and Inuit Art Centre at the Department of Indian and Northern Affairs, and asks to see their collection. It contains some of his earliest and finest artwork, pieces he hasn't seen in thirty-five years. Recovering from knee replacements, moving slowly and painfully, he arrives at the headquarters on Wellington Street in Hull, Quebec, and meets Ace in the marbled foyer. He stands there for a moment, watching the bustling civil servants going about their business. Resplendent and mystifying as ever in a necklace of medicinal roots resembling tiny torsos, a medicine pouch, and an intense red-and-black northwest Haida jacket against his shock of long grey hair, Morrisseau waits for a response. In his hand he holds a walking stick, not just any ordinary cane, but a long staff with a carved grizzly bear head, below it a dangling bear paw clutching a translucent crystal, and below that rows of triangular rattles made from deer hooves.

He waits for a reaction, but the numbed office workers glance at him at best. And that's when he begins pounding his great staff on the granite floor. The deer hooves rattle as each strike fills the stone interior with thunderous sound, and all activity around him jolts to a halt. As the bystanders stare at him, bewildered, he stares back at them without an inkling of self-consciousness, and then turns to Ace and says, "There, now I have their attention! Let's go and have some tea." Like everyone around him, Ace is taken aback, yet simultaneously drawn into Morrisseau's outrageous performance.

From there they proceed up to the glass and concrete Indian and Inuit Art Centre where Indian Affairs' vast collection of Morrisseau's work is stored. Purchased from Selwyn Dewdney's estate in 1985, it consists of manuscripts and personal correspondence along with drawings, paintings, baskets, carvings, and other miscellaneous items. As Ace pulls out box upon grey archival box of material, Morrisseau tells him that one of the paintings on two fragments of birchbark, stitched together with spruce root, is in fact a remnant of a birchbark scroll that originally belonged to his grandfather Potan, who was a Midewiwin elder. Taking it delicately in his hands, he runs his fingers over the incised figures and lines scratched into the surface, and says, "this was my grandfather's, and I painted this on top," pointing to the acrylic symbols and imagery painted on the incised markings. Morrisseau is deep in thought, and Ace cannot help but wonder what must be going on in his mind, what it must be like for him to see and hold the early years of his life. And so this is where Morrisseau spends the summer afternoon—happy that not everything was lost to constant upheaval—viewing for one last time the art that made him famous.

Two years later, in September of 1997, Morrisseau is again in the east, for what will be his last visit to the McMichael Gallery in Kleinburg. Coinciding with a solo show of the artist's work at the Kinsman Robinson Gallery (and the release of their full-colour art book *Norval Morrisseau: Travels to the House of Invention*), the McMichael Gallery opens the exhibition *Tradition of Change: First Nations Art at the McMichael*. Morrisseau has offered to perform an Earth Renewal ceremony for the institution in recognition of its long-time support of him and his work. Accompanying the artist are Gabe Vadas and former apprentice Ritchie Sinclair (Stardreamer). Ravaged by a stroke, knee surgery, and a broken hip the previous winter, plus the onset of Parkinson's, Morrisseau is feeble and supported by a wheelchair. Though only sixty-five, the painter is far from the vibrant giant of a man he once was. And yet, his determination to fly across the country and then drive from Toronto to Kleinburg is testament to his strength of character and sheer willpower.

When the ceremony is about to begin, Morrisseau scoots out on his motorized wheelchair to the edge of the manicured lawn of the gallery; thirty or so people have gathered around the perimeter to witness the spectacle. They watch and whisper among themselves while Morrisseau quietly addresses his two helpers. Always conscious of his dress, he is especially striking in a Haida and Anishinaabe inspired wardrobe: a bear claw necklace, a bear fur vest, a red-and-white mink headdress, and feathers, all combined according to his own artistic flair. Although nearly incapacitated by his disease, the artist guides his helpers into place around him. Finally, in a slow, measured motion, he looks everyone over, giving time for his apprentices to get ready, time for anticipation to build, and then formally signals the beginning of the performance. It is something he does with authority, making sure in the process to have everyone's rapt attention.

The ceremony itself is based on a traditional Anishinaabe Bear ceremony, and he has explained the idea of it to his apprentices. As Morrisseau beats a hand drum, Sinclair, wearing the requisite bear-skin, performs the role of a bear spirit—bends and growls, goes through the motions called for—while Vadas does an honour dance. At the end of the ceremony Sinclair removes the bearskin and lays it down on the ground, and with this action he symbolically returns to human form. The Grand Shaman, Morrisseau, then blesses him by placing his ceremonial headdress on Sinclair's head. He then removes Vadas's headdress and puts it on the head of the bearskin. Although neither of Morrisseau's apprentices is of First Nations heritage, nor do they speak the Anishinaabe language, for Morrisseau's version of the ceremony it really doesn't matter.

By this time, Morrisseau is barely able to speak himself, and the words coming from his mouth are little more than a faint jumble of sound. In another time and place the oratory associated with the ceremony would have made a world of difference. Would have been central to the ceremony. But here it is of little importance. Although this ritual is still a solemn affair, with all the mystery and cultural significance on display to keep the audience mesmerized, Morrisseau has changed the rules. He is well aware that the people watching are outside of his world and will soon be dashing off to appoint-ments, to dinner—that they have only stopped in momentarily. He has thought about it carefully and the objective here is to present a semblance of the old ways, to show them what it was and what it is today, even if it means taking some artistic licence on his part.

It is a sight to behold, and despite being bound to a wheelchair, the shaman-artist, the master of ceremonies, gives his audience what they want. What he wants. A journey back to the drama and theatre

at the roots of shamanism. When it is over, those who have watched
the ceremony, including Robert and Signe McMichael and Donald
Robinson, enthusiastically congratulate Morrisseau. He is then led
into the gallery, where together everyone tours the current exhibition of his work. Soon it is time to leave and he is thanked again for
coming, and for performing his ceremony, and he wheels off back to
the car, which takes him back to Toronto. And finally to the airport,
so he and Vadas can fly home to the west coast.

Fortress Morrisseau

FOR NORVAL MORRISSEAU life is without permanence, and this is once
again demonstrated when he leaves the two-storey oceanfront glass and
cedar studio that Vadas has built for him on the Semiahmoo Reserve,
and moves to the small town of Nanaimo on Vancouver Island. Vadas
remarks that "it just became too much," referring to the number of
people who want to visit the artist. He also suggests that Morrisseau's
family wouldn't leave them alone. The groupie-fuelled lifestyle suited
Morrisseau way back in Vandorf, Ontario, and even for a while living
on the Semiahmoo Reserve, with the steady stream of guests, but now
there is a difference: Morrisseau's lifestyle has caught up to him, he is
ill, and he looks and feels much older than his sixty-seven years.

There is a photograph taken during this time that shows Vadas,
bearded and youthful at thirty-three, kissing Morrisseau on top of
his white Santa Claus head. The old painter is staring directly into
the camera and there is a slight smile on his face. It is a look of satisfaction that you see, as though he is telling his audience that despite
incredible odds that most could never fathom, that saw him eating
garbage as a kid, saw him come out of residential school scarred for
life, saw him lose his mind and everything else more than once, that
despite everything he's been through somehow he made it—but
there's been a price to pay. He is wearing a bone breastplate and his
hair is long and grey and untidy. His thick body is frail and his lower
lip droops. His hands shake so severely he can barely hold his carved

cane. He struggles when he speaks. As though trying to find something positive to say, journalists remark that his dark eyes still sparkle with playfulness and humour, but then go on to describe the artist as a mere shadow of his former self.

Much has happened to Morrisseau throughout his life and career, some good, some bad, but what troubles him most is that he knows his painting days are coming to an end. In an act of will he holds his trembling hands over a sheet of paper to show everyone that he can steady them. It is more an act of defiance. Desperation. "Even with Parkinson's I've been painting for the last three years. My hands don't shake when I hold a brush," he says. Whatever power he calls upon, he manages to glide one hand smoothly over the sheet of paper—as though the paper is a magnet pulling it down. But his fear is real and palpable because he knows that even this gesture will be inevitably taken away from him. How long will he be able to keep it up before the disease consumes him like the dreaded Windigo? And so he hurries to fill dozens and dozens of canvases with dazzling colour, as if to paint himself back to health. "They say to eat is to live," he says about his art. "For me, to do art is to live." For Morrisseau the inability to paint is akin to death, and he cannot help but wonder if he is paying the ultimate price for living a life without restraint. Wonders if his grandfather's warning about his incomplete vision of Bear all those years ago has anything to do with it. When asked, he mumbles that it really doesn't matter because "If I had the chance, I'd do it all over again. I wouldn't change a thing."

Tucked away in Nanaimo, out of range of unwanted guests, Morrisseau knows that the fortress that Gabe Vadas has built around him is for his own good. He also knows that some things you can't keep out. Like dreams. There are always dreams of his blood family appearing in a storm of accusations, accusing him of abandoning them, reminding him that while he was living the high life they were going without food and clothes. Running shoes in winter. Windbreakers to shield snow. Scrounging for handouts. Sent off to residential school like their own father. He remembers reading that the Poplar Hill Development School, run by the Mennonites as part of their Northern Light Gospel Mission, had been shut down in 1989 over a discipline controversy. By way of justification, they said they adhered to biblical principals, which allowed physical punishment, and he had wondered how his children had fared there, wondered about kicks and slaps and whippings, while he was in Toronto, or in Thunder Bay, passed out somewhere.

In his dream, he searches their adult faces for some inkling of recognition and the inevitable question surfaces: how do you deny something that is true? He tells him that he's got new teeth. He's on a freshly squeezed lemon diet. That he doesn't drink anymore. That he's never felt better. But his children are in no mood for listening. They bring him to remember every detail. His oldest boy asks about the marks on his body. Beads of sweat collect on his forehead and he offers them money. He shoves it at them, but it is not enough, it can never be enough. The cost of appeasing his own conscience is the price of his soul, and that price is too high. They say they will be back. Another night and more relatives also want their due. A niece holds up a burned hand. But it doesn't last. Morrisseau mastered the art of escape long ago and flies off to other planes of existence. Other places. Other lives. And when they return the house is empty and he is gone.

But unlike in his dreams, his new home in Nanaimo is filled with life—Gabe and Michele now have a second young son—and Morrisseau is happy enough to tell the press that "the most beautiful gift is my grandson." And yet he is torn, and sometime wonders what he is doing there when his biological children and grandchildren are so far away in Ontario. Then one night he wakes in a west coast storm, draws the curtains aside and imagines the rough waves assailing the shore, witnesses the flash of a thunderbird scrawled across the night sky. And in an act as much imagination as reconciliation, he decides that he wants to return east to be with his birth family. And as if he had been chanting an Ojibway "calling-in-song," three of his sons fly in from Ontario for a short visit, and ask their father to return with them. Morrisseau agrees to go for a visit, telling Michele and Gabe that he'll be back. Gabe warns him against it, but the old painter loses his grip on the present, believing that he can slip seamlessly into the lives of the family he left so long ago—his sons in Thunder Bay, his daughter Victoria up in Keewaywin, all of them with their own children, all of them strangers.

The visit lasts a few months and he is back in Nanaimo. A part of him wanted to stay, and he even shed tears when he left, but the rest of him knew he couldn't. It told him to look in the mirror. And one night, smoking pot as though it were a drowsy charm to ward off the booze, he rolled his wheelchair to a full-length mirror and what he saw surprised him. He was too old and feeble, and too sick, for their kind of social living. Families of big men and big women, friends, dealers, collectors, neighbours, admirers, acquaintances, hustlers, like a whole troupe of acrobats and clowns dropping in at all hours. And always someone trying to strike up a deal. On top of it the rambunctiousness of grandchildren, names he mostly didn't know, running and jumping and screaming as kids do. Everybody a player in a merry-go-round circus, and all because of him, and for him. By this time he is used to silence, a small rose garden, a stroll in his wheelchair along the waterfront. What he longed for was the round-the-clock care he had been receiving from Vadas and his wife, the nurses he constantly fought with, the quiet of a few friends.

Not that his blood family wanted him to leave. On the contrary. Gabe Vadas calls Morrisseau's departure a clandestine rescue, in sharp contrast to the family members, who call it a kidnapping. Morrisseau is alone when Vadas pulls up in a rental and hustles him into it and hightails it to Winnipeg, where they board a plane and the old painter is whisked back to the west coast. Because Morrisseau is still selling his paintings to the Kinsman Robinson Gallery in Toronto, and Vadas is in regular contact with them, we can assume that he had no trouble finding Morrisseau. What is for certain is that in the few months Morrisseau was in Thunder Bay he also sold paintings to Steve Potosky at the Art of the North Gallery, at a time when it is questionable whether he could hold a paintbrush.

The way Potosky tells it, he shows up at the Landmark Inn, a little nondescript motel near a busy stretch of highway, and in the room there are nearly a dozen paintings. "I chose the pick of the litter," he says later. The rest he assumes will be sent to Kinsman Robinson, or some other gallery. Looking at the old man slouched over in his wheelchair, his hands jerking like gunfire, Potosky naturally has doubts about Morrisseau's ability to paint. And yet there they are, canvases spread across the room. Placed side by side, the variations of style and substance catch Potosky's eye like a hook and make him cringe and doubt their origin.

With a nod that encircles the room, Potosky gets right to the point. "How the hell can you paint?" he asks the old painter point blank, wanting to know how he could possibly do all these paintings, wanting to make sure he is not purchasing something done by someone else. Morrisseau is quick to take offence. Nobody crosses him. Nobody dares. Although Parkinson's has become a noose around his neck and holds him to his chair, his presence nevertheless fills the room. When one of Morrisseau's sons tries to deflect the question, the artist holds up a trembling hand to indicate he will speak for himself, as he has always done. He then goes about struggling with his blunt tongue to get the words out. Morrisseau challenges Potosky. He tells him to hold his hand over a canvas and they will see whose hand moves first. He looks Potosky in the eye. Takes the hook of doubt and yanks it as hard as he can. Potosky is surprised when the old painter manages to steady his hand over the canvas. To stub out any last sign of lingering doubt, he goes even further and explains his philosophy about painting and says that as in the days of the old masters, he too has apprentices. Apprentices as far back as he can remember. In his strongest voice, which Potosky still has to bend forward to hear, he says that if he even touches a canvas with a pencil mark it is still his. It is still an original Morrisseau. This before coughing and spitting up into his tin cup. Before gesturing to his sons that he's had enough. Before signing Potosky's certificate of authenticity.

The question of Morrisseau "fakes" will soon make front-page headlines and will escalate as more and more people become involved. Among others, former northern Ontario schoolteacher Joseph McLeod, the owner of Maslak McLeod Gallery, will eventually find himself embroiled in the controversy, and a disgruntled customer will sue him. This also happens to another Toronto gallery, Artworld of Sherway. In a similar vein, collectors, galleries, and artists will write blogs, or be quoted in articles, that will add to the cloud of distrust and the general suspicion over the authenticity of Morrisseau's paintings. Interviewed by Ritchie Sinclair (Stardreamer), Anishinaabe painter Blake Debassige, based on Manitoulin Island, tells of the time when a dealer from Winnipeg showed up at his Kasheese Studios with a suitcase of about forty Morrisseau paintings. He says that he refused to buy them and told the dealer that they were fakes. According to Debassige, the dealer then sold them to another gallery located on the island. To make matters even more complicated, Karl Burrows, an apprentice of Morrisseau's in the 1990s, has gone on record to say that he not only painted on the artist's behalf but even signed Morrisseau's name.

On the other hand, there are those dealers—including Joseph McLeod and collectors like Ugo Matulic and Joseph Otavnik—who believe that the issue of fakes is really a non-issue, a trumped-up conspiracy by Kinsman Robinson and Gabe Vadas to corner the market. In an attempt to put the issue to rest, impartial experts familiar with Morrisseau's work from various periods, and endorsed by the artist, form the Norval Morrisseau Heritage Society in 2005, with a mandate "to catalogue and ultimately verify authentic paintings in order to create a catalogue raisonné." The society, however, goes dormant, effectively having its legs cut from under it due to threats of litigation by stakeholders.

You would think the last word on any painting would go to

Morrisseau himself, who allegedly declared that he did not paint *Grandfather Speaks of Great Ancestral Warrior*, a work attributed to him, and sold by Edmonton's Bearclaw Gallery. But that's not what has happened. According to *The Ottawa Citizen*, "Mr. Morrisseau's word… when he was seriously ill with Parkinson's disease was not accepted as gospel by everyone. So maybe the painting is real, after all. It depends on who you believe." To date, then, even Morrisseau's own opinion has held little weight, and whatever the truth, the current storm of accusations and litigation shows no sign of dispersing. No sign of light.

The National Gallery of Canada

ALWAYS IN THE THICK of controversy. Always opening doors. Or breaking them down. In 2006, Morrisseau is again in the centre of the Canadian art scene. In the centre of Canadian consciousness. That year the National Gallery of Canada hosts a long-overdue retrospective of the artist's work, *Norval Morrisseau: Shaman Artist*, and in doing so puts him on the front page of nearly every major newspaper in the country. Full-page colour spreads of art along with full-page articles expound on his turbulent life and the virtues of his art. The exhibition captures the imagination of Canadians, who flock to see it. There they witness fifty-nine pieces carefully selected from Morrisseau's vast body of work, which art historians and curators speculate must be around three thousand paintings. From a career spanning five decades the gallery selects work ranging from small monotone birchbark sketches to massive technicolour murals (the lack of any trace of his large body of homoerotic paintings is notice-able to be sure). And the public bears witness to what Jack Pollock proclaimed four decades earlier: that what distinguishes Morrisseau from any so-called primitive artist is his "incredible capacity for constant growth and development."

And so Morrisseau is both the only Canadian painter credited with creating a whole artistic movement, the Woodland School, and the first Native painter to have a solo exhibition in the National Gallery of Canada. Claimed as Canada's own, he sits in his trusty wheelchair in the gallery surrounded by a crowd of art critics, well-wishers, and the curious public who have come to witness the Shaman's triumphant return from the alcohol-hazed streets of Vancouver, which they still talk about. Ever the Trickster, his transformation has been no less than a miracle—at least this is what he hears above the cacophony of voices crowding the room.

His mind like a little bird circling overhead, he perches on the frames of the paintings, taking it all in:

The silver-haired woman, wealthy, serious, scented, in her raw-silk suit, explains that she owns three of Morrisseau's paintings. She emphasizes that all of them are from the early 1970s when he was still living in the north and still close to the land. She enjoys the prestige she associates with buying his work when he was just starting out and needed a patron. Purchased them from Jack Pollock himself, she says, and goes on to describe a pattern of entwined loons and what she calls an X-ray bear. Similar to the one in the current exhibition, she points out, but different. The other she owns is more mythical, a kind of prehistoric water creature. She loves the earth tones, the forest green and burnt sienna. These new paintings are so different, she whispers with her brow furrowed, the colours are so glaring, hot pink and orange, not really traditional, are they.

The straight look of a banker catches his eye—Morrisseau moves in closer when he sees a suit, because it has always meant a sale.

The tall white-haired man in the three-piece lives in a world undeniably focused on one thing and one thing only: wealth. With his face almost close enough to taste the painting, he examines it thoroughly. *The Land (Land Rights)*. Indeed. Let's see: Acrylic on canvas, 1976. An early one. He considers its value. What it would have sold for originally. What it would cost to buy today. The percentage of profit. Much better than most dividends. The question is how much it will go up in say ten, twenty years, when the artist is long gone. It doesn't occur to him that he too will be long gone. Perhaps like King Tut, he dreams he will bring his gold with him to the next world. Noticing *Observations of the Astral World*, he suddenly forgets about the facts and figures and stands in awe of the spectacle. He marvels at the size, 93 by 202 inches. The dazzling array of colour. But his captivation is fleeting, barely seconds. Astral World? Indeed. It must be worth a pretty penny.

A flash of colour catches Morrisseau's eye. Rare in a crowd that wears black like a sign of belonging, and he shifts his gaze.

The thin woman with long red hair wearing a purple shawl patterned in a dream-catcher motif looks like she is on the verge of starvation. She stands in front of *Untitled (Two Bull Moose)*, communing with the power in the image of two males locked in combat over a female, and Morrisseau thinks she could use a good feed of moose meat. Looking away from the painting, she remarks to her companion that the last time she ate red meat was over ten years ago. After a moment, she exhales deeply and moves on to *Artist in Union with Mother Earth*—and instantly becomes red-faced at the sight of sex. Having trained herself in creative visualization, she can feel the sexual energy travel through her body, making it tingle. Embraced by what she calls the divine dance of love, she wishes she had brought her talisman, her sacred feather, to calm herself down. She would close her eyes and travel into inner space. There she would call upon her spirit helper, remove her conscious mask and get in touch with her authentic self.

Leaving the spectacle of her, Morrisseau hovers in midair. He darts over to the man with the big voice.

Examining *Untitled (Horned Snake Ojibway Medicine Society)*, a middle-aged man, greying hair, jeans, black turtleneck, sports jacket, turns to his blond companion. "Did you know Morrisseau's stylistic and iconographic sources were the sacred scrolls and the pictographs found in the Great Lakes region? That his pictorial and narrative mode reinvented the original templates by stamping his own evocative personality and rupturing past and present through innovative abstract symbols? Consider his rich palette indicative of his modus operandi, though of course intentionality remains unresolved." His young friend is impressed by his knowledge, and he lays it on thick for her. He tells her that he's been into Morrisseau's work for some time now and has read extensively on the Ojibway culture. Morrisseau is bored and decides to look elsewhere.

Then he spots him, a young man who looks to be in his mid-twenties. Ponytail, checkered shirt, jeans, boots, standing in front of *Untitled (Migration)*—it's a theme Morrisseau is fond of revisiting. Anishinaabe, Morrisseau thinks, and smiles, watching him stand in front of the painting, taking his time, contemplating it, which makes Morrisseau wonder if he knows anything about his own culture. If he knows the stories. If he speaks his language. He wonders if he will be the one to carry on the teachings. He remembers his grandfather Potan telling him a lifetime ago that their culture was like a cup of spring water that was cracked and slowly leaking out. He hopes and prays that this triumphant moment, probably his last, has brought him a step closer to his goal, always his one and only goal, to inspire his people to again achieve the greatness of past glories. But he cannot dwell on this need, this hope, because the very thought of all that has been lost is like a hand ripping his heart from his chest.

And so he flies into himself, closes his eyes, and leaves the gallery altogether.

Conjuring

All I ever wanted was for the people to know this art. That's all I ever wanted.

—NORVAL MORRISSEAU

FROM HIS GRANDFATHER Moses Potan Nanakonagos's teachings, Norval Morrisseau has taken what is left of the old ways and has buried it all in his heart. It is a belief system that goes back long before the parade of missionaries, when his people believed in ceremonies that looked at the rumbling sky and saw claws of black cloud, lightning eyes, heard thundering wings and prayed for benevolence. In a gesture reminiscent of reaching up to the sky to wrestle down a cloud with his bare hands, he says to the press and anybody else who will listen that he uses what he's managed to salvage from the priests, who set out to destroy "that thing that existed," to create his art.

Having studied the patchwork of his own culture since childhood, as an anthropologist of his own people, and absorbing what is left of the traditional teachings, the old language, the broken interpretations of the sacred scrolls of the Midewiwin, the faded pictographs of ancient shaman ancestors, plus everything possible about Western art, synthesizing vast amounts of information on artistic materials, techniques, art history, even the art market, he nonetheless believes that without the help of the spirit world, all this information would be useless. It is the tools of shamanism that are most important to him. And he has used these tools to conjure helpers, people he knows and does not know, people he passes on the street and those he has never met before. With the help of his Bear totem and the spirit forces of his ancestors, they have indeed come.

Morrisseau awakes into the dream of life and finds himself locked in a cage of bone. Unable to move his body, everything as steady and monotonous as the time for feeding—a slice of ham, green beans, mashed potatoes—the time for bed. The white walls make him want to reach out with a brush. If he could he would smear them red, orange, turquoise. Instead he tries to stretch his wings. But he cannot. They feel stapled to his body. No matter how hard he struggles he cannot make them grow. They no longer obey his command, no longer greet Nokomis, Mishomis, Grandmother Moon, Grandfather Sun, stretch and soar. The single room is what they know.

The tubes of paint are hardened. The paper is lying in the corner. Everything grows still. Everything grows calm. Except him. He looks down with his X-ray eyes through his pajamas into his beating heart. Struggles with all his force to lift his arm and drop it down upon his chest. It comes down with a thud, and he pulls his fingers apart and digs down inside himself, and retrieving his hand, holds what is left of himself. His beating heart. He examines the scars. Wonders how it could possibly keep beating after all he's been through. The pulses of it run through his hand and down his arm, telling him he is still alive.

He cannot admit to himself that his painting days are over. The reason he lived for so long, gone. The reason to keep going, gone. As quickly as his dancing brush once moved across the canvas, everything has gone. His body aches and he is tired. He thinks maybe he has lived too long. He tries to move his mouth. But it occurs to him that even if he did speak out in his language, there wouldn't be anyone who could understand him. To laugh at his joke. The painting on the wall at the foot of his bed has been removed for safe keeping, or stolen, so he looks out the window. Watches a cloud for a while that shifts into a giant Thunderbird, its darkening shadow moving across the face of the sky like a coastal storm. Getting closer.

And again he is riding high astride his beloved Thunderbird, each swoop of its massive wings cracking open the sky as he looks down through the gathering cloud to the small earthlings below. Portrait of the Shaman Rider, long flowing hair tied back in a band of leather, jade and ruby necklace, squawking birds either thrown asunder or perched royally, watchful, vigilant, bound to the gift of the Spirit. Portrait of the painter himself, who once spent twelve hours soul-travelling the higher plains up to the seventh level of the astral world, where he allowed it to reflect in his mind like a mirror, allowed himself to be used by the greater consciousness to paint what simply is. Much to everyone's surprise or disregard or disbelief when he tried to explain. But he doesn't care anymore, because he is so far out of range in his medicine dream, there is no turning back. His soul wanders the starry milky way, path of death, beacon of life, sliding through the multi-layered worlds of the universe, as galaxies explode and unfold before his eyes in radiant living colour.

Descending to earth, he never knows where he'll be, back in his little red asphalt shack in Beardmore, waking up in Thunder Bay at the Sea-Vue Motel with all his paintings gone, or maybe he's in Red Lake hawking a sketch at the Snake Pit for a quart of beer, or bent over a table in the basement of Okanski's What-Not-Shop unrolling a sheet of kraft paper, or maybe painting upstairs in the Sears store on the main drag. Maybe he sees himself waking up between Harriet's thighs, thinking life is good, little Victoria and her baby brother in the next room, or maybe he's back in Toronto with Pollock after that first show, yelling about greed and deceit in a white-tabled restaurant, startling onlookers. Maybe he's drugged and naked with a beautiful Italian boyfriend, or maybe drunk in Vancouver in a smoke-filled room, the skin melting from his back. But he's had his share of pain, and he tries to avoid such thoughts before setting down on solid ground.

This time he's painting in Tom Thomson's shack at the McMichael Gallery in Kleinburg, and it reminds him of his childhood at Sand Point on Lake Nipigon. He can already see them, his grandparents, speaking in Anishinaabemowin, the kerosene lamp and woodstove throwing a soft glow across the log cabin. He's on the floor near the fire snuggled in a thick blanket, listening to them. Outside it is the first snow of winter, and he is warm and happy, his little finger tracing the shadows on the wall beside him.

When Morrisseau opens his eyes he is on a plane flying from Nanaimo to Toronto to defend Gabe Vadas, and himself by implication, in the Ontario Superior Court of Justice from a claim of ten thousand dollars. It is a winter day in 2007, and he is above the clouds and the sky is bluer than he remembers ever seeing it, and he starts to think about its colour—bird blue, intense blue, robin's egg blue, turquoise blue, maya blue, columbia blue, sky blue—when Vadas leans over and quietly says that they will be meeting with the RCMP about the fake paintings. Morrisseau looks back out the window.

He cannot understand exactly how things have got to this point, why they have to go to court, why someone would say that he doesn't care about his past work. He thinks about that, and remembers going to the Indian Art Centre in Ottawa and explaining it to the young curator there: "A lot of people ask me if I remember doing a particular painting, and I tell them of course I remember doing that painting, and I remember exactly what I was thinking about at the time when I was doing it." He now sees his twisted reflection, a face that is no longer his face, and he knows he is close to leaving his body. If he could move his mouth the way he used to lap up the world, he would use it to speak—something he misses almost as much as painting. He would say that it's strange that the man who never gave a shit about money, who gave it away as fast as he made it, is being sued for money.

Then again, he would also have to say it's true that once upon a time he couldn't have cared less about where his art went, the paintings flowing from his fingertips, the days and nights endless. Couldn't have cared less how much he drank and smoked and screwed around. But now that he is old and sick it is a different story. And maybe in the end money is all anyone really cares about anyway. "Even the Indian forgets how to be an Indian—how to create and maintain his environment," he once told Donald Robinson. But now his thoughts are getting jumbled, and it pains him to think like this, and again he closes his eyes.

And he sees himself in a better place, among a stand of birch in the spring when the sap is running through their veins; he puts down his tobacco and slices wet sheets from the trunks and flattens them with stones positioned on each cardinal point. The heavy bark dries in the sun. He sees himself fashion brushes from moose hair. Gather whatever paint he can salvage from the dump. Root for discarded pens and pencils. Without any direct models to mimic, without a teacher to instruct him, without art books to guide him, without access to galleries, he chooses to paint what comes to mind. From his grandfather's stories images rise like a faint mist over Lake Nipigon: *Misshipesheu the Water Lynx, Creation Turtle, Horned Snake of the Ojibway Medicine Society, Thunderbird in Transformation.* And he staggers in their direction, falls and gropes for them, stands and tries again. Using sheer willpower he tries to render, interpret, filter them through his own consciousness, stamp them with his own name. These first emotional forays into the mythic are naive, child-like—crude, brutal assaults, Pollock will say—examples of the artist working his way into another world, another reality, the objective first and foremost to get it down.

Of all of Morrisseau's painting from his early period one stands out among the others. Its subject and perspective are unique. In *Ancestors Performing the Ritual of the Shaking Tent, 1958–60* the viewer stands outside the ceremony gazing upon three hooded Midewiwin members in the midst of the mysterious and powerful Jeesekum, the Shaking Tent ceremony. Of the two standing figures, one is drumming. The second, who is turned away, is presumably shaking a rattle. The third figure, whose back is also towards the viewer, is sitting, perhaps praying. Centred in the background is a wigwam stitched together firmly from hide or bark. Staked to the ground. Ostensibly there is a fourth figure we do not see. This is the figure inside the tent, the blessed shaman—the one who makes things tremble, the one sanctioned by gift, the one who is bound hand and foot, and provides the questions for Mikkinnuk, Turtle, to interpret for all the other spirits. Mikkinnuk is no ordinary turtle but a spirit embodied in the shell of a turtle. After the appropriate ritual, the prayers and songs of praise and humility, and if the spirits approve, if the ceremony is strong enough, Mikkinnuk will enter the tent first and blow away the shaman's bindings, then whoever or whatever may be follows, the spirits exuding such power that each response they give will literally lift the tent off the ground, their cacophony of voices slamming into it with the force of a storm. In another time and place, it is Norval Morrisseau inside the tent.

The plane touches down in Toronto and its engines roar in reverse, and Morrisseau wakes with a jolt from a deep dream that is as vivid as one of his technicolour paintings. He is sitting up at the front in business class, and Gabe Vadas and a stewardess immediately unbuckle him and help him out of his seat and into his wheelchair. But he is still elsewhere, thinking about that one elusive question he was supposed to ask Mikkinnuk. If a person could ask the spirits any question at all, what would it be? Morrisseau has come full circle. He is back in the city where it all began, but it feels to him like he has come to the end. Like he is meant to be here, now. He will go to his condo on the waterfront, which Vadas has bought as an investment, he will see old friends, and he will do what has to be done. But he is not thinking about any of this, as he is helped off the plane.

Indian Canoe

Behind the blink of a dream
the shaman paints himself
into voyage
and travels
with the people
who have been paddling all their lives
for centuries
back to the source
of religion

Misshipesheu
water manitou, spirit guide
swims the underworld
spiralling out of a whirlpool

Sign of medicine power
and presence
a prayer
for calm water

Loon shapes the canoe
in an elegant song
of loyalty
and beauty
head held high
to the distant horizon
vigilant for the people

Sturgeon supports
the fragile vessel
master of deep water
strength

and sweet flesh
given in self-sacrifice
beloved
totems

And the four aboard
Man, Woman, Child
Shaman (paddle or brush in hand)
painted in red ochre on stone
and bound together
transformed
innumerable times
by innumerable artists
so that the people might continue.

About Norval Morrisseau

Norval Morrisseau, Copper Thunderbird, was born in 1932 in the isolated Ojibway community of Sand Point in remote north-western Ontario, and having lived a tumultuous life of extreme highs and lows, he died in Toronto in 2007. Critics, art historians, and curators alike consider him one of the most innovative artists of the twentieth century and arguably Canada's greatest painter. Among his many awards and honours are the Order of Canada and an Aboriginal Achievement Award. Referred to as the "Picasso of the North" by the French press, he was the only Canadian painter invited to France to celebrate the bicentennial of the French Revolution in 1989. A self-taught painter, Norval Morrisseau came to the attention of the Canadian art scene in 1962 with his first solo and breakthrough exhibition at the Pollock Gallery in Toronto. This sold-out show announced the arrival of an artist like no other in the history of Canadian art. In the first-ever review of his work, *The Globe and Mail* art critic Pearl McCarthy declared him a genius.

Drawing initially on the iconography of traditional First Nations sources, in particular the sacred birchbark scrolls and the picto-graphs of the Algonquian-speaking peoples, Morrisseau would go on to incorporate a wide array of contemporary influences in his art, ranging from the techniques of modernist painters and the imagery of comic books and magazines to New Age philosophy. Continually evolving and developing as a painter, he would quickly eschew the label "primitive artist" and become renowned for his daring experiments with imagery, scale, and colour, which critics would come to call no less than extraordinary and visionary. Extremely prolific, Morrisseau is credited with having executed some three thousand paintings in his lifetime.

Following on the heels of his incredible success, a younger generation of painters, both Native and non-Native, followed in his style and became known as the Woodland School of painters, the only Indigenous school of painting to emerge in Canada. Additional information about Morrisseau's art can be obtained from the National Gallery of Canada, private galleries, and visual arts organizations.

Norval Morrisseau at home in White Rock, BC, 1996. *Courtesy Aboriginal Art Centre, Aboriginal Affairs and Northern Development Canada, Fred Cattroll photo*

Acknowledgments

I WILL BEGIN by acknowledging Norval Morrisseau, for giving me his "shamanic blessing" and challenging me to "not to leave anything out," which turned into a monumental task. I would also like to thank Gabe and Michele Vadas for arranging my meeting with Norval and for talking freely to me.

I would also like to thank the following people, who either met with me personally and allowed me to draw on their memory or provided valuable information through secondary sources. Without your invaluable input I could not have written this book: Brian Marion, Robert Lavack, Barbara Stimpson, Brian Schieder, Eva Quan, Barry Ace, Duke Redbird, Mary Okanski, Galal Helmy, John Newman, Donald Robinson, Daphne Odjig, Stan Somerville, Tom Hill, Bryant Ross, Peter Dewdney, Chris Dewdney, Richard Baker, Karl Jirgens, Joseph and Esther Weinstein, Ruth Phillips, Greg Hill, Robert Houle, Robert Checkwitch, Michele Alderton, Joseph McLeod, Roger Obomsawin, Ritchie Sinclair, Victoria Morrisseau, Christian Morrisseau, Ronald Morrisseau, Frank Morrisseau, Alice Olsen, Duncan Mercredi, George Maroosis, Angie Littlefield, Jeanne Pattison, Francis Carlstrom, Sandra Sweeney, Agnes Bugera, John Vincent, Hazel Fulford, Vivian Gray, Tom Hill, Jean Versteeg, Steve Potosky, Jennifer Bullock, Merv Farrow, Simon Brascoupé, Peter George, Heather Pullen, Jessica Wilson and Michael Whetung.

I would also like to thank Heather Macfarlane for her editorial insight, and Frances Itani and Parker Duchemin, who read the manuscript at stages and provided encouragement. A thanks goes out to Carol and Jim Macfarlane as well, who let me take over "the shed," where much of this book was written. I am indebted to the people at Douglas & McIntyre, to Brianna Cerkiewicz for locating photographs, and especially to Anna Comfort O'Keeffe, who was so helpful in getting this book off the ground and for connecting me with my editor, Pam Robertson, whose attention to detail pushed me to write the best book possible. There are others associated with the publisher who were also very involved, and I would like to publicly thank them all from the bottom of my heart.

Having grown up with an Ojibway mother who was born about the same time as Norval, I naturally drew on what she told me growing up to understand the era that Norval was born into. And so once again I acknowledge her presence. I also need to acknowledge the presence of the land in this book. I made every effort to visit the places that I have written about and soak up as much as I could.

If I have missed anyone please forgive me. In saying this, I would also like to acknowledge the numerous scholars, curators, writers, filmmakers, and journalists who have written books, essays, and newspaper articles and made films about Norval Morrisseau, which have been important sources of information. A few of these sources come to mind: Norval Morrisseau's own *Legends of My People: The Great Ojibway* (Selwyn Dewdney, ed., McGraw-Hill Ryerson, 1965); *The Art of Norval Morrisseau* (Jack Pollock and Lister Sinclair, eds., Methuen, 1979); *The Paradox of Norval Morrisseau* (Henning Jacobsen and Duke Redbird, NFB, 1974); *The Sound of the Drum: The Sacred Art of the Anishnabec* (Mary E. Southcott, The Boston Mills Press, 1984); *Norval Morrisseau* (Kinsman Robinson, 1997 and 2005); *The Art of Norval Morrisseau, the Writings of Basil H. Johnston* (Glenbow Museum, 1999); "Norval Morrisseau: Artist as Shaman" (Barry Ace, Aboriginal Curatorial Collective, 2005); *Norval Morrisseau: Shaman Artist* (Greg Hill, ed., National Gallery of Canada, 2006); *Norval Morrisseau and the Woodland Artists: the Red Lake Years, 1959–1980*

(Red Lake Regional Heritage Centre, 2008); *A Separate Reality* (Paul Cavallo, 2006). Chi-Miigwetch to all.

Excerpts of this book have appeared in one form or another in *Norval Morrisseau: Shaman Artist* (National Gallery of Canada), *The Malahat Review, Zócalo Poets, Rampike, EVENT, Canadian Literature,* and *Poetry Ireland Review.*

And, finally, I would like to thank the Canada Council for the Arts, and the Cultural Funding branch of the City of Ottawa, where I was living at the time of writing, for supporting this project.

Index

Page numbers in **bold** refer to illustrations

Ace, Barry, 281–83

Agnes (medicine woman), 42–43

Art Gallery of Ontario, 186, 236

Bearclaw Gallery, 242, 245, 259–60, 291

Beardmore, ON, 13, 39, 65, 83, 131, 212

"Biography—Life's Thoughts of Copper Thunderbird" (diary), 168

Bugera, Agnes, 242, 245, 260

Burnford, Sheila, 118–19, 120

Burrows, Karl, 276, 290

Checkwitch, Bob, 182, 205, 241

Cochenour, ON, **55**, 57, 59, 96, 150

Coghlan Art Studio, **255**, 262, 264, 268

Debassige, Blake, 237, 290

Dewdney, Irene, 74, 104–8

Dewdney, Selwyn, 11, 12, **55**, 68–79, 81, 86, 104–8, 122–23, 124–25, 174

documentary of Morrisseau, 1968, 131–33, 170

Farrow, Merv, 148–50

Frogg, Simon, 137–38

Gallagher, Father, 27, 44

garden party, **163**, 209–19, 222

George, Peter, 225, 227–28

Grosart, Allister, 11–12, 85–86, 94

Helmy, Galal, 241–50, 259–60, 61

Hill, Tom, 170–72, 237

Houle, Robert, 211, 213, 217, 231

Indian Group of Seven, The, 184–187, 236

Indians of Canada Pavilion at Expo 67, 125–27, 171, 185

Jacobsen, Henning, 170, 172–77

Kakegamic, David, 46–47

Kakegamic, Goyce, 182, 240

Kakegamic, Harriet, 46–47, 176, 279
  fights with Morrisseau, 123–24, 141, 151–52
  marriage, 58, 98, 108–10, 120, 157, 158, 171, 273
  poverty and neglect, 84, 105, 107, 125, 140, 148
  separation from Morrisseau, 146, 150, 156, 160–61, 187

Kakegamic, Henry, 182, 240

Kakegamic, Joshim, 144, 156, 182, 237, 240

Kinsman Robinson Gallery, 271–72, 273, 281, 283, 288, 290

Klee, Paul, 61, 76

Kritzwiser, Kay, 211, 237

Lavack, Robert, 133–39, 140–46, 150–54

Legends of My People: The Great Ojibway (book), 74, 79, 101, 122–23, 130, 176

Lorenzia, Sister, 25–26, 44

Maligne Canyon, AB, 242–44, 246, 247, 250

Marion Scott Gallery, 250, 252, 259

Marion, Brian, **163**, 191, 213–14, 218, 231–32, 233, 236, 276

McCarthy, Pearl, 13, 102, 108, 111, 303

McMichael Gallery, 191–93, 220–24, 283, 297

McMichael, Robert, 191–93, 221, 285

Morrisseau, Abel, 23, 38–39

Morrisseau, Benjamin, 246

Morrisseau, Christian, 227, 274

Morrisseau, David, 89, 97, 227, 297

Morrisseau, Eugene, 108, 227, 274

Morrisseau, Michael, 227

Morrisseau, Norval

    career: exhibitions (*see* Indians of
      Canada Pavilion at Expo 67;
      1962 solo exhibition; *Norval
      Morrisseau: Shaman Artist*; *The
      Shaman's Return* exhibition);
      forgery accusations, 246, 277,
      289–91, 297; reviews, 13, 93,
      108, 128–29, 222, 237, 251;
      technique, 77–79, 106, 194,
      268, 291

    early life and upbringing:
      birthdate, 2, 266; Copper
      Thunderbird (spirit name), 13,
      43, 46, 95; Ojibway heritage,
      14–15, 23–24, 45, 123, 133,
      146, 294; residential school (*see*
      St. Joseph's Roman Catholic
      Residential School)

    family: adopted family (*see* Gabor
      Vadas; Michele Vadas; Robin
      Vadas); brothers (*see* Ronald
      Morrisseau; Wolf Morrisseau);
      children, 89–90, 160, 223,
      227–28, 236, 244, 274–75,
      286–87 (*see also* names of indi-
      vidual children); father (*see* Abel
      Morrisseau); grandchildren,
      244, 277, 287–88; grandfather
      (*see* Moses Potan Nanakonagos);
      grandmother (*see* Veronique
      Nanakonagos); mother (*see*
      Grace Nanakonagos); wife (*see*
      Harriet Kakegamic)

    honours: honorary doctorate from
      McMaster University, 224–28;
      Order of Canada, 210, 221, 222,
      225, 249

    personal life: alcoholism, 97–98,
      119, 124, 141, 248–50, 275–76;
      homelessness, 250–53, 257–60,
      277, 281, 292; clothing, 212,
      218, 266, 282, 283; cross-
      dressing, 39–41, 84–85;
      sexuality, 41, 197, 215, 223, 291;
      Parkinson's disease, 280, 283,
      286, 289, 291

    spirituality: Christianity, 21–22,
      29–30, 142–43, 167, 178, 239;
      Eckankar, 196–98, 220, 226;
      shamanism, 37, 44, 230, 239,
      272, 284–85, 295

Morrisseau, Pierre, 227, 274

Morrisseau, Ronald, 37, 50

Morrisseau, Wolf, 183, 214, 276

Morrisseau Kakegamic, Victoria
    childhood, 97, 100, 108, 109, 132,
      188, 190, 227
    neglect, 89–90, 105, 107, 160
    adulthood, 236, 244, 277, 279, 288

Morrisseau Meekis, Lisa, 227

My Year with Norval Morrisseau (cata-
    logue), 259

Nanaimo, BC, 14, 285, 286, 288

Nanakonagos, Grace, 23, 38–40,
    41–42

Nanakonagos, Moses Potan
    apprenticeship of Morrisseau, 16,
      17–18, 19, 23, 30–36, 44, 282
    influence on Morrisseau, 92–93,
      122, 127, 198, 278, 294
    storytelling, 64–68, 80, 81, 130,
      146, 196, 298

Nanakonagos, Veronique, 20–22, 28, 38, 41–42, 81, 167

National Gallery of Canada, 1, 3, 5, 186, 268, 291–92

1962 solo exhibition, 1, 11, 14, 91–94, 190

Nipigon, Lake, 13, 15, 18, 23, 39

Norval Morrisseau: Shaman Artist (exhibition), 1, 5, 291–94

Norval Morrisseau: Travels to the House of Invention (book), 283

Odjig, Daphne, 183–87, 237, 247

Ojibway Art Circuit, the, 140–44, 154

Okanski, Marianne, 157

Okanski, Mary, 154–55, 158

Okanski, Paul, 154–55, 157–58, 159–61, 297

Olsen, Alice, 155–56, 187–90, 234

Olsen, Doris, 187–90

paintings by Morrisseau

A Tribute to My Beloved Daughter-In-Law, 278

Ancestors Performing the Ritual of the Shaking Tent, 299

Androgyny, 233, 235

Artist and His Four Wives, The, 204, 220

Artist in Union with Mother Earth, 158, 293

Artist's Wife and Daughter, The, 193–94

Children, The, 236

"Christ's Head", 29

Creation Turtle, 298

Daughter-in-law Holding Raven Granddaughter, 236

Door to Astral Heaven, 197

Earth Mother with Her Children, 127

First Son of the Ojibway Loon Totemic Clan, 167

Fish Cycle, 167

Grand Shaman and His Apprentice the Blond Person Tala, Sunshine For the Group, 230

Grandfather Speaks of Great Ancestral Warrior, 291

Horned Snake of the Ojibway Medicine Society, 298

Indian Jesus Christ, 145, 169, 178

Joseph with Christ Child and St. John the Baptist, 167

Land (Land Rights), The, 204, 220, 292

Levels of Consciousness, 197

Loon Cycle, 167

Man Changing into Thunderbird (Transmigration), 200, 205–8, 220

Man Who Changed into a Thunderbird, The, 111

Manifesting from Within Childlike Simplicity, 223

Medicine Bear, The, 33

Merman and Merwoman, 204

Misshipeshoo—Earth Monster, 191

Misshipeshu the Water Lynx, 298

Observations of the Astral World, 268, 269, 293

Ojibway Family, 236

Ojibway Shaman Receives the Sacred Fire from the Third Heaven, 167

Phallic God in Disguise, 158

Portrait of Christ in Sacred Robes, 167

Portrait of the Artist as Jesus Christ, 29, 178

Power Emanating From Ancient Spirit Vision, 167

Sacred Bear from Vision, 33

Sacred Bear Quest, 33

Self Portrait Devoured by Demons, 124, 178

Self-Portrait, 193–94

Self-Portrait, Devoured by His Own Passion, 178, 189

Shaman and Disciples, 224

Shaman Protected by Bear Power, The, 33

Shaman Rider, 157–58

Shaman's Apprentice, 230

Some of My Friends, 204

Soul in Form of Fish Swimming the Cosmic Sea, 222

Spiritual Self Emerges, 197

Spiritual Self Looks Beyond, 197

Storyteller: The Artist and His Grandfather, The, 198, 220, 236

Thunderbird in Transformation, 298

Thunderbird with Serpent, 111

Untitled (Horned Snake Ojibway Medicine Society), 293

Untitled (Migration), 294

Untitled (Two Bull Moose), 293

Victoria and Family, 236, 277

Virgin Mary with Christ Child and St. John the Baptist, 167

Warrior with Thunderbirds, 167

Paris, France, 266–68, 277

Picasso, Pablo, 61, 63, 76, 100, 184, 239, 267–68

Pollock Gallery, 11, 14, 83, 89, 91, 102, 110, 191, 201, 209, 228–30

Pollock, Jack, 11–13, **55**, 82–84, 87–91, 229–30

    as agent to Morrisseau, 94, 99, 157–59, 170–76, 203–8, 209–11, 213, 218

    conflict with Morrisseau, 110, 147–48, 155, 201–2, 219

Professional Native Indian Artists Inc., *See* The Indian Group of Seven

Quan, Eva, 195–96, 211, 231

Ray, Carl, 98, 126, 135–40, 142, 143, 144, 156, 185–86

Red Lake, ON, 46, 50, **55**, 57, 76, 94, 123, 130, 155

Redbird, Duke, 176–77

Richard, J., **163**

Robinson, Donald, 271–73, 281, 285, 298

Ross, Bryant, 261–68, 276

Ross, Susan, 84, 87, 89, 110, 118–21, 183

St. Joseph's Roman Catholic Residential School, 22–30, 44, 125, 142, 225, 239, 285

Sandy Lake Reserve, 46, 100, 119, 150

Schreyer, Edward, **163**, 218

Schreyer, Lily, **163**, 218

Schwarz, Herbert, 127–30

Shaking Tent ceremony, 19, 35–36, 129, 196, 226, 299

Sheppard, Constable Robert, 68–71, 74, 79

Shingoose (musician), 176–77, 223

Sinclair, Lister, 218, 219, 222

Sinclair, Ritchie (Stardreamer), 232, 235, 240, 283–84, 290

Sweeney, Doreen, 114, 115

Sweeney, John, 112–115, 117, 147

The Art of Norval Morrisseau (book), 218–19, 222

The Paradox of Norval Morrisseau (documentary), 170–74, 237

The Shaman's Return exhibition, 272, 281

Thomson, Tom, 221–24, 297

Thunderbird Poems, The, 5

    "Indian Canoe" 301–2

    "Indian Jesus Christ" 169

"Life Scroll" 6

"Observations of the Astral
World" 269

"Thunderbird and Inner Spirit"
199

"Thunderbird and Snake" 52

Thunderbird School of Shamanistic
Arts, 230, 232, 262

thunderbirds, 18, 43, 52, 66, 80,
199–208

Timberwolf Gallery, 247, 259

Toronto, ON, 11, 93, 102, 108, 175,
191, 233, 246

Vadas, Gabor (Gabe), 3–4, 257–62,
268, 275–76, 280, 283–87, 290,
297, 299–30

Vadas, Michele (née Richard), 265,
275–76, 280, 287

Vadas, Robin, **255**, 273, 275–76, 278

Vancouver, BC, 1, 179, 180, 250–51,
261, 277

Vandorf, ON, 230, 232–33

vision quest, 15, 30–33

Volpe, Albert, 230–31, 233–35, 246

Volpe, Paul, 233, 235

Volpe, Violette, 230, 233–35, 246

Weinstein, Esther, 14, 59–64, 76,
100–101

Weinstein, Joseph, 14, 59–64, 76, 79,
84, 100–101

White Rock, BC, 273, 276

Windigo and Other Tales of the Ojibway
(book), 129–30

Woodland School, 194, 198, 238, 240,
291